Eminent Nuns

Eminent Nuns

Women Chan Masters of
Seventeenth-Century China

Beata Grant

University of Hawai'i Press

Honolulu

14 13 12 11 10 09   6 5 4 3 2 1

LIBRARY OF CONGRESS CATALOGING-IN-PUBLICATION DATA
Grant, Beata.
    Eminent nuns : women Chan masters of seventeenth-century
China / Beata Grant.
        p. cm.
    Includes bibliographical references and index.
    ISBN 978-0-8248-3202-5 (hardcover : alk. paper)
    1. Buddhist nuns—China—Biography. 2. Monastic and
religious life (Zen Buddhism)—China. 3. Zen Buddhism—
China—History—17th century. I. Title.
    BQ9298.G73 2008
    294.3'9270820951—dc22

                                    2008010177

Designed by University of Hawai'i Press production staff

Printed by The Maple-Vail Book Manufacturing Group

BQ
9298
.G73
2009

Contents

A Brief Preface

Caroline Walker Bynum, referring to religious women of medieval Europe, remarks that "the stories men liked to tell about women reflected not so much what women did as what men admired or abhorred. . . . It is crucial not to take as women's own self-image the sentimentalizing or the castigating of the female in which . . . men indulged."[1] The only way to begin to redress the imbalance, she continues, is to take into consideration "works in which women wrote about their own visions and mystical experiences and about life among the sisters in their households, beguinages, and convents."[2] This book represents a preliminary effort to heed Bynum's advice and to begin to redress the imbalance in the study of Buddhist nuns in premodern China. It does so by making primary use of the closest thing we have in Chinese to the kinds of materials she recommends studying: the handful of extant collections of "discourse records," or *yulu,* composed (either orally or in writing), recorded, and compiled by nuns themselves.[3]

In the Chinese Buddhist tradition, only acknowledged Buddhist masters (the overwhelming majority of whom were men) were considered qualified to leave such collections, which were regarded as constituting their primary religious legacy to posterity. The heart of most discourse record collections are the formal and informal Dharma talks and "encounters," supposedly delivered spontaneously and recorded in situ by their disciples. The collections also include such things as letters, poems, colophons composed for paintings, and usually biographical and even autobiographical accounts or records of activities. In addition, they are usually accompanied by prefaces, stupa or funerary inscriptions, and other types of texts composed either by fellow monastics or, as is most often the case, by well-known literati figures.

Nevertheless, as many scholars have pointed out, these types of religious writings, including the seemingly "spontaneous" Dharma talks, must be read primarily as highly crafted texts, even primarily as literary texts, rather than as historical documents. This is true, of course, of many Western materials as well. The European cloister chronicles studied by Anne Winston-Allen, for instance, despite all the factual, historical, and financial data contained in them, are "literary fictions just as much as they are 'documents,' a distinction that New Cultural historians have for the most part abandoned as moot, if not meaningless."[4]

The "fictional" nature of these texts is, however, only part of the problem. Even more problematic, when it comes to the discourse records of Chinese women Chan masters, is that these writing nuns were subject to the same double bind to which writing women in most premodern cultures were subject: "As long as women remain silent, they will be outside the historical process. But, if they begin to speak and write *as men do,* they will enter history subdued and alienated."[5] Seventeenth-century women Chan masters were no exception to this rule. They generally wrote "as men do," having largely internalized and duplicated the patriarchal language of Chan Buddhism. In fact, most were regarded by others, and to a certain extent regarded themselves, as honorary men, or, to use the Chinese term, as *da zhangfu* (great gentlemen). Nevertheless, on the most fundamental level, an exploration of the discourse records of these seventeenth-century women can provide us a perspective much like the one Bynum describes as being provided by the cloister chronicles and other writings of medieval European Catholic nuns:

> [As] participants in the same institutional system, the female writers reflect and vary the ideological views that produced these institutions. Their perspective on institutional ideology differs significantly on one point, however, from that of the master narrative: in all of these texts women are at the center rather than at the margins or in the background. They are active and not passive agents."[6]

As the pages that follow will abundantly demonstrate, a great deal can be gleaned from these texts. What this gleaning requires, however, is a willingness, in the words of Sidonie Smith, "to grapple with the formal constrictions and rhetorical presentations, the historical context and psychosexual labyrinth, the subversions and the capitulations of women's self-writing in a patriarchal culture that 'fictionalizes' [women]."[7] The challenge is to avoid creating yet another fiction, however well meaning, in its place.[8] The scholar's task is not unlike that of an archaeologist who painstakingly brushes away the dust and dirt to reveal the sculpted faces, however fragmented. As with the archaeologist's findings, the piecemeal nature of the scholar's textual artifacts often make it necessary to engage in a certain amount of reconstruction. Ideally, however, that reconstruction will be based on the artifacts themselves combined with the scholar's understanding of the "horizon of possibility"—that is, what makes most sense given the historical, literary, and religious context in which these texts were produced.

This book, then, is one person's attempt to grapple with the discourse record collections of seven women Chan masters of the seventeenth century. My aim has been to present rather than represent or re-create the women whose legacy they are, which is why I have purposely retained as much of their own literary voices, in translation, as possible. Theirs may not have been the dominant voices or the most influential, but there is no question that, in their own way, these women Chan masters contributed as much to the religious landscape of seventeenth-century China as did many of their more well-known male counterparts.

Acknowledgments

This study has been a number of years in the making, and I am greatly indebted to the many who so generously offered their encouragement, friendship, and support along the way. My greatest debt of gratitude goes to Wilt L. Idema of Harvard University for his vast knowledge, collegial advice, and unflagging encouragement. Although I am sure he thinks I should have finished this book a long time ago, it is largely due to his support that I have completed it at all. I am also grateful to Jiang Wu, whose pathbreaking research on seventeenth-century Chan Buddhism has served both to inspire and to inform, and to Miriam Levering, with whom I have long shared a deep interest in the female Buddhist tradition in China. Here at Washington University in St. Louis, my deep appreciation goes to my friend and colleague Robert E. Hegel, who did much to keep me afloat when I was feeling overwhelmed. And I would be most remiss if I did not express my gratitude to Tony Chang of the East Asian Library at Washington University, who found a way to procure an entire reprint edition of the Jiaxing Buddhist canon for our library, knowing that I would be making intensive use of it. I am also immensely thankful to Patricia Crosby of Hawai'i University Press for her for expert editorial guidance and to Rosemary Wetherold for her meticulous copyediting. The book itself I would like to dedicate to my mother, Carolyn M. Grant, who offered to read the final version and, besides catching numerous elusive typos and infelicities, greatly lifted my spirits when she commented, "It kept me reading to the very end!"

Abbreviations

J. *Jiaxing Dazangjing.* 40 vols. Reprint of *Zhonghua dazang jing di er ji.*
    Taipei: Xinwenfeng chubanshe, 1987.

T. *Taishō shinshō daizōkyō.* Edited by Takakusu Junjirō et al. 100 vols.
    Tokyo: Daizōkyōkai shuppan, 1922–1933.

Z. *Shinsan dai Nihon zokuzōkyō.* 90 vols. Tokyo: Kokusho kankōkai,
    1975–1989. Originally published as *Dainihon zokuzōkyō,* 750 vols.
    (Kyoto: Zōkyō shoin, 1905–1912).

CHAPTER ONE

Setting the Stage
Seventeenth-Century Texts and Contexts

E very reader of premodern Chinese fiction, and indeed of medieval and early modern Western fiction as well, is probably familiar with the image of nuns (usually depicted as being both young and beautiful) who, left unsupervised by male kin behind surprisingly permeable convent walls, become either hapless sexual prey or seductive vampires.[1] Nonfictional sources, such as legal cases and miscellaneous records of various kinds, also tended to focus on the slanderous, the sensational, or the simply curious. In fact, for all their cultural and theological differences, this is the one thing that Buddhist nuns shared with their Catholic counterparts in premodern Europe: the sheer difficulty of escaping, whether in their own eyes or in the eyes of the world, their anomalous status. Whether associated with the absolute purity of the Virgin Mary or the lustful concupiscence of the harlot, such women were always—in the words of Jo Ann Kay McNamara, author of a history of Catholic nuns over two millennia—an "embarrassing anomaly," which in part explains why "[p]eer pressure, slander, seduction, and rape have been mobilized to neutralize women who choose a life without sex."[2] As early as 1896, Lina Eckenstein in her book *Women under Monasticism* notes with dismay the ubiquitous medieval depictions of the nun as "a slothful and hysterical," not to mention "dissolute," character.[3]

In China, as in the West, a religious vocation has always been one of many—and perhaps even the least—of motivations behind women entering a convent. More often than not, in a time and place that afforded few other options for women, the convent was a last resort for those with family, health, or economic problems that could not be otherwise resolved or at least contained. That these women should bring their problems (and their less than purely religious motivations) with them—and create new ones—is not surprising: it is these problems that often became explicitly the subject not only of fiction but of law cases as well. There is also no question that Buddhist convents—like Daoist ones—often provided an option for those women who boasted beauty as well as artistic talents to make use of both to entertain members of the opposite sex, monastic and lay. During periods known for a rich and romantic "courtesan culture"—and the late Ming dynasty was certainly one of these—the line between nuns and prostitutes could be very tenuous indeed. The Luminous Cause Convent (Mingyin an) in Hangzhou, for example, was one of the largest and most well-known convents in the Jiangnan or Lower Yangzi area. It flourished in the Southern Song period and continued to flourish throughout the late imperial period. In the Southern Song, however, it had the reputation for being a *nizhan* (nun station), where monks, literati, and officials would regularly call upon the youngest and most beautiful of the resident nuns for entertainment.[4] And it is in the Ming-Qing period that we see the emergence of the term *huachan* (flower-Chan), used in reference to nuns who entertained male visitors: among the most sought-after of these were the Wu-Yue *nüseng* (female monks of Wu-Yue), that is, the nuns of Suzhou, Songjiang, Changzhou, Jiaxing, and Huzhou.[5] In fact, one Chinese scholar, in a recent article (the translated title of which—"An Analysis of the Secular Mind-set of the Nuns of Premodern China"—gives a good idea of the author's perspective) claims that it was in the Ming-Qing period that "the transformation of nuns into prostitutes reached its zenith."[6]

Although these sorts of establishments certainly existed in actuality, in the profoundly anticlerical world of late imperial vernacular literature there were very few nuns (and, to be fair, monks as well) who were not dissolute, and very few convents that were not actually brothels in disguise. Endless examples could be cited as evidence for this, but a few should suffice. The first is a story by the famous late-Ming author Ling Mengchu (1580–1644). This particular tale—entitled "Adding Wine to Wine, Old Nun Zhao Leads a Beauty Astray; With Trick after Trick, Scholar Jin Avenges a Grievance"—takes place in a convent where Abbess Zhao serves as an unscrupulous and greedy go-between in the seduction of a married woman. The first two lines of the poem concisely summarize the dominant motif of this and other such stories: "When it comes to sex, monastics are like hungry ghosts; nor have those bedecked as nuns ever been any better."[7] Nor is it only in vernacular fiction that we find such perfidious nuns. If the following poem is any indication of his thoughts on the matter, the noted scholar, lyric poet, and bibliophile Zhu Yizun (1629–1709)—whom we will meet again later—seems to have been convinced that the entire history of nuns in China was one of dissolute licentiousness.

> In the Jin dynasty, nuns first appeared on the scene;
> By the Liang they'd become irredeemably worldly.

With ease they get involved in monastic dalliances,
Always putting on a show of being coy and docile.
Once they enter the gates of a wealthy household,
Words meant for inside only are carried out the door.
Arm in arm, they wander together over lake and hill,
Piling up the gold coins to build temples and stupas.
Their nunneries proliferate over a hundred districts;
Even the official bureau cannot keep them in check!
Spreading licentiousness in their monastic quarters,
They fill their bellies with the best monastic cuisine.
In this way, they sully people's customary ways;
How will an end be put to all of their mischief?
For women there is that which is women's work,
The essence of which is sericulture and weaving.
How is it then, in their monastic patchwork robes,
That they sally forth from their Jetavana gardens? [8]

In this poem, Zhu Yizun makes use of a number of special religious terms, the associations of which are not easily conveyed in translation. What I have translated as "monastic quarters," for example, in the original Chinese is *qingdou fang* (green-bean quarters), a reference to simple and austere monastic cells. By the same token, the term translated as "the best monastic cuisine" in the original is *xiangji fan* (accumulated-fragrance food), which in chapter 10 of the *Vimalakirti Sutra* refers to a special food that "is like the medicine called 'delicious,' which . . . is not digested until all the poisons of the passions have been eliminated." And the Jetavana garden, a reference to the first Buddhist monastery in India and a term commonly used to refer to monasteries in general, when combined with the word *sotuo,* which I have translated here as "sally," evokes more a pleasure garden than a center of monastic discipline.

Zhu Yizun's deliberate use of these terms suggests an intentional parody, of a sort that Andrea Goldman, rightly I believe, ascribes to "the late Ming literati preoccupation with unveiling duplicity . . . than it does with an outright attack on Buddhism." [9] Goldman also points out that not all Ming-Qing depictions of nuns were as vicious. In her excellent study of the various versions of the story and operatic piece entitled *Longing for the Secular Life (Sifan),* she notes that the portrayal of the nun Zhao Sekong "is quite sympathetic." [10] Nevertheless, the character is a young and beautiful nun who has been placed unwillingly in the convent by pious parents, and as such the religious life represents a site of physical and emotional incarceration rather than of liberation.

The important point is not that these stories, whether from late imperial China or medieval Europe, are all false or even purely fictional, but rather that they are one-sided. In the case of Catholic nuns, McNamara writes:

> Protestants prided themselves on "rescuing" women condemned to lan-guish without husbands, and modern historians have habitually ignored the clear testimony of the women who resisted their assaults. Enlighten-ment fantasies of the perverted sex to which innocent virgins were sub-jected behind convent walls are still published, but not the rebuttals of women who went to the guillotine rather than give up their cloisters. . . . Even today, the true or fictional accounts of renegade nuns readily gain a popular market. The accounts of women who founded new communities or flourished in old ones are too often left to private presses with limited circulation.[11]

The aim of this study of seventeenth-century Chan Buddhist nuns is not to show that all Buddhist nuns were actually spiritually transcen-dent and physically virtuous and all male accounts a matter of fiction and fantasy if not self-righteous slander. Neither is this book about the denizens of the world of flower-Chan. Rather, it about a group of women Chan masters who appear to have entered the religious life not out of compulsion but out of choice, although in many cases they did so only after losing a husband. Moreover, although many of them also engaged in the writing of poetry and were visited by male literati and officials, their primary objectives appear to have been not to entertain but to enlighten. Most important, all of these nuns left written records, including sermons, poems, letters, and, in some cases, autobiographical accounts, that provide the basis for, if not a detailed historical study, at least a series of portraits or representations that more fully reflect how these women themselves preferred to have been remembered. In other words, the purpose of this book is to redress the one-sidedness of the popular perception of nuns in premodern Chinese culture by presenting the far more multidimensional perspective reflected in the collected discourse records (yulu) of a group of seventeenth-century women Chan masters. Although originally circu-lated independently, all of these records were fortunately preserved in a privately printed edition of Buddhist scriptures and other texts known as the Jiaxing canon. For our purposes, these discourse record collections can be said to be equivalent to today's "private presses with limited circu-lation." McNamara notes that, as such, they may not have been as avidly consumed as materials designed for a more popular market; rather, they offer a different, and certainly far less one-dimensional, picture of the Buddhist nun in late imperial China.

Scholars have long noted that the mid-seventeenth century was a time when, in the words of historian Timothy Brook, "only the extremes were available: devoted involvement *(jingshi)* to the point of self-destruction or complete withdrawal *(chushi)* in the style of the Buddhist hermit-monk."[12] Many literati who, for one reason or other, did not give up their lives as loyalist martyrs retreated to their home districts, dedicating the remainder of their lives to the care of widowed mothers and orphans and making use of their literary talents to praise and lament the death of family, friends, and the dynasty itself. Others went so far as to actually take the tonsure and become ordained Buddhist monks, a few even rising to the ranks of eminent masters. For although it was by no means immune or indifferent to the political exigencies of the time, it was the Buddhist world that managed best to provide a measure of institutional stability in a world of constant change, as well as a hope of solace, if not transcendence, in a time of failed hopes and ruined ambitions.

Of course, the lives of women were also often dramatically affected. Many wives and mothers were left widowed, frequently in severe financial straits and with children and aged parents and in-laws to support and care for. Others found themselves facing a life without either husband or children, morally reluctant to marry someone else when the man to whom they had been promised suffered an untimely death. Not a few women, as the grim lists of *liefu* (heroic women) in the regional gazetteers from this period attest, chose to commit suicide rather then face a future both alone and under an alien regime. As Wai-yee Li points out, during the chaos and turmoil of the Ming-Qing transition period, "the favored literary topos is the heroic woman whose courage, valor, or victimhood adds dignity and pathos to the cataclysmic turmoil of the mid-seventeenth century."[13]

Some elite women, especially if left widowed or without children, could, like their male counterparts, also choose to enter a convent or hermitage, with far less social opprobrium than before. Some women simply retreated to a room in the family compound or to a specially built family cloister to devote themselves to religious pursuits; others took more active roles. An example of the former is Xia Shuji (*zi* Longying).[14] She was the daughter of the loyalist martyr Xia Yunyi (1596–1645) and the sister of Xia Wanchun (1631–1647), a brilliant poet who died at the hands of the Qing troops two years after his father. Her husband, Hou Xun (nephew of Hou Dongceng, 1591–1645), had led a failed campaign of resistance in his native district of Jiading but was captured by Qing troops, who promptly decapitated him and hung his head on the city wall.[15] Xia Shuji became a recluse—together with her sister-in-law Yao Guiyu, the daughter of Minister of Culture Yao Ximeng and the widow of the loyalist martyr Hou Yan (1560–1636)—and took the religious name of Shengyin; Yao Guiyu became Zaisheng.[16] Neither of these two women was formally ordained; in fact, there seems to be some confusion in the sources as to whether they were Buddhist or Daoist nuns. The important thing is, however, that their life of seclusion and renunciation represented an active response to the political and social turmoil of the times and paralleled that made by their counterparts among the male literati. In fact, after the fall of the Ming, Hou Jing, a son of the martyr Hou Dongceng and related by marriage to both Xia Shuji and Yao Guiyu, himself took the tonsure at the Lingyin si (Soul's Retreat Monastery) in Hangzhou.

A more active turn to the religious life as a response to the political turmoil of the time is exemplified by the younger sister of Tianran Aozheng (1608–1685), a Caodong Chan master and Ming loyalist from Guangdong.[17] Tianran Aozheng began as a Confucian degree-holder but, after being introduced to Buddhist teachings, left home to become a monk. Before long, due in no small part to the turmoil of the times, his parents, his wife, and his siblings also decided to take the tonsure. Of these, his younger sister, who took the religious name of Jinzai Laiji, had from an early age been known for both her strength of character and her precocious intelligence. She took the tonsure in 1647, around the time she was expected to marry. She and her mother visited with several eminent Caodong masters of the day, and Jinzai Laiji herself soon gained a reputation for her combined practice of Chan (meditation) and Vinaya (discipline) practice. She also devoted herself to building a convent for women, which, after more than ten years of arduous fund-raising (the "piling up of gold coins" referred to so sarcastically by Zhu Yizun) and strenuous effort, was finally completed in 1697. It soon became one of the largest convents of the time and an important refuge for women who had become dislocated during the turmoil of the late Ming and early Qing. After Jinzai Laiji's death, the convent continued to be run by successive generations of her students, and it remains active to this very day.

Both of these examples illustrate an important point: during this period of social and political dislocation, leaving home to enter the religious life became an acceptable, and even honorable, option for educated men and women from the gentry class. Indeed, it was a decision that, while perhaps not quite as admirable as actually giving up one's life for the loyalist cause, was still seen as an expression of heroic resolve. And, most important, definitions of heroism became, by necessity, jolted from their traditional gender categories as men and women alike were forced by the times into situations and circumstances that often required drastic responses. For women in particular, as Wai-yee Li notes, the designation of *nü yimin* (female remnant subject) "placed women beyond gender-specific virtues."[18]

In 1658 we find the scholar-official and Ming loyalist Gao Yiyong (*zi* Zixiu, *jinshi* 1613)[19] musing that, in his experience, it had been mostly "heroic and valiant men with steely-fierce characters" who were able to walk the path of enlightenment successfully and thus become models of religious achievement. Women, however, associated primarily with "fragrant inner chambers and embroidered fans, and being for the most part fragile and docile," had been set up as models, not of fierce determination, but rather of "great gentleness":

> If one looks for [women] who have taken refuge in the Dharma groves and transmitted the lamp [of the Dharma] down through the generations, one will not find very many. Could this not be due to the mutual incompatibility of steely-resolve and gentleness? Or is it due to the scarcity of [women] who have been endowed with this gift?[20]

Gao Yiyong goes on say that although such incompatibility may indeed be true in most cases, he had himself heard of many such religiously heroic women in his own hometown of Jiaxing. In fact, he knew of two such women in his own immediate family.

> Since the fall of the previous dynasty, in my district the women's quarters of prominent families have [produced] many who have sacrificed themselves and saved others. Some were able to abandon illustrious glory and [find] resonance with the Dao; others had different aspirations and donned the dark robes of the Buddhists. . . . Their brilliance vies with those of past and present; as models they illuminate both those who came before and those who will come after!

Jiaxing was located in the heart of Jiangnan, which during the late Ming and early Qing was a center of not only fervent and sustained political loyalism but also—despite and even because of the transitional turmoil—an extraordinarily rich cultural life. In particular, the Jiangnan area was a major site of a flourishing women's literary culture, which began in the late sixteenth century and continued on into the seventeenth, a period some scholars have termed "the first high tide" of women's writing in China.[21]

The last decades have seen the emergence of an exciting and increasingly sophisticated and detailed body of scholarship on women writers of the late imperial period, work represented by scholars such as Dorothy Ko, Grace Fong, Kang-i Sun Chang, Ellen Widmer, Susan Mann, Patricia Ebrey, Wilt Idema, and many others. The unprecedented numbers of highly educated Chinese gentry women (as well as, in the late Ming, highly educated courtesans) during this period created a new class of both readers and writers. The growing urbanization, along with the commercialization of printing and publishing, led also to an avid interest in compiling, printing, and publishing both individual collections of poetry by women and anthologies devoted exclusively to women's poetry.[22] Although it was largely male publishers and editors who took the lead in this endeavor, in 1667 we see the publication, to great acclaim, of an anthology entitled *Classic Poetry by Famous Women (Mingyuan shiwei)*, a collection of approximately fifteen hundred poems by over a thousand women compiled, edited, and annotated by the noted woman writer and Ming loyalist Wang Duanshu (b. 1621).

As Dorothy Ko has persuasively argued in her pathbreaking book, *Teachers of the Inner Chamber,* an important dimension of women's increased literacy and publication was the formation of social and literary networks among women, sometimes within a single extended family, sometimes among different families. In other words, these educated women began to do what their male counterparts had long done: participate in literary coteries and "poetry clubs" through which they were able to engage in intellectual discussions, exchange poems, and even take excursions together to nearby gardens or temples. Clearly, this phenomenon of widespread female literacy is extremely relevant to our study of seventeenth-century nuns, all of whom were highly educated and many of whom had acquired reputations for their literary and other artistic talents even before entering the religious life. For these nuns, entering the convent did not mean cutting all their ties with other elite men and women. In fact, as we shall see, during this period in particular the convent became for elite laywomen what the monastery had always been for male literati: a place they could go not only for religious sustenance and spiritual comfort but for intellectual and aesthetic inspiration as well. It also meant that poetry writing continued to be a primary form of expression for these Buddhist nuns, more often than not used for religious instruction and elucidation, but also composed with an understanding of the traditional conventions, demands, and subtle nuances of literary expression. In fact, it would appear that their intellectual and literary talents and inclinations were largely responsible for attracting these women to Chan Buddhism, with its (theoretically) playful and (ritualistically) iconoclastic and paradoxical use of language to help people overcome their attachment to language, rather than some of the more purely devotional forms of Pure Land practice. It is in Chan Buddhism as well that we find the most ubiquitous expression of the need for heroic determination as opposed to merely pious devotion—in part because the goal was not rebirth in the Pure Land in another life (and, in the case of women, in a male body) but rather enlightenment in this very life and in this very body (which, in the case of women, meant the female body that in so many Buddhist texts was equated with impurity).

This brings us to a third major factor behind the emergence of the women Chan masters: the vigorous revival or, as Jiang Wu calls it, the "reinvention" of Chan Buddhism. The revival began early in the century and continued for several generations until it finally lost momentum at the beginning of the eighteenth century.[23]

The prospects had seemed good for Buddhism when the first Ming emperor, who had himself spent some time as a Buddhist monk, ascended the throne. Although astute enough to realize the importance of exercising a firm control over its institutions, he was in general favorably disposed toward its activities: an edition of the Buddhist canon was reprinted on his command and distributed to many of the larger monasteries. Buddhism continued to flourish under subsequent emperors as well, and the numbers of temples, monasteries, and clergy grew rapidly. During the sixteenth century, however, with the ascent of the Jiajing emperor (r. 1522–1566) to the throne, Buddhism went into eclipse. Although the emperor appears to have been completely obsessed with his desire to obtain Daoist immortality for himself, a number of dedicated Confucian officials took advantage of their emperor's undisguised anti-Buddhist feelings to impose what were often quite draconian measures on the many Buddhist establishments that dotted the Chinese physical and social landscape. The ubiquitous presence of convents particularly offended the orthodox Confucian sensibilities of many of these men. One of the most egregious examples of this is the official Huo Tao, who in 1536 took it as his personal mission to clean his home city of Nanjing of its nuns and nunneries. A year later he announced: "Now all of the nuns fifty and below have been returned to their natal families; their pernicious influence has been mitigated, and there are no longer any cloisters or temples into which people's wives and daughters can secretly repair."[24]

The death of the Jiajing emperor put a halt to this persecution, and after a hiatus of nearly a century, Buddhism began to flourish again in the mid-sixteenth century. The so-called wild Chan *(kuang Chan)* of the late Ming, associated primarily with iconoclastic figures such as Li Zhi (1527–1602), advocated the spiritual (and artistic) values of intuitionalism and spontaneity. Although highly influenced by Chan notions of sudden enlightenment, this movement was not primarily a religious one. Promoted largely by the literati, and in particular the immediate disciples of Wang Yangming (1472–1529), the members of the so-called Taizhou

school of Confucianism, it was marked by an outpouring of often marvelous poetry. However, no major Chan monasteries and few eminent Chan
masters were associated with *kuang Chan*. In fact, the most well-known
Buddhist teachers of the period, monks such as Yunqi Zhuhong (1535–
1612), Zibo Zhenke (1543–1603), and Hanshan Deqing (1546–1623),
derived much of their religious authority from opposing the extreme
antinomianism (which many equated with moral corruption) that they
associated with the Chan school. That is, although they certainly did
teach meditation, they placed equal, if not greater, emphasis on devotional practices, scriptural study, meritorious works, and moral discipline.
They also, to a large extent, advocated a more traditional role for religious women: preferably the pious performance of devotional practices
within the privacy of the home's inner quarters or, in special cases, within
the cloistered confines of a convent.[25]

Just as active during this time, although far less well known today,
was Chan master Miyun Yuanwu (1566–1642). Together with his twelve
Dharma successors, he embarked on an energetic attempt to revive what
he called the "orthodoxy of the Linji school" *(Linji zhengzong)* and to
recover what he considered to be the true spirit of the great Tang master
Linji Yixuan (d. 866) This endeavor involved primarily two strategies. The
first was a renewed emphasis on nonverbal teaching methods, in particular the "blows and shouts" *(banghe)* that were said to have been used, with
apparently extraordinary results, by Linji and his immediate disciples.
It was these "blows and shouts," he felt, that represented the very heart
of the method of Linji himself. Huang Duanbo (?–1645), a well-known
Ming loyalist and a follower of Miyun Yuanwu, who wrote a preface to his
teacher's collection of discourse records, notes admiringly: "He makes
use of blows and shouts alternatively, leaving students without the opportunity of opening their mouths. Everyone follows after him, and regards
him as Master Linji come again."[26] Indeed Miyun Yuanwu's Chan Buddhist revival found many adherents among the literati, who took great
intellectual pleasure, if not spiritual inspiration, from the dramatic performance of "blows and shouts" and the tantalizing intellectual challenge
of the encounter dialogues. Others, however, were less impressed. The
famous scholar-poet and Buddhist layman Qian Qianyi (1582–1664), who
considered himself primarily a follower of Yunqi Zhuhong, regarded all
of this shouting and hitting as little more than the theatrical antics of
little boys:

> The Chan of today is not Chan. . . . If a smile is called for, then just smile;
> if wall-gazing is what is required, then just gaze at the wall; if beating and
> shouting are necessary, then just shout and beat. . . . Today [Chan masters]

draw analogies freely and lecture to just anybody. The demonstration in the Dharma hall can be compared to actors ascending the stage; the paying of homage and the bestowal of certification of enlightenment are like performances enacted by little boys. They boast to each other about the number of followers they have, the extent of their fame, and the wealth of their profits and patronage.[27]

Another primary characteristic of Miyun Yuanwu's revival was a renewed emphasis on the vital importance of official Dharma transmission between an authentic, living Chan master and his disciple, between spiritual father and son. This emphasis—one could say obsession—with verifying, claiming, and establishing lines of legitimate Dharma transmission, as Jiang Wu's magisterial study persuasively demonstrates, often resulted in the spilling of an extraordinary amount of passionate and polemical ink, both among Miyun Yuanwu's own students and between different schools of Buddhism. This period also witnessed the establishment of the Dharma-transmission monastery *(chuanfa conglin)*, a new kind of Chan institution whose abbots were selected on the basis of their membership in certain Dharma transmission lineages. One of the consequences of this concern for reviving and strengthening what was believed to be the authentic orthodox Linji lineage was a veritable explosion of Dharma transmissions. Miyun Yuanwu's twelve Dharma heirs legitimated no fewer than 495 of their own Dharma successors, and by the third generation, there were 1,168 Dharma heirs in Miyun Yuanwu's line. And, most important, a small but significant number of these Dharma heirs were women. In fact, Gao Yiyong's relative, and the nun for whom he wrote a preface, was one of these female Chan masters. Thanks to a particular historical confluence of causes and conditions, these women were not only able but expected to travel and study with eminent Chan masters and then take on disciples of their own, as well as to engage in active fund-raising and convent building, to deliver public religious discourses, and especially to have these discourses, as well as other writings, compiled, printed, and circulated. As recognized (though sometimes hotly disputed) members of the Linji lineage, they were also able to transcend the purely local. They took their place, if only temporarily, in a religious context that was said to reach back to Linji and other great Tang masters and was part of a larger religious and textual community extending over much of seventeenth-century China.

As this study will show, a significant number of these women took their roles as Chan masters very seriously, mastering the classical Chan textual tradition and drawing with considerably authority and ease on this tradition for their own formal and informal Dharma talks, as well as for their letters, poems, words of instruction, and other writings. These women Chan masters, all of whom served as abbesses of at least one or more convents, devoted unstinting time, effort, and energy to fund-raising, to building and expanding their respective convents, and to meeting the various needs—whether for food, ritual services, or spiritual counsel—not only of their own monastic communities but of lay and monastic visitors as well. They also took very seriously their duty to maintain, strengthen, and ultimately pass on both convent and lineage to qualified women successors. And finally, they labored, with the help of their disciples and lay supporters, to assure that their teachings and contributions would be remembered by future generations, by taking full advantage of the Chan master's prerogative to have his or her words preserved in collections of discourse records.—whether written, recorded, or, as was often the case, a combination of the two.

This brings us back to a point made earlier about the extraordinary expansion of printing and publication that characterized the late Ming and early Qing periods in particular. As we have seen, one of the most significant new categories of publication was women's writings, whether as privately published collections designed largely for family consumption or as large, commercially marketed anthologies. Another important category of publications was that of Chan texts, including genealogical histories, or "histories of the transmission of the flame [the Dharma]" *(chuandeng lu),* as well as hundreds of discourse record collections. Among the latter were not only reprints of the discourse records of the great masters of the Tang and Song dynasties but also compilations of new ones by seventeenth-century Chan masters. A large selection of these collections, both old and new, came to be included in a privately printed edition of the (expanded) Buddhist canon known as the *Jiaxing dazang jing.* The carving of the blocks for this collection began in 1579 on Mount Wutai, at the instigation of Master Zibo Zhenke. After his death in 1603, the work was transferred to the Jiangnan area, and it was not until 1677 that the first complete edition was printed at a monastery on Mount Jing near Hangzhou. The primary distribution center for this new collection was the Sūramgama Monastery (Lengyan si) in nearby Jiaxing, which is why it is often referred to as the Jiaxing canon. Additions continued to be made to this collection up until 1719. The Jiaxing canon contains more than five hundred titles not included in any previous editions, public or private, of the Buddhist canon. Some of these additions were expanded or previously unpublished texts from earlier periods, but the majority were texts associated with seventeenth-century Chan Buddhist masters. Because it contains texts found nowhere else, the Chinese scholar Lan Jifu goes so far as equate the significance of the Jiaxing canon for the study of seventeenth-century Chan to that of the more famous discoveries at Dunhuang.[28]

It is noteworthy, although not particularly novel, that a significant number of nuns and laywomen were involved in sponsoring the carving and printing of the discourse record collections of male Chan masters included in the Jiaxing canon; in some cases, in fact, the primary sponsors were women rather than men. Exactly one-half of the thirty fascicles of discourse records of Linji Chan master Baichi Xingyuan (1611–1662), for example, were sponsored by Buddhist nuns, usually single-handedly, sometimes with the help of a laywoman. And the printing of the entire fourteen-fascicle discourse record collection of Linji Chan master Feiyin Tongrong (1593–1661), Baichi Xingyuan's teacher and one of Miyun Yuanwu's most well-known Dharma successors, was sponsored primarily by his female Dharma heir, the nun Fajin Xinghao, with the help of a laywoman, Madame Cheng. What is novel, however, and extremely noteworthy is the inclusion of seven discourse record collections, each collection from one to five fascicles in length and ascribed to a different female Chan master of the Linji lineage. There are also two additional collections of writings—a compilation of poems and other writings published by one of the seven nuns after the compilation of her discourse records, and a collaborative collection of religious verses composed by two of the other nuns.

This is not to say that these are the first such writing nuns in Chinese history. In fact, from the very beginning of female monasticism in China there have been nuns known for their intellectual acumen, preaching skills, and literary talents.[29] Nor are they the first women Chan masters. In the Song dynasty, as Miriam Levering describes it,

> women for the first time are able to be fully imagined as teachers and lineage members, serving as abbesses, preaching sermons, and teaching by entering into dialogues and Dharma combat. . . . They behave ceremonially as men teachers do, ascending the Hall, as Buddhas to teach. . . . They leave the same marks on the world as men do: in the case of several of the women . . . we are told that records of their sayings, activities and poems circulated in the world.[30]

The person credited with doing the most to legitimize women's participation in the "public" sphere of Chan religious life was Linji Chan master Dahui Zonggao (1089–1163), whose reprinted discourse records, not incidentally, were particularly popular in the seventeenth century. Dahui Zonggao was acknowledged as one of the greatest Buddhist figures of his day and credited with the perfection of the cultivation technique known

as *kanhua Chan* (investigation of the critical phrase). According to Levering, the religious effectiveness of this technique was validated primarily by Dahui Zonggao's women disciples, in particular the three women
who were to receive his official Dharma transmission: the laywoman Lady
Qinguo and two women who left married life to become nuns and Chan
Buddhist masters, Miaodao and Miaozong.[31]

Although Dahui Zonggao's women disciples were the first to be officially acknowledged as Dharma successors (which, as we shall see, was of
considerable symbolic and practical significance to seventeenth-century
women), they were not the first "eminent nuns" in the Chan tradition.
The unofficial "female lineage," revived if not actually created in the
seventeenth century, goes back to Zongchi, who tradition (and mostly
likely legend) counts among the four senior disciples of Bodhidharma.
Although she is said to have attained only the "flesh" of his teaching—her
fellow student, the monk Huike was said to have attained the marrow and
was thus deemed worthy of inheriting the title "patriarch of Chan Buddhism"—she did acquire an informal role as "matriarch" over the centuries. (In tracing the Chan lineage to its Indian origins, Mahakashyapa is
often referred to as the first person to have received the "special" wordless
Dharma transmission from the Buddha, and thus the first Indian patriarch of Chan. The Buddha's aunt and step-mother, Mahaprajapati, traditionally credited with having persuaded him—with the intervention of
his male disciple Ananda—to agree to the formation of a female sangha,
regarded as the first in a parallel female Chan Buddhist lineage.)

From Zongchi, there is a big leap to Chan Buddhist women of the
Tang dynasty—or more accurately, to the stories of Tang-dynasty Chan
practitioners recorded in various texts compiled during the Song and
early Yuan. Many of these women are nameless and advanced in years—
such as the old woman of Taishan who manages to confound the disciples
of Linji and, apparently, even Linji himself. Another noteworthy female
figure is Liu Tiemo, or Iron-Grinder Liu. She was a disciple of the famous
Chan master Guishan Lingyou (771–853), whose Chan practice was
described as "precipitously awesome and dangerous" and who features in
case 60 of the *Blue Cliff Record (Biyan lu),* a collection of a hundred Chan
stories published in the Song dynasty and also exceedingly popular during the seventeenth century.

Although there are numerous references to wise old women in Buddhist texts claiming to be records of Tang Chan history (most of which
are Song-dynasty creations), one Tang-dynasty nun—Moshan Liaoran—is
actually given a record of her own in the important *Jingde chuandeng lu*
(Transmission of the Lamp of the Jingde Period), one of the first collections of biographical accounts of Chan-lineage monks, compiled in

1004.[32] The famous story of her Dharma encounter with the querulous and skeptical monk Guanxi Zhixian (d. 895) is referred to again and again, often as evidence of women's religious potential, in the discourse records of both male and female Chan masters of the seventeenth century. Indeed, one of the highest compliments that most male Chan masters could think to pay a Chan nun was either to refer to her as a reincarnation of Moshan or, at the very least, to assure her that she was worthy of carrying on the Moshan lineage. In this story, Guanxi Zhixian asks Moshan, whose name means "Summit Mountain," what this summit is like, to which Moshan Liaoran replies that it "does not reveal its peak." The monk persists, asking who the owner of Summit Mountain is, to which Moshan Liaoran replies, "Its appearance is not male or female." At this point, Guanxi Zhixian changes direction and asks, "Why doesn't it transform itself?" Moshan Liaoran's response is immediate: "It is not a god and it is not ghost, What should it transform itself into?" Her reply echoes that of the nameless nun who was a disciple of Linji Yixuan's and, when challenged by the monk Tankong to manifest at least one transformation, retorted, "I am not a wild fox spirit. What should I change into?" The point, of course, was that "maleness" and "femaleness" are not essential attributes—indeed Buddhism denies any such unchanging essence or "own-being." In the end, Guanxi Zhixian has the grace and the wisdom to recognize Moshan Liaoran's superior wisdom and even goes so far as to work as her gardener for three years.

There were also a fair number of eminent Chan nuns in the years following the Song dynasty. In the early Yuan, the eminent Linji Chan master Gaofeng Yuanmiao (1238–1295), whose discourse records were also an exceedingly popular reprint in the seventeenth century, followed Dahui Zonggao's practice of naming female Dharma successors. One of them was Pugui Wuwei, the orphaned daughter of an official who died while on a government mission to Japan. She eventually acquired a reputation for the eloquence of her Dharma talks, as well as her *songgu,* or poetic eulogies on the ancient precedents, or cases, of the great Chan masters. We are told that these eulogies were so beautifully written that they were often memorized and recited. She died in 1322 and was said to have left behind five-colored relics *(sarira),* the traditional sign of extraordinary spiritual accomplishment.[33] Another of Gaofeng Yuanmiao's female Dharma heirs was Wenjian Guxin, who was also known for her eloquent and persuasive preaching. She established a large convent in her hometown, and later was invited to the capital in Beijing, where she became the abbess of two major convents. She also died in 1322.[34]

Many of these earlier women were known for their impressive command, not only of Buddhist literature, but also of the Confucian classics and Daoist texts. As Chan masters, several of them also left collections of discourse records, which may well have been printed and circulated during their lifetimes. The Song-dynasty nun Miaozong (1095–1170) was particularly highly regarded for her literary and poetic talent. Although her discourse record collection is no longer extant in its entirety, forty of her poetic eulogies on ancient cases remain and, as we shall see, were the source of both spiritual and literary inspiration for our seventeenth-century Buddhist nuns. In fact, Miaozong's name will appear over and over again in our story of seventeenth-century women Chan masters, who as practitioners are exhorted to follow her example and as realized Chan masters are often praised as being her equal, if not her actual reincarnation. The seventeenth-century Linji Chan master Baichi Xingyuan, for example, in his instructions to the nun Zhixue, recounts the story of Miaozong's enlightenment upon overhearing an exchange between Dahui and a male disciple. Baichi Xingyuan then remarks, "If you rely on Miaozong as an exemplary model, then when you encounter others, you will not have to sheathe your talons and claws!" [35]

The problem is, of course, that for most of these earlier nuns, very little, if any, of their own writings still exist. For others, we have a handful of poems and a few sermons. But for none of them do we have any extant discourse record collections, such as the one we are told was left by Miaozong. Even the handful of seventeenth-century Chan nuns for whom we do have extant discourse records represents a fraction of the actual number of such that may have been in circulation at the time. I have so far found references to nearly two dozen discourse record collections by seventeenth-century women Chan masters, all of which are said to have "circulated in the world" *(xingshi)*. In other words, the women who are the subject of this study, while certainly constituting a minority within the larger world of seventeenth-century Chan Buddhism, were not necessarily as marginal or even as exceptional as one might presume.

CHAPTER TWO

Images of Nuns in the Writings of Seventeenth-Century Monks

This study is primarily concerned with the perspectives and representations of religious women as articulated by religious women themselves—since it is precisely these that have been so conspicuously lacking from previous studies of Chinese nuns. However, a brief look at the descriptions and images of nuns found in the writings of seventeenth-century male monastics and Buddhist laymen—as opposed to writers of fiction—will help illuminate the variety of male views of women religious.

Even a cursory perusal of the discourse records of the seventeenth-century male Chan masters included in the Jiaxing canon reveals the significant presence of women as both disciples and patrons. Some of these writings, it is true, contain little more than a handful of Dharma talks delivered on the occasion of the funeral or death anniversary of a female devotee, usually the mother or wife of a lay patron. In some cases, the deceased is a nun, and often the nun in question was also the mother of the monk. In yet other discourse records, we find many more references to Buddhist nuns, although, again, primarily in the context of funeral or death anniversary rituals. Many of these nuns are referred to explicitly as abbesses of such-and-such convent; others note that the request to perform the ritual and deliver the Dharma talk comes from female disciples. In a significant number of these collections, however, we find references to Buddhist nuns in a far greater range of contexts, including "words of instruction" *(shi);* letters, tomb (as opposed to funeral) inscriptions designed to be carved into stone, portrait inscriptions, elegies, and poems commemorating such occasions as tonsure ceremonies, birthdays, the beginning or conclusion of solitary retreats, and the inauguration of new nunneries. Many of these discourse records are of eminent Chan masters associated with so-called reinvention of Linji Chan Buddhism, such as Miyun Yuanwu and his successors. In the discourse record collection of Miyun Yuanwu's Dharma heir Poshan Haiming (1597–1666), for example, there are no less than eighteen texts addressed to named Buddhist nuns, and just as many to laywomen disciples. And in the discourse records of Baichi Xingyuan, a second-generation Dharma successor of Miyun Yuanwu, there are over two dozen texts addressed to or composed for named nuns.

The quantity and range of these texts point to the active participation of a significant number of educated nuns and laywomen in seventeenth-century Chan Buddhist circles. They also give us some indication of how such women were regarded by at least some of their male monastic counterparts. These views are, not surprisingly, considerably more positive than what one finds in fictional texts (although one might well interpret the complete absence of any mention of women at all in some monks' discourse records as a clear example of androcentric if not explicitly misogynist attitudes). The texts that do refer to women are varied and diverse, however, and by no means free of ambivalence and contradiction. They range from a conviction that the best place for a woman to seek liberation was within the home, to an explicit use of Buddhist-nun-as-symbol to make one or another polemical or doctrinal point, to what appears to be a genuine concern for nuns' religious practice and aspirations as well as high praise for their ultimate achievements.

Although in-depth study of the images of religious women in seventeenth-century Buddhist writings is beyond the scope of this study, a general overview of these three major viewpoints may be useful as a context for our subsequent discussion of these women's own self-representations. Some Chan Buddhist monks—especially, perhaps, monks such as Hongzan Zaican (1611–1681), who belonged to the Caodong lineage and who entered the monastery only after having had a thorough immersion in the Confucian classics, clearly held very traditional attitudes about the role that religious piety should play in the lives of women. A Guangzhou native, and one of many literati men who became a monk after the fall of the Ming, Hongzan Zaican studied with several eminent Chan masters in the Jiangnan area, finally receiving Dharma transmission from Caodong master Xueguan Zhiyin (1585–1637), who advocated a parallel emphasis on Chan meditation on the one hand, and discipline, sutra study, and Pure Land devotional practice on the other. Hongzan Zaican's Confucian background, coupled with the emphasis on moral discipline and Pure Land devotional practice, may help explain the viewpoint he articulated in a letter he wrote to the wife of a high official, a certain Madame Yan who, given that she had already adopted a religious name (Xuxian *daoren*, or "person of the Way" Xuxian), was quite committed to her religious practice and perhaps even considering leaving the home to become a nun. In his letter, Hongzan Zaican sets out to convince the woman that it is by staying home and carrying out her household duties that she can best fulfill her aspiration to understand "the great matter of life and death," as well as fulfill the Mahayana Buddhist imperative to work for the liberation of all sentient beings rather than just oneself.

A woman who [has a female body] and yet has the determination to investigate deeply in hopes of fully understanding the great matter of life and death, can be said to possess completely the wisdom of a man *(zhangfu)*. The Lady's determination to investigate and study the [matter of] life and death is to study the Way. [Both] those who study the Way and those who study Buddhism take the task of liberating sentient beings as their mission, but to liberate sentient beings, one does not need to neglect that which is near and seek out that which is distant. Those who encircle and face the Lady—husband, sons, daughters, and maidservants—are all sentient beings. To serve one's husband with respect and not to do anything to cause him to become enraged is the same as liberating the sentient being that is your husband. To instruct one's children in righteousness and not to do anything that will encourage their ignorant mind is the same as liberating the sentient beings that are one's sons and daughters. . . . If one neglects sentient beings and does not liberate them and seeks to investigate and study [the great matter] of life and death, this is then to know the head but not to know the tail.[1]

Hongzan Caican appears to have advocated domestic piety primarily as a logical extension of his own teaching and practice. However, in some cases the presence of Buddhist nuns who had left the domestic sphere—and, in particular, women who claimed the status of Chan masters—provoked a considerably amount of polemic ire. As noted earlier, the revival of Linji Chan in the seventeenth century was accompanied by often very vitriolic polemical debates, whether between advocates of a "pure" Linji Chan and those who espoused a more syncretic (and less antinomian) type of Buddhism, or between different views within the Linji Chan school itself. Women Chan masters do not appear to have participated directly in these debates—in fact, when they do mention the sectarian wrangling, it is to lament its foolishness. Yet they were unable to completely keep out of the fray, especially since they sometimes found themselves used, by men both within and without the Linji revival movement, as symbolic weapons in this larger polemical battle. For some of the most acerbic examples of this, we turn not to a male Chan master but to the Buddhist layman Qian Qianyi, who, as we have seen, did not think much of the performative re-creations of the "blows and shouts" advocated by Miyun Yuanwu. He was also highly critical of what he called an "indiscriminate" proliferation of Dharma transmissions, which he saw not as proof of the revival of Chan Buddhism, but rather as further proof of its degenerate state. Significantly, he presents as evidence of this the fact that women were among those receiving such Dharma transmission and assuming the title and authority of Chan masters:

> In these latter days of the Dharma, the Chan school has lost its way. Witch-like nuns [*yaoni*] and their demonic kin [*mojuan*] ascend the [Dharma] hall, preach to the congregation, and circulate their discourse records. This is all due to a generation of heterodox teachers and blind Chan followers who indiscriminately bestow the seal of transmission. Oiled heads and rouged cheeks wrangle over who will grasp the fly whisk; untouchable slave girls are elevated to the status of lineage masters.

As is well known, Qian Qianyi was by no means unsympathetic to female aspirations: he edited a substantial anthology of women's writings, with the help of his wife, the famous late-Ming poet and ex-courtesan Liu Rushi, and was in general quite supportive of women who pushed the social and cultural envelope. However, we also find a similar vitriolic polemic against female Chan practitioners elsewhere in his writings. In one instance, he again rails against the "women of today . . . who seek the Way of leaving the world":

> [Some] in seeking it, cling to appearances, paying homage, reciting prayers, exhorting zealously and distributing alms. Their mouths are like lotus flowers, but their hearts are like thorns and thistles and all of their womanly appearances are still in place, not to mention [the questions of life and death]. [Some] in seeking it shatter appearances: abandoning propriety and regulations, they plagiarize [others'] words and phrases and plunder the expedient teaching devices of the old women [of the Chan texts] and collect together all of their words and talks. [In so doing,] they plummet into hell as swiftly as an arrow: they certainly cannot be said have escaped [the wheel of] life and death.[2]

Although this passage does seem to indicate the limits of Qian Qianyi's tolerance for women's active participation in religious activities, it is clear that his primary target was not women per se but rather the antinomian Chan practices espoused by Miyun Yuanwu and his circle, which included not only the "blows and shouts" but a renewed interest in re-creating the dialogues and discourses found in Chan texts. Qian

Qianyi himself espoused the combined practice *(shuangxiu)* of Pure Land and Chan as taught by Yunqi Zhuhong and others, which preserved the focus on pious devotion, good works, and—in the case of women—a praiseworthy death with the promise of rebirth sans the female body in Amitabha's Pure Land. It certainly did not encourage women to abandon their traditional religious roles as models of piety, much less to ascend the dais and publicly play the role of Chan master. We see an explicit articulation of this view in a funerary inscription that Qian Qianyi composed for Chaoyin, a nun who entered the religious life only after having raised a family and conscientiously served both her parents and her in-laws. In this inscription, Qian Qianyi draws a sharp contrast between Chaoyin and other types of nuns who, like their male Chan counterparts, appear to Qian to be more interested in public performance than in private practice:

> Nowadays, there are so many women who have taken the precepts in the Chan school and vie to assume the honorary position of priests [*ācāryas*]. Their dressing cases are filled with discourse records and religious poems *(gatha)* all mixed up with their rouge and powders. Some have [even] received the Dharma verification of eminent masters, and establish branch sects of the transmitted lineage. This is not the way to be a nun *(biqiuni)* [who should] flee the marketplace and distance herself from vulgar people and should not broadcast her karmic affinity for traveling to visit [religious teachers *(canfang)*] or [claim to be the eminent] successor in the lineage of an eminent monk. [Rather] she, with every single sound of the Buddha's name, [devotes] ten thoughts to [his compassion, thus ensuring that she will appear] on the list of those destined for rebirth [in the Pure Land]. In the latter days of the Dharma this is very difficult, and there are few [who can accomplish it]. . . . Layman Xu Bo has spoken highly of Chaoyin, saying: "When the Honored One preached the Dharma, all of the four divisions of the sangha [monks, nuns, laymen, laywomen] assembled together; and it has been recorded that at the Lotus Assembly there were nuns among the various major disciples who attained Buddhahood. However, this is no longer true today. Now [women] stick out their heads and expose their faces almost as if they were acting in a play; blindly investigating and ignorantly [transmitting the Dharma] seal, they dispense with the Buddha Dharma.[3]

No doubt Qian Qianyi would have emphatically agreed with the early seventeenth-century Spanish theologian Bartolomé de Medina, who declared that Teresa of Avila and her nuns would be better off "in their convents praying and spinning,"[4] or, in the Chinese equivalent, pursuing their devotions in the privacy of the inner quarters or, in exceptional cases, the cloister. As the Jesuit priest Rodrigo Niño, in a 1627 sermon in honor of Teresa of Avila's nomination as co-patron of Spain, remarked, "Sanctity in women usually consists in being quiet, obeying, staying in a corner and forgetting about oneself; O new miracle and rare prodigy! Not by keeping quiet, but by speaking, teaching and writing; not only by obeying, but by ordering, commanding, governing; not by observing enclosure but by traveling, disputing."[5]

We see a somewhat more thoughtful critique of Miyun Yuanwu and his practices proffered by the monk Yongjue Yuanxian (1587–1657), a monk from Fujian who received a thorough Confucian training (the influence of which appears throughout his writings) before deciding to take the tonsure when he was forty years old. He studied with various masters, including Wuyi Yuanlai and Wengu Guangyin (1566–1636),[6] and was ordained by Yunqi Zhuhong, all of whom taught a combination of Chan and Pure Land, with a strong emphasis on moral regulation and monastic discipline. What is interesting is that this critique appears in a letter responding to a request for instruction from a nun named Jing-guang.[7] In the letter, Yongjue Yuanxian explains that there are two major flaws in Chan teachings that have contributed to its degenerate state. The first is that it is so unpolished and vulgar *(longtong)*, the primary example of which is the way in which "in a spirit of empty arrogance, when [the masters] encounter people, they mindlessly shout and recklessly hit." He also resents the way (and here he is clearly referring to Miyun Yuanwu's claim to orthodoxy) they "set themselves up as the hegemon over other schools and sects [which] is simply intolerable—they really are nothing but common pole-carrying laborers!" The second flaw he sees in Chan is its "bias and marginality" *(zhili),* and here his primary target appears to be the almost exclusive focus that some of Miyun Yuanwu's followers placed on the study and re-creation of encounter dialogues, not to mention "blows" and "shouts." Although they engage in a lot of mental work, he says disparagingly, "they remain as black as lacquer buckets, and are only good enough to become officials of iron and salt." Yongjue Yuanxian ends with some advice to Jingguang, whose religious practice he does seem to take quite seriously:

> If you wish to avoid the corrupt practice of the unpolished and vulgar, it will not be through finding liberation in this teaching of deliberation [*shangliang xue*]; if you want to avoid the corrupt practice of marginality and irrelevance, it will not be through idiotically clinging to a single post. You must step beyond the tip of the hundred-foot pole, and then the sun will naturally take its place in the sky, and the mountains and rivers will not

remain hidden. . . . How then will you not be at ease! The so-called two corrupt practices will leave no mark and will naturally disappear. The nun Jingguang from Taiqian wrote a letter requesting some Dharma words, and so I casually wrote these in order to exhort her.[8]

This perception of the corrupt state of Chan Buddhism was by no means limited to critics of Miyun Yuanwu's Linji Chan revival. Obviously, although they had very different ideas of where the problems lay, those involved in this revival also believed themselves to be confronting this corruption and doing something about it. What is interesting is that, again, we find religious women being used to make a polemical point. In this case, however, women are used primarily to illustrate the qualities of determination, heroism, and renunciation that the authors see sadly lacking in many of their male counterparts. Muchen Daomin (1596–1674), one of the most influential of Miyun Yuanwu's twelve Dharma heirs, was, unlike his teacher, a highly educated man who had received a thorough training in Confucian scholarship and the literary arts before entering the monastery.[9] He was an extraordinarily prolific writer (Jiang Wu notes that he may even have been the ghostwriter for most if not all of Miyun Yuanwu's polemical screeds). What is of interest here, however, are some of the texts written about and to Chan Buddhist female practitioners in his various collected works.

In one of these texts, we find Muchen Daomin warning a certain laywoman named Madame Hu against the predations of monks who falsely claim to be Chan masters and who glibly produce fictitious encounter dialogues and claim to be able to authenticate people's realization. "It is truly deplorable," Muchen Daomin writes, "how many among the masses of 'beards and whiskers' [take advantage of the] ignorance of women. Isn't this lamentable! This is [because] women of the inner chambers are particularly inclined to 'otherworldly feelings' [chushi qing]." He then exhorts Madame Hu not to forget "the ultimate truth of [the saying that] the Great Way has neither the face of a man nor that of a woman, which transcends everyday understanding [changqing]" and to always keep in mind the example of the Dragon King's Daughter, whose realization was such that she was able to attain Buddhahood in the snap of a finger.[10] Here Muchen Daomin, somewhat like Qian Qianyi, would appear to be blaming not the women (who he believes are gullible and ignorant and also more religiously minded) but rather the men who improperly claim Dharma transmission and just as improperly transmit it.

Another interesting text by Muchen Daomin is a fairly lengthy funerary inscription written to be carved in stone and placed at the gravesite of the nun Daxian of the Chanding Convent in Huzhou. It is one of the longest funerary inscriptions composed by a monk that I have come across. Muchen Daomin opens by noting that the way of the Great Hero *(Da xiongshi)*, that is, the Buddha, is not divided into male and female or even into the educated and the ignorant. Rather it is a question of being able to put one's realization into actual physical practice *(shenti er lixing)*. Only by embodying one's realization, as it were, can one be assured of escaping the wheel of samsara. Unfortunately, Muchen Daomin laments, when it comes to upholding religious discipline in these corrupt times, laypeople are far ahead of monastics, and women are just as good as men, if not better. He complains that it has become more and more difficult to know when people are acting out of sincere realization, and when they are just acting. Not only that, but because "true inscriptions and sham texts are nowadays all mixed up and no distinction is made between them," there is no way of verifying the truth of what is written of those said to have embodied the teachings. With this as a prologue, Muchen Daomin then sets out to provide a "true" account of the life of a woman he believes truly did embody the teachings and, in so doing, put to shame both male monastics and men in general.

From the selected details that Muchen Daomin provides about the nun Daxian's life, we can see that what he admires in religious women is, first, their adherence to Confucian feminine virtues and, second, their ascetic practice and moral integrity. We learn that Daxian was born in 1561 to a literati-official family from Wucheng, in Huzhou country. She was the second of three children; both her elder and younger brothers held official posts. Not much is said of her childhood, except that she was diligent, accommodating, and obedient; and she appears to have exemplified these same virtues after her marriage to a certain Ni Chengji. Muchen Daomin tells us that even after her marriage, Daxian maintained a vegetarian diet, wore simple clothing, and did not have the slightest interest in cosmetics and other adornments. In fact, she early on vowed to spend her life as a laywoman *(upasika)*. However, when her husband died unexpectedly while on an official posting, she decided to become a nun instead. This was in 1593, when she was thirty-two years old. According to Muchen Daomin, Daxian first studied under Yunqi Zhuhong and then under his own teacher, Miyun Yuanwu. Her primary practice was the dual practice of Chan and Pure Land and consisted primarily in meditation on the phrase "Who is the one who is reciting the name of the Amitabha Buddha?" She then built herself a simply thatched hut in the wilds, where she lived in ascetic solitude, "sometimes eating only once every two days, and sometimes not leaving [her room] for weeks at a time." Although family members tried to get her to give up her ascetic lifestyle, she refused. An example of her moral integrity and detachment from worldly things,

Muchen Daomin notes that when thieves came to her house, there was nothing for them to take, and so she herself turned all the storage jars upside down in search of grains of rice to give them. "Her compassion for people and love for beings was of this kind," the monk observes.

Muchen Daomin describes Daxian's death in terms familiar from other such descriptions of the passing of pious women. In 1624, on a day that she herself had predicted, she sat in the lotus position and, reciting the name of the Buddha, peacefully passed way. The room was filled with a sweet scent, and her body remained unchanged for an entire week. Muchen Daomin then explains that nearly twenty years after her death, in 1643, her husband's younger brother, a monk by the name of Shux-ian, converted her retreat into a monastery. Daxian's tomb, by this time overgrown with weeds, was cleaned up, and Muchen Daomin was asked to compose a tomb inscription so that her memory would not be forgotten. He relates the primary reason he agreed to do so: "In these latter days of the Dharma, people are lazy and indolent. In the beginning they suffer difficulties and labor fiercely, but in the end, they [get caught up in the search for] wealth and fame."[11]

We can see from Muchen Daomin's inscription that he was not all that interested in the nun Daxian's doctrinal affiliations (even though, in other contexts, he himself was very much a defender of "pure" Linji ortho-doxy). Rather, what he found most admirable was Daxian's unwavering determination to pursue the path and her total detachment from worldly concerns. In other words, she evinced the qualities of a great gentleman *(da zhangfu),* which were lacking in many of her male counterparts.

The revival of Chan meant also a revival of the emphasis both on the nondual nature of ultimate reality and on the (sudden) realization of enlightenment in one's very body. In other words, it meant the revival of the so-called rhetoric of equality as well as the "rhetoric of heroism. In her important 1992 article, "Lin-chi (Rinzai) Ch'an and Gender: The Rhetoric of Equality and the Rhetoric of Heroism," Miriam Levering notes that it is only with the records of the two prominent Song-dynasty Chan/Zen teachers, the Linji master Dahui Zonggao and the Zaodong master Hongzhi Zhengjue (1091–1157), that we find frequent mention of the notion of religious equality.[12] As Dahui states, "[Regarding] this matter [of enlightenment], we do not speak of male and female, of high class and low, of large and small. In equality, all are one."[13] Levering asso-ciates the increasing use of this rhetoric of equality to the presence of a growing fcmale audience of women students and donors who "elicited from these masters an affirmation of their equal potential for enlighten-ment."[14] Dahui Zonggao himself, as we have seen, had twenty-four women students, and of these, six received his official Dharma transmission, the

most well known being the nuns Miaozong and Miaodao and the laywoman Lady Qinguo. Nevertheless, while Dahui Zonggao affirms often
and in no uncertain terms that realization does not hinge on whether one
is a man or a woman, he also is quick to remind his listeners that it does
require the heroic determination and virile spirit of a great gentleman.[15]

The term *da zhangfu* can be traced back as far as Mencius and, whenever it appears, is always strongly gender-marked; it "means man, a manly
man."[16] Since Mencius, the term was often used to refer to virtues or talents considered to be inherently or essentially masculine, be they heroic
valor or extraordinary literary talent. In Chinese Buddhist texts, the term
was also used as a translation of the expression *maha purusha,* which has
a long history in Hinduism and Buddhism. In the latter, *maha purusha*
means "great or supreme male"—it was often used to refer to enlightened
beings or gods—it is, for example, one of the names of the deity Vishnu.
In Buddhism the term was also used to refer to men of advanced spiritual
insight and, if not of gods, then of bodhisattvas. *The Treatise on the Great
Gentleman (Da zhangfu lun, T.* 1577), translated in the early fifth century
by the monk Daotai and attributed to the Indian teacher Tibolo Pusa of
the Northern Liang (397–439), provides this definition: "Those who are
only able to cultivate merit, but are lacking in wisdom and compassion
may be called 'gentleman.' Those who possess merit and wisdom may be
called 'good gentlemen'; if one cultivates merit, cultivates wisdom, and
cultivates compassion, one may be called 'a great gentleman.'"[17]

Dahui Zonggao and other Buddhist teachers and preachers realized,
of course, that the term *da zhangfu* was strongly gendered and as such
might well vitiate, however unintentionally, the claim of absolute spiritual equality. As Levering points out, they tried to resolve the problem
by insisting both that men had to earn the title of *da zhangfu* as much as
women did, and that women who exhibited the qualities of a *da zhangfu*
were to be regarded honorary men.

According to Levering, the frequent use of the rhetoric of gender
equality in the writings of Song-dynasty masters such as Dahui Zonggao
reflects an unprecedented public acknowledgment that there were (and
probably always had been) a significant number of women who aspired
to spiritual enlightenment, whether as nuns or as laywomen. However,
there were certainly precedents to this rhetorical use of gender. We find
it, for example, in the great Huayan master Fazang (643–712). In his
Huayan jing tanxuan ji (Plumbing the Mysteries of the *Huayan Sutra*),
Fazang writes of who do not understand true principles of the teachings
of the *Huayan Sutra,* stating that "although they are men, they cannot be
called gentlemen" *(sui yue nanzi buming zhangfu).* Not only that, he adds,
but "those women who turn around and [aspire] to transcendence may

be called gentleman" *(nü yi fanshang ji ming zhangfu).*[18] He then elaborates: "Even though one is a woman, if one is able to have faith that the Buddha nature dwells within oneself, then one can be [considered] a great gentleman. If there are men who do not understand that the Buddha nature dwells within themselves, those men, I say, are equivalent to [being] women."[19]

Chengguan (738–840), the Huayan master considered to be Fazang's spiritual heir (although he never actually studied with Fazang), quotes those lines from Fazang in his magnum opus, the eighty-fascicle exegesis of the *Flower Garden Sutra* entitled the *Dafang guangfo Huayanjing shu.* However, instead of saying that a man who does not realize his own Buddha nature is "like a woman" *(you shi nüren),* Chengguan simply says that such a man "is nothing but a woman" *(jishi nüren).*[20] Chengguan also repeats Fazang's reference to the seven principles *(qi yi)* of the *zhangfu* as, according to Fazang, they are laid out in Yogacara teachings. Among these seven we find such things as a long life free of sickness and anxieties; eloquence; intelligence; and being blessed with the body of "neither slave nor woman nor hermaphrodite."[21] Chengguan's lack of concern at the double message this might conceivably be sending can be attributed to his studied avoidance of contact with women, if indeed he kept to the third of the ten vows he is said to have made when he entered the religious life, which was to avoid ever laying eyes on a woman *(mu bushi nüren).*[22]

Song-dynasty Linji Chan master Dahui Zonggao, of course, not only laid eyes on women but took them on as disciples and declared a number of them his official Dharma successors. This was true also of a number of Buddhist masters in the subsequent centuries, and in particular in the seventeenth century with the Chan Buddhist revival (and not incidentally, the reprinting of the Dahui Zonggao's discourse records), as well as the renewed interest of at least some elite women in serving not only as lay disciples and donors but as Dharma heirs and religious leaders. It is perhaps not surprising, then, that we should find eminent seventeenth-century Linji Chan monks such as Muchen Daomin echoing Dahui Zonggao in their own writings: "In the Way, there is no high class and low class, there is no male and female, there is no old and young, there is no educated and ignorant, there is no monastic and lay. It is only those who have not realized the Way who make all these different kinds of distinctions."[23] Indeed, we find variations of this claim over and over again in the discourse records of these seventeenth-century Chan masters, especially in discourses addressed to lay literati who, to a large extent, provided the economic and spiritual capital upon which Buddhist institutions of the time so completely depended, and in discourses addressed to or referring to laywomen and nuns. These various sets of binaries are not all the same,

and simply placing gender among a larger group of binaries does not
obviate the fact that it implies a wider (and more deeply rooted) range of
social and cultural traditions, tensions, and ambiguities than any of the
others. Thus, if (male) Chan Buddhist writers employed this "rhetoric of
equality," they also had to find ways to deal with the issues it brought up.
It is here, I suggest, that we can perhaps begin to see some of the various
nuances of response to the more visible participation of women—and
especially of Chan Buddhist nuns and even Chan masters—in the early
and mid-seventeenth century.

For many of these men, it is clear that for a woman to become an
honorary man, she must renounce the supposed "weaknesses" of her
sex, including attachment to family and to sensual pleasures, especially
beautiful clothes and adornments. Perhaps because portraiture inevitably
raised issues of physicality and the body, some of the best examples of
this view of female renunciation are found in inscriptions composed for
portraits of nuns. The following inscription, written by the seventeenth-
century Chan master Xixin Shui for a portrait of a nun by the name of
Liaofan, states,

> She leaps out of the Red Dust, establishing herself in Chan.
> Wearing out the meditation mat, no more "yeses" and "noes."
> She bequeaths a fragrant name that will continue on another day,
> And she leaves a pearly luster that will shine another time.
>
> Sweeping away [notions of] self and other, time becomes sparse:
> Cutting through the bonds of attachment, space becomes spare.
> Partial to her nun's robes, she emulates the Buddha and
>   patriarchs
> And doesn't keep even a single thread from her bridal
>   trousseau.[24]

We find a similar admiration of a woman's rejection of the womanly
pleasures in another portrait inscription, this one composed for the nun
Daoyu by the early seventeenth-century master from Sichuan, Yinyin
Faxi.

> Her old granny spirit [*laopo qi*] is extraordinary,
> Such that men would find it difficult to compete.
> She takes no pleasure in combs, makeup, or embroidered gowns;
> Instead she shaves her head and dons the formal robes of the
>   sangha.

> If originally there is emotional attachment, why struggle to cut it off?
> If one lacks worldly sentiments, what need [is there] for rules and
> regulations?
> So don't imagine that the only completeness is between a mother and
> son.
> Uniformly correct in her work, one day she'll touch her mother-given
> nose
> And then she will be the equal of the nun Moshan of yesteryear.[25]

The penultimate line in the above poem is an allusion to the "Shijiu" song from the *Classic of Poetry (Shijing)*, the first verse of which reads: "The turtle dove is in the mulberry tree, / And her young ones are seven. / The virtuous man, the princely one, / Is uniformly correct in his deportment. / He is uniformly correct in his deportment. / His heart is as if it were tied to what is correct."[26] Although in the *Shijing* text the subject is clearly a man, under the section "matronly models" in the *Biographies of Exemplary Women (Lienü zhuan)* we find the notion of uniformly correct deportment used to refer to the Mother of Wei, who is praised for her single-minded devotion. As the editor informs us, "The turtle dove with a single-minded heart raised her seven young ones; the gentleman *(junzi)* with a uniform deportment nourishes the myriad things. With a single heart one can serve a hundred gentlemen; with a hundred hearts one cannot serve even a single gentleman. This is what this means."[27] In this inscription by Chan master Yinyin Faxi we find yet another twist: this single-minded attention need not be focused only on one's maternal duties. If a woman wants to count herself on a par with the famous Tang-dynasty nun Moshan Liaoran, then she must apply that focus to her religious practice.

This brings us to a particularly prominent motif in the representation of religious women during this period. Although women were labeled and lauded as *da zhangfu*, or great men, they were compared not to men in general but to "honorary men" of the past, both mythical and historical. The most common comparisons to mythical women were to the Dragon King's Daughter from the *Lotus Sutra* and the Heavenly Goddess from the *Vimalakirti Sutra;* the most ubiquitous references to historical women are to the sixth-century Zongchi, the Tang-dynasty Moshan Liaoran, and the Song-dynasty Miaozong. Xiuye Minglin (1614–1660), a Chan master from Sichuan who was first ordained by Miyun Yuanwu, for example, exhorts the nun Jiyun Xiang to cultivate a true realization so that she can effectively maintain the "bloodline of Moshan's way" *(Moshan daomo).*[28]

Combining both the rhetoric of heroism and the call to join the female lineage of exemplary women, another Linji Chan monk, Xing-

kong Xingtai (1608–1678), begins a Dharma talk delivered on the occasion of a nun receiving the tonsure as follows: "Having discarded the white
[clothes of a layperson] and donned the black [clothes of a monastic],
she has distanced herself from worldly dust. Although a woman, she [now
can be regarded] as having the body of a man [*nüzhong que you zhangfu
shen*]." Xingkong Xingtai then refers to examples of previous women who
had also accomplished this feat, including not only the Dragon King's
Daughter, Moshan Liaoran, and Miaozong but also the Tang-dynasty nun
Shiji, who visited the monk Juzhi in his mountain retreat but refused to
remove her hat unless he could reply satisfactorily to her questions. He
couldn't. Xingkong Xingtai then exhorts the newly tonsured nun: "Only
if you are able to achieve this sort of marvelous efficacy [*miaoyong*] will
you be able to benefit yourself and benefit others, and only then will you
have achieved realization and inherited the way. . . . With a thousand
chisels, one can break open the waters of the Three Gorges; but even with
nine carts, it is difficult to hold back the heart of a *zhangfu*." [29]

In other words, although these women Chan masters were considered to be—and, what is most important, considered themselves to be—
legitimate inheritors of the lineage of Linji, they were at the same time
considered to be—and considered themselves to be—inheritors of the
female lineage represented by women from Mahaprajapati to Moshan to
Miaozong. In other words, although they were in some ways considered
to have "transcended gender," their gender remained an important mark
of identification.

One of the most important sources of this notion of a dual lineage
is the story of Moshan Liaoran and the monk Guanxi, who, having been
bested by the nun in Dharma debate, admitted defeat and worked as her
gardener for three years in order to learn from her—one of the few examples we have in Chan textual history of an established male Chan master
actually studying with a female Chan master. The Moshan story is the basis
for a very interesting account found in the *yulu* of Chan master Baichi
Xingyuan, a Dharma grandson of Miyun Yuanwu. This text presumably
records a Dharma dialogue that took place at the Cloud-Dwelling Convent (Yunzhu an) in Shanghai, where Baichi Xingyuan had been invited
to inscribe and install a special name plaque for the convent. Those gathered for the occasion included not only the prioress *(shangzuo)* Zhaoyun
and her nuns but also various male lay donors, one of whom, Lingmin,
opens the dialogue by raising the following question: "I have heard that
the monk Guanxi once said: 'I obtained a half dipperful from Grandfather Linji [Linji *yeye*] and a half dipperful from Grandmother Moshan
[Moshan *niangniang*], which together make a full dipperful.' What does
he mean by combining the two to make a full dipperful?" When Baichi

Xingyuan responds only that "the one who eats understands the compassion [of those who feed]," the layman raises the question that he probably finds most puzzling: "If the *zhangfu* [e.g., Guanxi] had already penetrated the Way of Heaven [*tianlu*], why then did he bow his head and for three years work as [Moshan's] gardener?"[30] From the subsequent dialogue, it appears that what this layman is trying to do is construct parallels between Moshan and the abbess of the Cloud-Dwelling Convent, and between Guanxi and Baichi Xingyuan, who in this case has taken the trouble to travel to this convent, thus, in the eyes of certain beholders, implying a degree of subordination. Baichi Xingyuan, in typical Chan-master fashion, consistently refuses to answer these questions directly, but it is clear from what he does say that he rejects this perception of hierarchical duality. What is most important, however, is this notion of a dual parentage: Linji as grandfather (or patriarch) and Moshan as grandmother (matriarch). Although there are a number of instances where this notion appears in discourses directed solely at monks, it is primarily applied by these male Chan masters to Chan women practitioners.

A related motif found in these texts is that of *laopo Chan*, or Grandmother Chan. There are many well-known references in Chan texts to nameless old women who nevertheless possess a superior understanding. For instance, one of the most famous koans in the Chan Buddhist tradition revolves around Linji and his monks' encounter with the old woman of Mount Tai. As Ding-hwa E. Hsieh notes, the frequent appearance of these "humble and yet spiritually advanced female figures in [Chan] encounter dialogues helps to illuminate the need to renounce all kinds of dualistic thought in the pursuit of religious attainment."[31] She notes as well that, in the Song dynasty, "[Chan] masters probably also used these stories to inspire their male students to make greater efforts in their practice: if a lower-class old woman could attain the highest goal of the [Chan] path, why could they not do so as well?" While there is no question that these stories of enlightened old women were used in much the same way in the seventeenth century, what is different is that they were also used to inspire women to make greater efforts; for example, if this humble old lady could do it, why not a relatively well-educated woman from the gentry class like you? We had a glimpse of this new trend through the rather negative lens of Qian Qianyi, when he groused over the growing popularity of Chan Buddhism among women who not only abandoned propriety and regulations but plundered "the expedient teaching devices of the old women [of the Chan texts] and took them for their own." A more positive spin is provided by Baichi Xingyuan. In his "words of instruction" addressed to a certain Huang *daopo* ("old woman of the Way" Huang), Baichi Xingyuan refers to the high spiritual achievements of Ling *xingpo* (old woman postulant Ling), who is mentioned in the *Transmission of the Lamp of the Jingde Period* as someone who engaged in Dharma debate with, and ultimately served as teacher of, the Tang-dynasty Chan master Foubei. Baichi Xingyuan then exhorts Huang *daopo* to follow in the footsteps of Ling *xingpo* and exert herself in the search for enlightenment, for if she is successful, Huang *daopo* will become eligible for the title of "gentleman among women" and for "serving as a great model for the world" (*shijian zuo da bangyang*).[32] In short, just as a female religious practitioner might be praised for her *da zhangfu qi* (great gentleman-like spirit), she might also be praised for her *laopo qi* (old granny-like spirit), as in the portrait inscription of the nun Daoyu quoted earlier.

Closely related to this is the use of the term "granny compassion" (*laopo xin* or *laopo xinqie*) to refer to Chan masters who had a deep enough love and compassion for their students to make use of seemingly ruthless, even violent, devices to awaken their minds. Perhaps the most famous example appears in the story of Linji Yixuan himself. Having been struck several times by his teacher Huangbo Xiyun (d. 850), Linji finally fled in frustration to the temple of Master Dayu. When he complained about his ill treatment at the hands of Huangbo Xiyun, Dayu, instead of commiserating with Linji, rebuked him. Dayu said that Linji was most fortunate to have found a teacher like Huangbo, who was "such a kind old grandmother [*laopo*], wearing himself out on your account, and then you come here and ask whether you did something wrong or not!" Upon hearing this, Linji attained enlightenment, crying out, "There really wasn't anything so hard about [Huangbo's] Buddhadharma. Ah, there isn't so much to Huangbo's Buddhadharma!" Linji then returned to Huangbo to continue his training, saying, "It's all because of your grandmotherly kindness [*laopo xinqie*]."[33]

As Ding-hwa E. Hsieh notes, this and other related terms (such as *laopo Chan,* or Grandmother Chan) were particularly popular in Song-dynasty Chan circles. She speculates—rightly, I believe—that the use of such terms may reflect the self-perception of Song Chan monks: "In addition to their nurturing role as teachers, [Chan] monks may have seen themselves—at least compared to their Confucian male counterparts—as powerless and marginal. Yet their description of themselves as 'humble old women' was used positively to express their renunciation of worldly prestige and power."[34] Such use of these terms for male monastic self-legitimation certainly continues into the seventeenth century. In fact, in the spirit of "re-creation," there are accounts of these seventeenth-century masters' own encounters with such nameless old women.[35] However, we also find these terms used in reference to women Chan masters. Hsieh notes that "the vivid, and sometimes vulgar, exchanges between the lower-class old women and monks" may have been attractive to potential Song-dynasty female donors because "they demonstrated the equal access to the highest goal of the [Chan] path and, at the same time, also vicariously acted out fantasies of rebellion on the part of these women of the inner quarters who were always told to behave themselves and be subservient to men."[36] Again, this is true in the seventeenth century as well: the main difference is that for many women, the "fantasies" were no longer nec-essarily fantasies to be enjoyed only vicariously. It is worth noting, for example, that the discourse records of many seventeenth-century mas-ters contain poems and "words of instruction" directed to various types of women practitioners, including nuns *(biqiuni)*, laywomen *(youpo yi)*, female believers *(xin nü)*, and, significantly, old women *(pozi)*, and old women of the Way *(daopo)*. These *pozi* and *daopo*, however, usually are not from humble stock, and most are provided with names. And while they may not be the spiritually enlightened old women of the Tang and Song texts, they are for the most part addressed as if they have the potential of becoming so.

In the case of Chan Buddhist nuns, the term *da zhangfu,* although applicable to both genders, meant that a woman had to abandon certain traits or activities traditionally considered feminine. On the other hand, the term *laopo Chan,* also applicable to both genders, meant that a woman did not have to abandon anything; she simply had to assume the role of the stern but loving grandmother. In other words, once she became a Chan master through the exercise of her "masculine" qualities, she was then authorized—and indeed expected—not only to provide the nour-ishing milk of the Dharma *(faru)* to others but also to practice the tough love of *laopo Chan.* As the mid-seventeenth-century Fujianese Chan mas-ter Lianfeng writes in a poem to the woman monk Sixiu (*nüseng* Sixiu):

> The meaning of Bodhidharma's coming from the West
> is of utmost mysteriousness:
> By drinking when thirsty and eating when hungry,
> you will realize the True Suchness.
> The fruit attained, you will be able to hold all of creation
> in the hollow of your breast;
> And when you deal with others, you will find yourself
> effortlessly speaking Grandmother Chan.[37]

This does not mean, however, that the ideal of complete transcen-dence of gender was abandoned. In the discourse records of Chan master

Yuan'an Benli (1622–1682), a Dharma successor of Muchen Daomin, we find four texts addressed to the abbess Fanjing Zong of Universal Radiance Convent (Puming an). One of these texts was composed on the occasion of the nun's going into solitary retreat; one was an inscription for a portrait; and two were eulogies written after her death, on the occasion of the sealing of the tomb (*fenggang*) containing her ashes. In the four-line poem written when Fanjing Zong was entering retreat, Yuan'an Benli again refers to the Linji/Moshan dual ancestry (the "lineage of Northern Ji [Beiji]" refers to Linji):

> The inner self originally has neither male nor female form:
> [Note how] Moshan that day kept the tip completely concealed.
> Sitting in retreat, you must cut off the road of "sage" and "commoner."
> Only then will you have profoundly penetrated the lineage of
>   Northern Ji.[38]

From the two extended eulogies, we learn that Fanjing Zong had become a nun—or Chan wife (*chanshi*), as Yuan'an Benli puts it—after the premature death of her husband and that she was sixty-eight years old when she died. In the first of these eulogies, we again find a reference to her transformation, if not outright rejection, of the traditionally feminine. He compares her to

> a [man] of whiskers and brows among [women of] the inner chambers, auspicious among those who wear the dark robes, mentally she transcended the clouds [*chaoyun*], and her masculine determination [*hanzhi*] was as pure as ice and frost. She saw through the [illusory] flowers [reflected in the] mirror on her toilette table, and early on she understood the clear purity of the moon [reflected] in the water and meditated upon emptiness [*guankong*] in her embroidered chambers [*xiushi*, i.e., young woman's rooms]. Alone she realized that which was truly permanent [*zhenchang*], and so when she lost her mate, she repaired to the emptiness chambers [*kongshi*, i.e., the convent] and became a Chan wife by transmitting the lamp of the [teachings] of the Deer Park [i.e., Buddhism] and serving as a bridge by which people might be saved from the bitter sea [of suffering].[39]

While the language of these eulogies is, as befitting the occasion, somewhat conventional and obviously hyperbolic, they do seem to indicate a profound and respectful admiration not simply for Fanjing Zong's exemplary virtues but also for her achievement of a freedom of mind and spirit, which Yuan'an Benli describes in terms of largely Daoist imageries of transcendence and immortality. It is also worth remarking that neither of these eulogies contains any mention of previous female exemplars— perhaps because, as the eulogies explicitly note, by the time of her death Fanjing Zong had gone beyond the need for such models and, indeed, had herself become a model, not just for women but for all those who donned the dark robes of a monastic *(zimen)*:

> When she was young, she lost her mate [after which] she determined to don the dark robes [of a nun]. Finding no joy in narrow and petty experiences [*bule zhaixiao jianwen*], she plunged deeply into the wide and vast world [*shenru guangda jingjie*]. She regularly took liberation [*jietuo*] as her Buddhist practice [*foshi*];[40] took being grave and stern [*zhuangyan*] as her Buddhist practice; took meditative silence [*chanji*] as her Buddhist practice; and took charity and giving [*shiyu*] as her Buddhist practice. She separated herself from the appearances of male and female [*nannü xiang*]; she separated herself from mental attachments to the external world [*xinyuan xiang*]; she separated herself from the phenomena of words and phrases [*yanyu xiang*]; and she separated herself from the [delusional] appearance of self and other [*biwo xiang*]. It was for this reason she was able to soar in the clouds over Taibai and travel through the moon over Rufeng, imbibing the breezes of Wulei and feeding on the snows of Ruiyan.[41] Although her Dharma family [*menting*] is scattered in all directions, the principle that they receive is just the one that leads to liberation. [As such] she is worthy of serving as a model for all monastics [*kanzuo zimen biaobang*].[42]

Although of necessity quite brief, this discussion of various male representations of seventeenth-century Chan Buddhist women does point to a few tentative conclusions. The first is that religious women, and in particular nuns, were far from constituting an invisible presence in Chan Buddhist circles during this period; rather, they traveled and studied with some of the most eminent of the male Chan masters of the time, received Dharma transmission and, in some cases, bestowed it on their own female Dharma heirs, presided as not only abbesses but also Chan masters over their own convents; and often left collections of their recorded discourses as well as their poetry, letters, and other writings. Some male Buddhists lamented the public nature of many of these women's activities; others lauded the women's fierce determination and *da zhangfu qi*. The male tendency was still to see these women as "honorary males," although relatively speaking, while exceptional they were not necessarily exceptions, as there were certainly quite a few of them. And, although they certainly acknowledged that officially designated women Chan masters had a right to take their place in the ranks of the patriarchal lineage, they also tended to place them in the female lineage represented by Zongchi, Moshan Liaoran, Miaozong, and others. And finally, there is no question that these religious women seem to have been unable to avoid both being compared to female models of the past and, in the end, being set up as models for women of the present and future. In short, even if they were able to escape the restrictions of traditional feminine rules and regulations, they were still not freed of the responsibility to serve as exemplary women.

CHAPTER THREE

The Making of a Woman Chan Master

Qiyuan Xinggang

Q iyuan Xinggang (1597–1654) can be considered the grande dame or, perhaps more appropriately, the matriarch of seventeenth-century women Chan masters, not only because she was the one of the first to set foot on the stage in that century but also because she left seven women Dharma successors, one of whom wrote a relatively detailed biographical account *(xingzhuang)* of her teacher's life.[1] Much like European vitae of the saints, that account was written not primarily as self-revelation but rather as a record of character and deeds that might serve as a model for later generations. This is true, in fact, of much of traditional Chinese biographical writing, particularly as related to women. Nevertheless, while largely exemplary in intent, these accounts can differ considerably as to detail and tone, depending on the subgenre to which they belong: *nianpu* (chronological records), *liezhuan* (biographies of exemplary persons), *lienü zhuan* (biographies of exemplary women), *xingshi* or *xingzhuang* (factual records of a life), *zixu* (self-written biography), *taming* (funerary stupa inscription), and so on. Susan Mann differentiates, for example, between the *lienü zhuan* and the *xingzhuang* as follows:

> The "factual record" is an intimate biographical form that could be written only by someone personally acquainted with the subject and/or her family. In contrast, the "exemplary woman" biography is what a scholar of the time might have considered a routine, even formulaic, writing assignment.[2]

It is significant, then, that some of the most valuable information about and insight into Qiyuan Xinggang's life is found in the *xingzhuang* compiled not by a male patron or disciple but by one of her own closest female disciples, Yikui Chaochen, who was indeed in a position to observe her teacher's everyday behavior (xing).[3] What this means is that although clearly the primary purpose of such writing remains exemplary, there is often a more "intimate" and thus somewhat more revealing tone than one might otherwise expect in a biography of this sort. It must be emphasized that even Yikui Chaochen's account does adhere fairly closely to established conventions of how a Chan master's life should be written. Nevertheless, when one considers that the descriptions are compiled and written by a woman about her female teacher, and that the activities described—including chastising male literati visitors for their superficial glibness—are being carried out by a woman Chan master, then they immediately acquire a new significance. And of course there are certain issues that are particular to the story of a woman religious, such as the questions of how to deal properly with marriage (especially when one is not so inclined), widowhood, and one's traditional obligations to kith and kin. Thus these biographical/hagiographical accounts are valuable not only for the information they occasionally provide, but above all for their descriptions of religious women's lives as related by religious women themselves.

Yikui Chaochen's xingzhuang is supplemented by another, shorter biographical text, in this case an inscription written in 1558 for Qiyuan Xinggang's funerary stupa by the well-known literati-official Wu Zhu (zi Dingwu, 1597–1682, jinshi 1618).[4] Wu Zhu was a personal acquaintance of Qiyuan Xinggang. Her discourse record collection includes several letters and poems addressed to him, and it is clear that he was an active Dharma patron. Moreover, his wife, Madame Qian, was a most devoted lay disciple of Qiyuan Xinggang. Thus his inscription is based on personal knowledge rather than secondhand information, as was often the case in such texts.

From these two major sources, supplemented by brief notices found in local gazetteers and other writings, we can reconstruct the following basic outline of Qiyuan Xinggang's life. She was born in Jiaxing, the only child of a retired scholar (jushi) by the name of Hu Rihua (his zi, or style name was Yangsu, or "nourishing the simple," a possible indication of his eremitic inclinations). It appears that her mother was Hu's concubine, Madame Tao, rather than his primary wife, Madame Gao, although from the wording of Yikui Chaochen's account, Qiyuan Xinggang regarded them both as her mothers. Although I have been unable to find any biographical information on Hu Rihua, it is quite likely that the motivation behind his retirement was political and that he was, like many if not most of the other literati men and women of this area, a confirmed Ming loyalist. It is not surprising to hear that Qiyuan Xinggang showed signs of her religious inclinations early on: Yikui Chaochen notes that even as a young girl, Qiyuan Xinggang was known for her earnest sincerity and her fondness for Buddha recitation *(nianfo)*. Religious precociousness is, of course, a standard feature of many hagiographic accounts, both Eastern and Western; in the Buddhist case, it is often attributed to the child's being born with a karmic predisposition for the religious life brought over from previous lives. We also learn that Qiyuan Xinggang, like many other women of her class, received an education; as an only child, she may even have been tutored by her father. Here too she showed a certain precocity; her name—in this case, "Miss Hu"—appears in a Jiaxing prefectural gazetteer under the section on talented women *(cainü),* or women noted for their literary abilities.[5]

When Qiyuan Xinggang was eighteen *sui,*[6] she was engaged to an aspiring degree-candidate by the name of Chang Gongzhen, who, however, unexpectedly died before the marriage could be formalized. In the Ming-Qing period it was expected of women left in this position that they would devote themselves to the care of their deceased fiancé's parents, and it would appear that Qiyuan Xinggang was initially prepared to do so. However, as Wu Zhu mentions in his inscription, Qiyuan Xinggang, even as a young girl, had not wanted to marry at all and had pleaded unsuccessfully with her parents to allow her to enter the religious life.[7] In time, the discrepancy between the self-effacing demands of adherence to societal patterns and the aspiration for individual self-realization and liberation made itself felt, and once again she pleaded with her parents to allow her to enter the religious life. Apparently they were still unwilling to give their consent, not because they hoped that she would remarry but because she was their only child. As Yikui Chaochen puts it:

> One day, she suddenly began to think about how quickly time was going by and that she was not making good use of her floating life in this world of Jambudvipa. When Death arrived, how could she be its master? She became more and more depressed every day and was ashamed of being unable to seek out guidance from knowledgeable teachers. Day and night she earnestly prostrated herself in the front of the statue of the Buddha and vowed that she would realize the true fruit of enlightenment in this very lifetime. Our Master was her father and mother's only child, and they cherished her as they would a pearl in the palm of their hands. However, when they forbade her to eat only vegetarian food, our Master simply stopped eating or drinking altogether. Her father and mother felt pity for her and finally went along with her wishes.

Although Qiyuan Xinggang finally gained her parents' approval, she still had to deal with her responsibility to her fiancé's parents before she could embark on the religious life she had so desired. She needed the permission of Chang's parents, to whom she owed a filial duty as strong as, if not stronger than, the one she owed her own parents.[8] From a letter written by Qiyuan Xinggang to Chang's father, it would appear that in this case she made use, not of the emotional blackmail she had used with her own parents, but rather more practical expedients:

> Knowing that the two of you are healthy and happy fills with me boundless joy. . . . What I wish to speak about is the matter of land. In the past, when I bid you farewell, I met with the two of you face-to-face and confessed to you my many faults. I was feeling acutely conscious that the matter of life and death was one of great importance, and that Death's messenger would arrive before much time had passed, and when he showed up, he would not wait. And so I vowed that I would get to the heart of this matter. Having left my family and abandoned the secular life, I am no longer in a position to conduct the [ancestral] sacrifices and am unable to fulfill the social norms of filial behavior. It is for this reason that I wish to take the several *mu* of land that I myself purchased and give it to the two of you for your own use. In so doing, I hope to express my feelings and to atone for the sin of unfiliality. In the future, you will then be able to bequeath it to your descendants, who will carry out the [ancestral] sacrifices and fulfill all of the duties to the Chang family that should have been mine. On the eighth day of the fourth month of last year, I closed the gates and put everything aside. The so-called transmission of the mind-seal of the Buddha and the following of the Buddha's wise command is by no means a trifling matter. That is why I am [resolved] to spend the rest of my days behind closed doors nourishing my not-knowing.[9]

This is a rather remarkable letter in many ways. First of all, it illustrates the extent of Qiyuan Xinggang's determination to pursue the religious life. Such a sense of urgency can be found in many Chan Buddhist writings, and as such is perhaps conventionally mandatory. In this case, however, we cannot help but note that it is contrasted with the alternative of having to spend the rest of her life in obedient service to her fiancé's parents. Still, fully aware of the filial duties she will be neglecting by entering the religious life, and having been unable due to the early death of her fiancé to furnish his parents with an heir, she provides Chang's parents with some land that she says she has purchased, probably with the money from her dowry. This land can then be given to other family members who will be in a better position to offer the ancestral sacrifices.

Qiyuan Xinggang, now twenty-six *sui* and having been a "widow" for over eight years, finally felt free to focus single-mindedly on her religious pursuits. She could have spent the rest of her life in her home, devoting herself to pious practices such as Buddha recitation as would be expected of a pious, but proper, widow. Instead, she took the initiative to seek religious instruction from an elderly teacher by the name of Cixing. It is difficult to say whether Master Cixing was male or female; nor do we know what kind of religious instruction Master Cixing provided Qiyuan Xinggang. We do know that by the time her father died four years later, Qiyuan Xinggang was beginning to feel the need for a deeper level of instruction. She waited for another two years and then took the rather momentous step of paying a visit to Chan master Miyun Yuanwu, who, in the spring of 1624, had assumed the leadership of the Linji Chan monastery on Mount Jinsu, in Jiaxing Prefecture just west of Haiyan city.

As we shall see, one of the primary characteristics of many of the seventeenth-century nuns that we will meet in this book is that they are all described has having been the ones to take the initiative to seek further religious training. Like Qiyuan Xinggang, most were from elite families who, although they may not have been particularly wealthy, certainly were not so poorly off that a widow such as Qiyuan Xinggang would need to seek refuge in a convent for economic reasons. Nor is there any indication in Qiyuan Xinggang's case that she would have been pressured by her parents to remarry. It is also important to note that in the beginning Qiyuan Xinggang (or Miss Hu, as she was still called at this point) was not particularly interested in entering a convent or becoming a nun. What she was interested in, rather, was a more intense and intensive form of religious practice. She was not resigned, as so many acclaimed widows appear to have been, to simply receding into virtuous, albeit pious, obscurity.

According to Wu Zhu's inscription, the first time Miyun Yuanwu met Qiyuan Xinggang, he regaled her with the story of Thirteenth-Daughter Zheng. As we have seen, it was common practice for male Chan masters to use such stories of successful female religious figures from the past to encourage or inspire their female disciples. Although listed as a Dharma successor of Changqing Da'an (793–883) in Wuming's *Liandeng huiyuan* (1183), there is no trace of Thirteenth-Daughter Zheng in later lineage records and genealogical collections.[10] In the two brief stories related by Wuming, Thirteenth-Daughter Zheng is described as a twelve-year-old girl from Fujian Province with "a tongue like a sharp sword whose words poured out like torrents of water." In these stories Thirteenth-Daughter Zheng is described as having entered her interview with the master (presumably Changqing Da'an) with complete fearlessness and confidence in her understanding of Chan. Although at first she is unable to win the master's approval and is summarily dismissed, she remains undaunted and undeterred. The stories appear to illustrate the unripe understanding of an intellectually precocious girl with considerable spiritual potential and fierce determination—her being listed as Master Changqing Da'an's Dharma heir is an indication that she did ultimately attain realization. Assuming that the use of this particular story is intentional, Miyun Yuanwu may have chosen to include it because when Thirteenth-Daughter Zheng has her first encounter with Master Changqing Da'an, she is still a laywoman. However, given that Thirteenth-Daughter Zheng is also several times dismissed unceremoniously by the master, Master Yuanwu may also have been using the story as a warning to this intelligent and articulate woman that she must not be overly headstrong or impatient. Hong Beimou, the modern author of a popular book on famous nuns of China, suggests that although Qiyuan Xinggang had wanted to become a nun, Miyun Yuanwu sent her home when he discovered that not only had she failed to complete the requisite three-year mourning period for her deceased father but also her mother was still alive.[11] If this was the reason (and the original sources I have seen are silent on this point), it would indicate a certain double standard on the part of Miyun Yuanwu, who himself had abandoned parents, wife, and children at the age of thirty to become a monk.[12] In any case, Qiyuan Xinggang bowed politely and returned home, where, alone, she grappled with the *huatou* that Miyun Yuanwu had assigned her: "Where is the place where I can dwell in peace with the will of heaven [*anshen liming*]?"[13]

As noted earlier, the method of *huatou* investigation, or *kanhua Chan,* was one that had been elaborated and perfected by the great Song-dynasty Linji master Dahui Zonggao, with the particular assistance of his female Dharma heir Miaozong. Miyun Yuanwu, despite his primary association with "blows" and "shouts" also advocated the practice of *huatou* and, even more important, held that it was a practice suitable for women. In the following letter Miyun Yuanwu wrote in reply to one he received from a lay female practitioner, we see him distinctly echoing Dahui Zonggao's emphasis on one-pointed concentration on the *huatou* throughout all of one's activities:

> In your letter you write: "A thousand *li,* but a single hall." But [I] fear that this is not an authentic realization. If it were truly a real understanding, then "one mind is the Buddha" and "returning to the other shore" would also be superfluous statements. So how can one say that it is in vain that one has been born in the human world, much less having been endowed with the form of a woman! If you truly wish to understand life and death,

you must observe the moment before thoughts are born; observe when walking, observe when standing, observe when seated, observe when lying down. When you have realized that lying down is not lying down, sitting is not sitting, standing is not standing, walking is not walking, then your words will be silenced and your activity become quiescent, and there is nothing you will not achieve. Therefore [at the point] where a thought has not yet arisen, the complete truth spontaneously manifests. How then could one any longer perceive male and female forms?[14]

Huatou investigation continued to be widely used in Chan circles down into the seventeenth century, and echoes, if not nearly verbatim reiterations, of Dahui Zonggao's instructions can be found scattered throughout the discourse records of many Chan masters, both male and female, of this period. It was, in fact, a form of Chan practice that was advocated (although never exclusively) by many late Ming masters as well, including Hanshan Deqing and Yunqi Zhuhong.[15] Miyun Yuanwu, known more for his seemingly single-minded and often strident emphasis on "blows and shouts" and performative encounters between teacher and student in the Dharma hall, was highly criticized by Buddhists such as Hanshan Deqing, who decried what they regarded as a reluctance to engage in the real (and often solitary) work of sitting on the meditation mat and engaging in difficult mental discipline. This certainly may have been true of many monks, and perhaps even many nuns, in the Linji revival. However, it is clear that while Qiyuan Xinggang (and later her women disciples) endured the blows and shouts of their teachers, and even went on—if we are to take the accounts in their discourse records literally—to employ these same methods themselves, their own primary practice, and the practice that they most strongly advocated for others, was *huatou* meditation. Furthermore, as we shall see later, these women's critiques of those who were more interested in showing off their quick wit and passing off their verbal cleverness as a product of an enlightened mind echo, sometimes almost verbatim, the criticisms made by Hanshan Deqing and even Yunqi Zhuhong. The latter lamented, "Nowadays, there are people who do not have any enlightenment in their hearts, but because they are quick-witted and clever with words, they sneak a look at various discourse records [*yulu*] and imitate some of the phrases."[16] In other words, although the polemical differences between Miyun Yuanwu and his critics were, as Jiang Wu argues most persuasively, very real, in terms of actual practice the boundary lines were far more porous—at least for the women Chan masters that are the subject of this study.

In any case, in the accounts of these women's own religious practice, the blows and shouts delivered by their teachers appear to be of less importance than the actual—and, in the end, solitary and arduous—work of *huatou* meditation. Thus we see that after returning home from her initial encounter with Miyun Yuanwu, Qiyuan Xinggang "made no headway at all and every day felt very depressed and unhappy, lamenting the fact that she was spending her time in vain." When a few years later her mother also passed away, Qiyuan Xinggang, to the consternation of many of her in-laws and family members, disposed of all of her own clothes, jewelry, and other possessions and moved into a small cloister that she had built for herself near her parents' tombs. There she settled in to work on her *huatou* meditation, vowing never again to return to the worldly life. It was not long, however, before she realized that, without further instruction and guidance of a teacher, she would probably not get very far. And so, at the age of thirty-five *sui*, she again sought out Miyun Yuanwu at Mount Jinsu. This time, in acknowledgment of her deeper commitment, she officially received the tonsure from him. Yikui Chaochen describes her teacher's exchange with Miyun Yuanwu as follows:

> "What kind of realization have you experienced?" Our Master said: "To be honest, I have not yet [realized anything at all]. That is why I have finally come to beseech you, Master, to have compassion on me and provide me with initial instruction." Master Miyun [replied by] striking her thirty times in succession, and our Master bowed respectfully and retired.

Although Miyun Yuanwu was known for delivering his blows literally (it is said that one of his senior disciples was left nearly crippled after one particular encounter), we do not know if he would have gone so far as to actually strike a woman disciple. As unlikely as it may seem, the imposition of thirty blows, even if only symbolic, indicated a certain amount of spiritual progress by Qiyuan Xinggang. On her previous visit, Miyun Yuanwu had not considered her even worth a single blow—blows which in the Chan Buddhist context are traditionally regarded as indications of a teacher's compassion.

Nevertheless, Qiyuan Xinggang does not appear to have established a religious connection with Miyun Yuanwu, and eventually she began to seek elsewhere for instruction. She first studied with an elderly teacher living in Haiyan by the name of Master Ergong Ci'an, who gave her yet another *huatou* to work on: "The myriad dharmas return to the One, but where does the One return to?" She worked on this *huatou* for some time but, again, made little headway. Finally, after a year of intensive study, Ergong Ci'an suggested that the two of them lacked the requisite karmic affinity and recommended that Qiyuan Xinggang study with one of Miyun Yuanwu's Dharma heirs, Shiche Tongsheng (1593–1638). By this time Qiyuan Xinggang was thirty-six *sui,* and almost exactly ten years had passed since she had first taken the tonsure.

Shiche Tongsheng, who was himself a native of Zhejiang Province, had become a monk at the age of twenty-six. After receiving Dharma transmission from Miyun Yuanwu, he had served as the latter's secretary for seven years before assuming the abbacy of the East Pagoda Monastery (Dongta si) in Jiaxing. He then took over Miyun Yuanwu's position as abbot of the Linji Chan monastery on Mount Jinsu in Haiyan. Although he acquired a reputation as an effective teacher, he does not appear to have exerted as wide an influence as some of Miyun Yuanwu's other twelve dharma heirs. Nor did Shiche Tongsheng have as many Dharma successors as did some of his fellow students. In fact, he appears to have had only had three official Dharma heirs, one of whom was Qiyuan Xinggang.

It is hard to tell what sort of relationship Qiyuan Xinggang had with her teacher, since the accounts of their exchanges are quite formulaic and differ very little from other contemporary accounts of exchanges between male disciples and their teachers. All one can say, perhaps, is that Shiche Tongsheng was not in the least sparing of her because she was a woman. In fact, as we can see from the following account of their first encounter, he makes liberal use not only of beatings but also of the rhetoric of heroism, calling her such a "smart and clever fellow" *(lingli han),* not a compliment in terms of Chan spiritual development, but a sign that at least he considered her to have the determination and courage normally attributed to a "fellow." Like her previous teachers, he also assigned her a different *huatou:* "What was your face before your mother and father were born?"

Returning to her small hermitage next to her parents' graves, Qiyuan Xinggang investigated this *huatou* for a full year. When she went back for an interview with Shiche Tongsheng, however, she still found herself unable to respond satisfactorily to his queries:

> Shiche said: "You have spent an entire year [with nothing to show for it]. What an example you've turned out to be! I am really not happy about this at all!" He added: "After you leave me this time, if you do not attain the great realization, then there is no point coming to see me again!

After this, Qiyuan Xinggang again returned home and, frustrated with her seeming lack of progress, gave herself seven days in which to achieve at least some measure of insight. One of the most crucial stages in the *huatou* meditation practice taught by Dahui Zonggao (as well as by late Ming Chan masters such as Hanshan Deqing) was the cultivation of a great existential "doubt," described in many Chan texts as having a ball of iron lodged in one's throat, unable to spit it out and equally unable to swallow it. This is how Yikui Chaochen describes Qiyuan Xinggang's experience at this important stage:

> Hating herself for being so stupid and clumsy [*zihen yuzhuo*], she faced the statue of the Buddha and wept bitterly. Plagued by nightmares, she took her ordination robes, and placing them on the top of her head, she knelt in front of the statue of the Buddha[, saying,] "Given that I have found that for which I have an affinity, I will not let it go." Day and night she labored and toiled, but still did not succeed in having a breakthrough. One day, just as she was seated in meditation, it was as though in that dark room she had a glimpse of a white sun, which was a second later obscured again by floating clouds. Her efforts were very strenuous, and she paid little heed to her physical body. Even though one day she spit up three bowls of red [blood] and could neither eat nor drink, yet still she refused to let up on her efforts.

This determined struggle appears to have led Qiyuan Xinggang to a moment of insight, although not yet to a full breakthrough. That came a little later, while on another visit to Jinsu. On this occasion she was sitting with the others in the Dharma hall, listening to Shiche Tongsheng's exchange with none other than her first teacher, Cixing, who happened to be visiting Shiche Tongsheng. According to Yikui Chaochen's account, when Shiche Tongsheng asked what *huatou* Cixing was working on, Cixing responded that she (or he?) was working on the *huatou* "Who?"—a pared-down version of the longer phrase "Who is the one reciting the name of the Buddha?" [17] As soon as Qiyuan Xinggang heard Shiche Tongsheng's query, and before Cixing had a chance to reply, she suddenly spoke up and took over the exchange:

> "Who is the one who is asking? Who is the one who is responding? Put on your clothes, eat your meal, and do what you will." Shiche asked: "Where is your lord and master who lives in peace with the will of heaven?" [Qiyuan Xinggang] replied by stamping her foot. Shiche asked: "When you are dead and cremated, how will you live?" [Qiyuan Xinggang] clenched her fist. Shiche then struck her. [Qiyuan Xinggang then] asked: "When [you, Venerable] Monk[,] are dead and cremated, where will *you* be?" Shiche replied: "The red dust rises from the bottom of the sea." [Qiyuan Xinggang] respectfully bowed.

What is important about this exchange is that it shows Qiyuan Xinggang beginning to gain enough confidence to throw her teacher's questions back at him. In fact, we are told that at this point Shiche Tongsheng acknowledged that she had indeed made progress but still had a way to go. All of this—the student's struggles and the teacher's unrelenting and seemingly unsympathetic discipline—was traditionally regarded as part of the travails expected of a sincere aspirant to enlightenment. In other words, the ability to undergo and survive these travails is what defined a *da zhangfu*, or "great gentleman." As the male Chan master Shuijian Bingzhen, a second-generation Dharma successor of Miyun Yuanwu, writes to one of his female Dharma heirs, the nun Shangji Mingben, "Only when things are difficult can one see the manly mind [*zhangfu xin*]; only when the season is cold can one see the [evergreen] of the pine and cypress."[18] And so once again Qiyuan Xinggang returned home, this time locking herself in and vowing that she would not leave until she had achieved her goal:

> For twenty-six hours she urgently investigated [her *huatou*], and as a result [she] gradually gained strength. She was just in the midst of a [great feeling of] doubt when suddenly she cracked open her *huatou*. She then composed the following gatha:
>
> > Before my mother and father were born:
> > Emptiness congealed silent and complete
> > Originally there has been nothing lacking;
> > The clouds disperse, revealing the blue sky.

Qiyuan Xinggang was now thirty-nine *sui*. Over the following months, Yikui Chaochen tells us, she had a series of increasingly deeper flashes of insight, the most profound of which occurred when, stepping down from a platform after having had her head freshly shaved, she suddenly felt "as if everything in front of her had split open, shattering both body and mind." It was not until the winter of 1638, by which time Qiyuan Xinggang was forty-three *sui*, that Shiche Tongsheng finally acknowledged her accomplishment. Yikui Chaochen re-creates this last exchange as follows:

> He asked her: "The divine true nature is not illusory. What was it like when you were [nourishing] the [spiritual] embryo?" Our Master replied: "It [felt] congealed, deep and solitary." Master Shiche said: "When you gave birth to the embryo, what was it like?" Our Master replied: "It was like being completely stripped bare." Shiche said: "When you met with the founder,

what was it like?" Our Master said: "I availed myself of the opportunity to
see him face-to-face." Shiche said: "Good! Good! You will be a model for
those who come after."

Here, it would appear that Shiche Tongsheng is reviewing the stages of
Qiyuan Xinggang's qualifying enlightenment experience, here described
in terms (borrowed from common Daoist imagery) of nourishing and
subsequently giving birth to the spiritual embryo, or Buddha nature. In
Chan practice, this nourishing of the spiritual embryo is considered a
fairly advanced practice that comes after having successfully mastered a
certain number of *huatou*.[19] While such maternal imagery was symbolically
gendered and was often used for male practitioners, that Shiche Tongsheng should make use of it at this point with his female Dharma heir, after
having treated her with such ferocity, strikes one as being rather poignant
and an indication, perhaps, of his profound trust of her ability to serve
as a model for future generations and in effect to carry on his lineage.
Indeed, it was not long after this that Shiche Tongsheng finally presented
her with a wish-fulfilling scepter *(ruyi),* a symbol of spiritual authority and
also, importantly, a symbol that she had taken her rightful place in the
lineage of Dharma transmission, as the gatha she wrote on this occasion
illustrates:[20]

> Now with scepter in hand, the lineage continues;
> No present, no past, it soars into the vast emptiness.
> If you still want to know what the true scepter is,
> The immovable Tathagata is in my hand.

Among Buddhists, the wish-fulfilling scepter was similar to the fly whisk
(or, as John Kieshnick notes, "the judge's gavel in present-day court-
rooms") in that it was both a tool of discourse used by monks when debat-
ing and lecturing, and a symbol of authority. Thus, the significance of the
transfer of the scepter as a symbol of the transmission of spiritual authority to a woman can hardly be underestimated.

Qiyuan Xinggang's newly bestowed authority as a Chan master and
Dharma successor was both spiritual and public. However, as Yikui Chaochen tells us (although, unfortunately, without providing very many
details), that authority did not go unquestioned:[21]

> At the time when our Dharma grandfather, the monk Shiche, was teach-
> ing at Jinsu, there were many senior monks in the community. Thus, when
> he bestowed the scepter on our Master, there were none among the Chan

brethren who were not skeptical and astonished. However, when they saw how our Master, by means of authentic practice and the genuine realization, demonstrated [her mastery of] great methods and great functions, they all acknowledged [her legitimacy] and apologized.

Yikui Chaochen refers to this episode again later in her account:

> When Jinsu [Shi]che was lying on his sickbed, among his disciples there was one who falsely claimed to be a Dharma successor in the lineage. But our Master was unafraid of the tigers and wolves, and alone she stood firmly for the Dharma. To this day, whenever Channists talk about the matter of the purity of the lineage, they sigh over her lofty talent and knowledge. Whenever I am reading discourse record collections [and come across passages that] deal with slander and accusation, I close the book without looking at them. It is said that the Three Teachings are a single school and originally do not differ in their [basic] ideas; how much more should this be true of Buddhist schools . . . with their shared rules and common principles.

This passage demonstrates that these women Chan masters were by no means oblivious to the acrimonious polemical debates that were swirling around them. It also indicates that being a legitimately acknowledged Dharma successor was very important to Qiyuan Xinggang, although, according to Yikui Chaochen at least, for genuinely religious reasons and not (as she intimates was often true for many of their male counterparts) for primarily polemical or political ones.

Another indication of how much it meant to Qiyuan Xinggang and other women Chan masters to be able to assume an official place in the traditionally male lineage is a literary one: a relatively new genre of sectarian religious writing known as *yuanliu song*, or transmission certificate eulogies. The term *yuanliu* (literally, the stream from the origins) refers to a form of Dharma transmission certificate that was apparently first used by Miyun Yuanwu's Dharma grandfather, Xiaoyan Debao (1512–1581), and continued to be used primarily by Miyun Yuanwu and his successors as proof of legitimate Dharma transmission. The certificate itself was in the form of a list of the names in the particular lineage or sublineage, followed by a notice of its official conferral on the individual concerned. Along with this form of certification, *yuanliu song* emerged as a new literary genre, consisting of a series of brief biographies of all of the lineage ancestors listed on the certificate; each biography was followed by a eulogy, often in poetic form, composed by the recipient of the certificate. This new genre reached its greatest period of popularity during the polemically tumultuous seventeenth century, with the *Verses on the Dharma Transmissions of the Caoxi [School] (Caoxi yuanliu song)*, published in 1636 by Feiyin Tongrong. This was followed by many more *yuanliu song*, the majority written in the latter half of the seventeenth century.

Qiyuan Xinggang's *yuanliu song* is among the three (as far as we know) extant examples written by women Chan masters.[22] It begins with the traditional first-generation "patriarch" of the Linji Chan lineage, Nanyue Huairang (677–744), and continues down through thirty-five generations (including Mazu Daoyi, 709–788; Huangbo Xiyun; Linji Yixuan; and so on), and ending with Miyun Yuanwu and, finally, her own Dharma master, Shiche Tongsheng. The understanding, of course, is that she herself is the next person in line, although her entry, along with the requisite verse of praise, is left to her Dharma heir, Yigong Chaoke, to compose when she writes her own *yuanliu song* several decades later.

Qiyuan Xinggang's religious training did not stop after she received formal Dharma transmission. In fact, immediately afterwards, she decided to embark on a solitary retreat, or *biguan,* in the same small hermitage near her parents' graves where she had begun her more focused religious life years earlier.[23] Although fairly common during this period, the practice of solitary retreat was not always looked upon with approval. The Zaodong monk Yongjie Yuanshan, for example, remarked that "even if you seclude yourself in a single room, there will still be a hundred thoughts buzzing around [in your head], so what is the value in sealing [the door]?"[24] And Yunqi Zhuhong also had mixed feelings about *biguan,* although it would seem that his primary objection was that many who engaged in the practice did so at the beginning of their spiritual training, when they were as yet spiritually immature:

> When a person has just left a burning house . . . he should not go into retreat right away. If he does so, he cannot know his mistakes, nor can he dispel his doubts. He may want to climb higher, but in truth he will fall lower. . . . I have seen quite a few beginners in Buddhist cultivation that built huts in some remote mountains and lived there alone. They regarded themselves as lofty and refined. Although they may not all go mad in the end, I am sure that they all lose much benefit.[25]

Qiyuan Xinggang, however, had already undergone a rigorous religious training under the guidance of Shiche Tongsheng and had had her first experiences of awakening. She spent nine years in solitary retreat, during which she engaged in fairly ascetic practices such as reducing her intake of food. Curiously, Yikui Chaochen skims over these nine years with little more than a brief reference to its self-denying asceticism. Qiyuan Xinggang's own description of her retreat experience, however, places less emphasis on the hardships suffered and more on the spiritual pleasures enjoyed:

> I lived in deep seclusion with few comforts but determined to persevere. My body [seated upright] with grave dignity, [I made no distinctions between] inner and outer. I pushed against emptiness, cutting off entanglements. Once the [distinction between] inner and outer [was gone], then all entanglements were dissolved. When there is neither shape nor form, one can then see one's [original] face and can gather up great eons of time in a single point and spread a speck of dust over the ten directions. [Then one experiences] no restrictions, no restraints, [and is] free to go where one pleases.[26]

One might also be tempted to say that in returning to her hermitage and locking the doors behind her, Qiyuan Xinggang was returning to where women were traditionally considered to belong: hidden away in the inner chambers. Certainly religion functioned in the lives of many lay and monastic Ming-Qing women as it did in the lives of Song-dynasty women, of whom Patricia Ebrey writes: "What is striking in women's biographies, however, is not the ways women used religious activities to escape the house, but the ways they drew on Buddhism to withdraw deeper inside."[27] While this certainly may have been true for many, and perhaps even most, women, it is important to allow for the possibility that a woman such as Qiyuan Xinggang had, through her years of intensive practice of meditation and mindfulness, reached the point at which, in the words of Anne Klein, "the silence of mindfulness comes from a capacity of mind, not a failure of speech. . . . The point is not that the mindful subject *is* silent—incapable of expressing herself—but that she deliberately *has* silence as a possibility."[28] This sort of mindfulness can also erase the conventional (and, in the seventeenth century, very real) boundaries between the public and the private, the inner and the outer. In Klein's words, "mindfulness eases the sense of being caught 'inside' oneself, of being isolated from the wider world. Its subjective space is not confined inside the body, because to go deep enough 'inside' is also sometimes to touch a point that connects with a vast neither-external-nor-internal-world."[29] After her retreat, it would appear that Qiyuan Xinggang took up residence at the Delighting-in-Mountains Convent (Leshan an) in Xinxing, in nearby Haiyan, perhaps intending to spend the remainder of her life in cloistered contemplation. This was, however, not destined to be.

In 1647, Qiyuan Xinggang received an invitation from a group of lay patrons from Meixi (Plum Creek, so called because of its abundance of flowering plum trees), which is known today as Wangdian village and is located in Xiuzhou District, Jiaxing.[30] They had heard of her spiritual attainments and wanted her to become the first abbess of the newly named Lion-Subduing Chan Cloister (Fushi chanyuan), which had been recently converted from a small family hermitage by the Dong family of neighboring Nanxun.[31] The Dong family had for more than a dozen generations been among the most eminent and prosperous families in the Jiangnan area. They had owned large tracts of lands and had a great many servants and "gold coins that piled up like mountains."[32] By the mid-seventeenth century, the Dong family fortunes had begun to suffer a setback, due to a combination of financial mismanagement and family tragedies. The family continued, however, as it had long done, to produce a number of both men and women remarkable for their scholarship, their literary talents, and their works of charity. Nanxun—today a small, quiet riverside town about two hours drive from Shanghai—was then a relatively new town that had become a center of the silk industry. It also appears to have prided itself both on its academic achievements and on its philanthropic activities. As late as the early seventeenth century, we find a local scholar writing a fund-raising appeal for the local Accumulated Good Works Convent (Jishan an), explaining that its name derives from the fact that although Nanxun is not a major metropolitan center, it has been blessed with great abundance and wealth. As a result, many of its citizens—officials, literati, merchants, and farmers alike—each in their own way, "compete in good works" and "contribute to the building of orphanages for the homeless and the collection funds to help bury the dead." He then notes that the nuns living in the Accumulated Good Works Convent all "diligently carry out the work of pure cultivation" and "are fully deserving of the generous support of those who take pleasure in giving."[33]

The Dong family itself had a long history of Buddhist patronage. Family members were responsible for building, refurbishing, or in one way or another patronizing a significant number of religious establishments large and small in Nanxun and neighboring areas. During the last quarter of the sixteenth century, Dong Bin (1510–1595, *jinshi* 1541) had been a Pure Land devotee and a follower of the famous late Ming Buddhist master Yunqi Zhuhong. Sometime during the Wanli period, with Yunqi Zhuhong's blessing, Dong Bin raised the money for the restoration and expansion of the Eastern Treasury Monastery (Dongzang si), a Chan institution in Nanxun. This monastery subsequently became an important center of local religious activities and was famous for its trees, which had been personally planted by Yunqi Zhuhong and whose seeds the resident monks used to make rosaries.[34]

One of the primary sources for information on the Lion-Subduing Chan Cloister is an inscription by Wang Ting (1607–1693, *jinshi* 1654), another local literatus and well-known Buddhist layman.[35] Wang Ting was himself a major contributor to the Lion-Subduing Chan Cloister, and his inscription, entitled "Account of the Repair of the Lion-Subduing Chan Cloister," provides a number of interesting details about the cloister's history. According to Wang, the credit for its initial establishment goes to Madame Li (d. 1632), the third daughter of Li Yuanzhong, an important literatus (and loyalist) from Meixi. Madame Li's husband was Nanxun native Dong Sizhao (*zi* Zhongtiao), one of Dong Bin's grandsons.[36] After passing the *jinshi* examinations in 1595 at the relatively young age of twenty-one, Dong Sizhao was appointed to a post in the Ministry of Rites in the capital. However, less than two months later, he succumbed to illness and died, leaving an eighteen-year-old widow and one child, a daughter. Madame Li, we are told, subsequently devoted her energies to the care of her daughter and her in-laws; she also actively engaged in works of charity and religious piety. In 1608, for example, she donated lands for use in helping to provide aid to needy members of the clan when the area suffered devastating crop damage, and in 1626 she provided much needed grain and other forms of aid to those less well-off than herself. Madame Li's daughter, perhaps traumatized by her father's death, early on expressed her desire to remain unmarried and, indeed, to become a nun. Her mother not only agreed to her daughter's request but, in 1644, purchased a house and converted it into a small cloister for her to live in. At the beginning, it was very sparingly furnished and was adorned only with an impressive iron Buddha image (said to have been three meters tall), which is why for a time it was called the Iron Statue Convent (Tiexiang an). However, it was more commonly known as simply the Dong Convent (Dong an).

After Madame Li's death, her daughter continued to live in the small cloister her mother had built for her until 1647, when, Wang Ting tells us, the decision was made to expand the cloister. Several buildings went up, including a kitchen, living quarters for nuns, and, most important, quarters for an abbess as well. As Wang Ting notes, it now had the "dimensions of a real Chan monastery [*conglin*, Chinese for *vindhyavana*]."

The initiative to convert a smaller, and in this case purely familial, hermitage into a larger convent open to women from outside the family appears to have come from Dong Hance (*zi* Weiru, d. 1693), who was the grandson of Dong Sicheng, and from Dong Hance's widowed mother, Madame Gu (d. 1656).[37] In the years after the fall of the Ming, Dong's primary claim to fame was that of a filial son and, together with his mother, active patron of Buddhist monasteries and convents, both large and small, in the Jiaxing area.[38]

Dong Hance was indubitably an active Buddhist donor, but there is also no question that much of the impetus for his temple-building activities, especially at the beginning, probably came from his mother, Madame Gu. She was from a well-established family of scholar-officials from Gui'an in Zhejiang. Dong Tingxun, Madame Gu's husband and Dong Hance's father, was awarded a *jinshi* degree at the age of twenty-one, after which he was appointed to an office in the Ministry of Rites. However, in 1632, at the age of only thirty-six *sui,* he fell ill and died, leaving Madame Gu to outlive her husband by twenty-four years. Madame Gu—whose name appears in the sections on filial wives in several local gazetteers—attained a reputation for her virtue and chastity and for having successfully raised her son, but also for her wise management of the household left in her care. She is said to have composed a highly regarded "Preface to Be Handed Down to the Family" *(Zhuan jia xu).*[39]

Madame Gu was also an active patron of Buddhist convents. In Nanxun she was directly responsible for the establishment of at least two religious establishments for women, the Myriad Good Works Convent (Wanshan an) and the Prajñā Convent (Bore an). In an inscription composed in 1689, some years after his mother's death, Dong Hance recounts how Madame Gu, together with some women friends of similar religious persuasion, went about establishing the Myriad Good Works Convent. She purchased an abandoned building and land just north of Nanxun and then, after having an elegant Dharma hall built as well as the requisite kitchen and bathhouse, invited Chan master Yangshan Songji to serve as abbess. When Yangshan Songji fell critically ill and died just two years later, Madame Gu, along with a larger group of lay patrons, invited the eminent master Zhiyuan Changyi from the Precious Longevity Convent (Baoshou yuan) in Jiaxing to become abbess.

Chan master Zhiyuan Changyi was known particularly for combining Pure Land and Chan practice and in many ways represented the kind of nun that men like Qian Qianyi most admired. In a different inscription, Dong Hance even refers to the tension between the more popular Pure Land practice of Yunqi Zhuhong and Miyun Yuanwu's "pure" Chan of blows and shouts.

> People say that great masters of the Chan lineage, if they are to be outstanding, must make use of the methods of citing verses, beating, and shouting. However, the Master was not at all like this. She specialized in Pure Land practice. Her style was somewhat like that of Yunqi [Zhuhong], and yet

she also emphasized study and investigation. For this reason people from far and near joined in to take refuge with her. In just a few years, the halls and buildings were wide and spacious, and the golden statues were shining and bright; later, land was cleared to the left of the convent for vegetable gardens, whereupon the fragrance filled the windows and halls and everything was complete. That was thirty years ago, and now if you look for it, it would appear that no one knows that there was a great master residing in the abbess quarters of the Accumulated Good Works Convent. She did not solicit donations or ask for favors from those living nearby; the Master only taught the so called dual practice of Chan and Pure Land, and she upheld it very closely. Truly, Chan and Pure Land are indeed not mutually incompatible; in fact they are mutually beneficial.[40]

While the Buddhist laymen and women of Jiaxing were clearly aware of the polemical disputes that marked the general religious milieu, such disputes do not appear to have affected their decisions regarding patronage. Thus, while Zhiyuan Changyi's practice had explicitly represented a combination of Chan and Pure Land, Qiyuan Xinggang, as we have seen, both regarded herself and was regarded as others as an "orthodox" successor in the Linji Chan lineage of Miyun Yuanwu himself. She assumed leadership of the Lion-Subduing Chan Cloister in 1647, although only after modestly insisting on her lack of qualifications and, interestingly enough, only after consulting with her "Dharma uncle" Chan master Muyun Tongmen (1591–1671), a Dharma heir of Miyun Yuanwu's Dharma brother, Yulin Tongxi.

After serving for many years as his teacher's personal secretary, Muyun Tongmen became abbot of the Southern Antiquity Monastery (Gunan si) in Meixi.[41] Known for his broad knowledge and poetic talents, he attracted a sizable following among the local literati, both Confucian and Buddhist, and the Southern Antiquity Monastery became a cultural center of sorts. He also had several tens of Dharma heirs, at least one of whom was a woman, Yuanjian Xingyuan (1601–1673).[42] In 1644, the year the Ming capital fell to the Manchus, Muyun Tongmen was away and did not return to Meixi until several years later, just in time to provide Qiyuan Xinggang with the advice she sought.

It was with Muyun Tongmen's encouragement and blessing, then, that Qiyuan Xinggang finally accepted the position of abbess of the Lion-Subduing Chan Cloister, although again, with seeming reluctance. It may be, however, that these expressions of modesty and even self-disparagement had less to do with her being a woman than with a realization of the troubles she would have in running a religious establishment in difficult and, in the eyes of many, religiously corrupt times. Not too long after she had assumed the abbacy, in an address to her congregation she spoke about why she finally made the decision to accept the position:

> Although I studied with the late Master of Jinsu (Shiche Tongsheng) and received his transmission, I regarded myself as ignorant and had resolved to live in seclusion. However, [given the extent to which] my late Master guided me and repeatedly, through the slash-and-burn method [encouraged the growth of my practice], I wanted to fulfill my vow to repay, at least in some small part, the Dharma nourishment he provided me. Because the Dong Convent was secluded and tranquil, I felt that it would be most suitable for me. The donors and laypeople strongly urged me to ascend the platform [*shang tang*], and although I refused several times, in the end I could not refuse to assume [the abbess's] seat in order to instruct the assembly. The days of release and restraint have already passed in vain with me at your head. The way of Chan has [become] dispersed and scattered; the demonic is strong and the Dharma is weak. If even those of great wisdom, great strength, and great merit are not up to the duties of the office, how much less can an unsophisticated person [like me] consider herself up to the task? This is a grave matter, and if one is not careful in the beginning, then things will surely go very badly in the end. If even our distant ancestor Fenyang [Shanzhao] was invited many times but refused to go, how could I, whose talents are slight and virtues slim, meet the confidence of the donors![43]

Chan master Fenyang Shanzhao (947–1024) was said to have traveled widely throughout China, seeking instruction from more than seventy teachers. Tradition also has it that eight times he was invited to assume the abbacy of a major monastery, and eight times he refused. Finally, when his teacher Shoushan Shengnian died, a fellow monk by the name of Qicong came to beg him to take over his teacher's position as abbot. At first Fenyang Shanzhao refused even to open the door, pretending to be asleep. But Qicong, reminding him of the important role their master had had in keeping the Linji school alive and vital, said to Fenyang, "You have the ability to carry on the great Dharma of the Tathagatas. This is not the time for taking a nap!" Fenyang then jumped up, packed his bag, and went back with Qicong to assume leadership of his teacher's monastery.[44]

Qiyuan Xinggang's reference to this story would indicate that it was out of a sense of responsibility for the well-being of the Linji school that she finally accepted the invitation to become the abbess of the Lion-Subduing Chan Cloister. Her implicit comparison of her situation to that of the great Song-dynasty figure Fenyang Shanzhao would also seem to indicate that, for all her protestations of inadequacy, she did not really feel that she lacked the qualifications.

It turns out that her own hesitancy was matched by some initial skepticism from others as to how the nun, who had just spent nine years in near-solitary retreat, would manage as the abbess of a fledgling convent. However, her dedication, skill, and evident charisma apparently soon laid their doubts to rest. As Yikui Chaochen recounts:

> When our Master arrived at the monastery, some said that she was the reincarnation of the nun Moshan [Liaoran], but that they were afraid she would not find it easy to transform the ways of this town. . . . There were also those venerable monks and lofty worthies who themselves were all heads of monasteries and did not consider her to be worth their attention, but when they heard about the Master's speech and actions [*daoxing*], there was not one who was not greatly moved, and they exclaimed that the Way had not completely disappeared [after all].

It was not long before Qiyuan Xinggang began to attract disciples, and she soon had nearly a hundred nuns living in her community. By then she had acquired a considerable reputation as a meditation master, and her retreats attracted nuns not only from the Jiangnan area but from many different parts of China, including Henan, Anhui, and even as far south as Fujian and Guangdong. All of these nuns would show up "undeterred by the small and cramped quarters." The Lion-Subduing Chan Cloister itself in time became regarded as one of the ten scenic sites of Meixi. Madame Li's daughter, for whom the Dong Convent had originally been built, now became Qiyuan Xinggang's first official disciple and was given the Dharma name of Yichuan Chaolang. Qiyuan Xinggang had become a full-fledged Chan master.

CHAPTER FOUR

Qiyuan Xinggang as Abbess, Dharma Teacher, and Religious Exemplar

Chan master Qiyuan Xinggang (1597–1654). From *Fushi Qiyuan chanshi yulu, Mingban Jiaxing dazangjing* (Taipei: Xinwenfeng chubanshe, 1987), 28:421.

The composite description of Qiyuan Xinggang provided by Yikui Chaochen's vita and Wu Zhu's stupa inscription give some indication of her energy and determination, qualities that are conveyed as well by the woodcut portrait of Qiyuan Xinggang that is reprinted along with her *yulu* in the Jiaxing canon.[1] In this portrait, Qiyuan Xinggang is depicted as a solid woman with strong features. Her head is covered with a short fringe of hair, rather than completely shaved, which may indicate that she had only recently emerged from her period of solitary retreat. One of her hands is hidden beneath her outer robes, and the other (a surprisingly delicate one, given her rather solid figure) firmly grasps the long, dark-colored scepter *(ruyi)*, which lies across her chest and rests on her left shoulder. As we have seen, the scepter was not only a symbol of many years of arduous personal religious cultivation but also a certification of her qualifications and indeed her duty, as a Chan master, to now lead others along the same path to realization. That she fully took on the performance role of a Linji Chan master as well is evident from two texts she wrote as colophons to a portrait of herself, quite likely the one described above. The second of these verses, according to a brief editorial note, was requested by two of her women disciples:

Qiyuan knows nothing of Chan: when hungry, she eats; when tired, she sleeps. When people come to ask her about the Way, she has nothing to say: thrusting forth her hand and clenching her fists, the marvelous mystery is complete.

In my hand I grasp the scepter,
Totally at ease, without a care.
As pure as jade, virtuous as ice,
The winter plum puts out buds,
Ah! The endlessly fragrant breeze stirs!
There is nothing that I am concealing from you.[2]

The last line in the above verse is originally from the *Analects* of Confucius, said to have been his reply to his students who, realizing that they could not even begin to match their teacher's understanding, asked if he was not withholding some secret knowledge from them. However, the reference to the fragrance of the plum in the preceding lines indicates that here Qiyuan Xinggang is alluding to the story of the encounter between the famous poet and Buddhist layman Huang Tingjian (1045–1105) and his teacher, the Song-dynasty Linji master Huitang Zuxin (1025–1100). According to this story, one day the two men took an excursion in the mountains. It was the season of blossoming trees, and when Huitang Zuxin asked Huang if he could smell their fragrance, Huang replied immediately that he could. Huitang Zuxin then said: "That which I see, that which I smell, is just the same as you. There is nothing that I can hide from you!" This is, of course, an archetypical Chan story; the fragrance of the blossoming trees is a reference to the Chan truth, which can be apprehended in the most ordinary objects and by anyone who has a deeper understanding. That Qiyuan Xinggang should make use of the story points not only to her own personal identification with the role of Chan master but also to the straightforward and direct manner for which she was known.

Interestingly, there apparently was also another official portrait, presumably no longer extant, of Qiyuan Xinggang standing together with Miyun Yuanwu and Shiche Tongsheng. We know of this "three-generation portrait" *(sanshi tu)* only because Muchen Daomin wrote a colophon for it, at the request of one of Qiyuan Xinggang's Dharma heirs, the nun Guding Chaochen. In this colophon, Muchen Daomin speaks of the ascendance and flourishing of the Mount Jinsu tradition—or, more precisely, the "family sound" *(jiasheng)*—under these three Linji Chan masters, all of whom, including Qiyuan Xinggang, he refers to in terms of their "father" and "son" relationship. He also refers to them all as heroes

and victors *(nai jie, nai ying)* and ends on a somewhat elegiac note. Judging from this colophon, Muchen Daomin clearly regarded Qiyuan Xinggang as a legitimate Dharma successor in Miyun Yuanwu's lineage. We see
yet another expression of Muchen Daomin's acceptance of Qiyuan Xinggang as a member of the religious family in a text, perhaps also written
as a colophon for a portrait, entitled simply "Chan Master Qiyuan Gang,
[Dharma] Niece." Like many of the other male-authored texts discussed
in Chapter One, this text draws on highly gendered imagery and includes
the now familiar comparisons to Moshan Liaoran, Miaozong, and the
Dragon King's Daughter. It is, however, possible to interpret Muchen Daomin's comment that she was "reluctant to settle for Moshan's half dipperful" as an acknowledgment that she was in possession of Linji's half
dipperful as well and as such was a full—that is, completely realized and
completely qualified—Chan master.

> [Among] those who take pride in jadelike faces and Heaven-bestowed tal-
> ents, are there any who[, like Qiyuan Xinggang,] can overcome the five
> obstacles [that keep women from Buddhahood] and command fame as
> a model [of religious attainment]? Her mind-flower, so resplendent and
> luminous, has opened up the Dharma of Jinsu. Hou! Zha! Suo! It resounds
> to the very corners of the sea. Reluctant to settle for Moshan's half dipper-
> ful, she chooses to imitate Miaozong's *"sulu"* and plant her heels solidly
> like the Dragon King's Daughter, who went south and became a buddha. A
> true gentleman [*zhen zhangfu*]![3]

As a highly respected Chan master who was herself from the Jiaxing
area, Qiyuan Xinggang had close connections with the Jiaxing elite. In
some cases her connections were with entire families of lay patrons—husband, wife, and often their offspring as well. Her biographers make a
point of emphasizing that this respect was well earned and was based
on a reputation for running a dignified and disciplined convent. At a
time when the corruption and decadence of Buddhist institutions were a
constant lament, such an emphasis was perhaps rhetorically essential. Wu
Zhu's 1658 funerary stupa inscription, although most certainly indulging
in a certain amount of hyperbole, does point to her immense popularity,
especially among the gentry women of the area.

> She established [monastic] regulations that were stern and lofty, and
> [because] the discipline was so dignified, both monastics and laity looked
> upon it with respect, and there was scarcely a single empty day [without
> visitors]. She treated everyone equally and was the same from beginning
> to end. When people came for [religious] interviews, [she would make

use of] painful blows and heated shouts. . . . There was not a single one of the women of the inner quarters from the gentry families of these times who did not rid herself of sin, purify and cleanse herself, and, facing north [toward the abbess, who, like the emperor, sat facing south], aspire to the Way. No matter whether they were educated or not, those who heard her [teaching] style would all salute her, saying: "She is the Buddha of old who has returned to this world."[4]

One of these gentry women was Wu Zhu's own wife, Madame Qian, who, as noted earlier, was one of Qiyuan Xinggang's most devoted lay followers.[5] In fact, it seems that Wu Zhu first met Qiyuan Xinggang when Madame Qian, having heard of the abbess's reputation, persuaded her husband to invite the abbess to their home for a private religious gathering. Several days before her arrival, Madame Qian dreamed that she saw the abbess arriving, accompanied by fluttering banners and covered with a magnificent canopy. Wu's wife had never actually met Qiyuan Xinggang before and was astonished that when the latter did arrive, she looked just as she had in the dream.[6]

It is important to note, however, that Qiyuan Xinggang's circle was by no means composed solely of nuns and wealthy widows. In fact, although many of Qiyuan Xinggang's discourses, letters, and poems are addressed to her own monastic disciples as well as to her female lay followers, it is striking how many we find that are also said to have been addressed either to laymen and laywomen as couples or to laymen alone. We find, for example, that at least eight among the twenty-one letters included in her collection are addressed to laymen. There are also at least that many poems written in response to, or using the rhymes of, poems sent to her by laymen; and nearly a dozen texts in the collection of eulogies and portrait colophons were composed for laymen. Among the latter is a colophon Qiyuan Xinggang wrote for a painting of Xu Zhike, a literatus from a gentry family who became a recluse farmer after the fall of the Ming. In her colophon to this painting, which appears to have depicted Xu tilling the fields, she praises his willingness to give up status and wealth for the sake of his moral convictions and for the "loyal heart and heroic courage" *(zhongxin lingjie)*.[7] Like other similar sorts of texts, this colophon illustrates that Qiyuan Xinggang's being a Buddhist nun by no means meant a withdrawal from society. As Wai-yee Li and others have noted, "although the question of service or withdrawal is irrelevant [during the transition period], women sympathetic to the loyalist cause often dwell on their political convictions."[8] Qiyuan Xinggang and other nuns were no exception in this regard.

Given her time and place, it is not surprising that many of Qiyuan Xinggang's primary lay supporters had loyalist connections. Wu Zhongmu (*zi* Fanxhang) was the son of Wu Linwei (1593–1644, *jinshi* 1622), who had served in a succession of high official posts, including that of vice-minister of the Court of Imperial Sacrifices, and valiantly fought the Manchu invasion of Beijing before finally committing suicide in 1644. After his father's death, Wu Zhongmu's mother, Madame Zhu, was awarded the title of Lady of Virtue *(shuren)*, and her name would later be included in the Virtuous Women section of the Jiaxing gazetteer under the category of "wise wives."[9] Wu Zhongmu himself attained only the level of first-degree candidate and dedicated his life to the preservation of his father's memory and the care of his widowed mother. Wu Zhongmu was primarily neo-Confucian in his intellectual orientation—he made his living as a teacher and was a close friend and companion of another high official turned loyalist recluse and farmer, Zhang Lixiang (1611–1674), and of the neo-Confucian scholar and loyalist martyr Liu Zongzhou (1578–1645). Nevertheless, it is clear that Wu Zhongmu, like many of his loyalist counterparts, also had many connections with Chan masters, including, in this case, Qiyuan Xinggang.[10] Wu's mother, Madame Zhu, became Qiyuan Xinggang's disciple and took the Dharma name of Chaochen; she is the lay female disciple referred to most often in Qiyuan Xinggang's *yulu* collection. In the following letter, Qiyuan Xinggang refers to Madame Zhu's grief over the death of her martyred loyalist husband and reminds her of the vital importance of setting her priorities straight, which means that the search for awakening should come before household duties and family concerns:

> When I received your letter, then I could tell that your worldly thoughts had gradually become fewer, and that your grief and sorrow are becoming completely purified. That makes me very happy, very happy. You must first resolve to set up enlightenment as your standard, and in this way see through the fame and profit of the world. As you ease up on your household duties, your thoughts of the Way will naturally become deep and strong. You must know that all karmic circumstances are created from one's own mind, and that if you are able to master the familiar habits associated with karmic circumstances, then you will not be entrapped by them. Focus single-mindedly and without cease on your *huatou* . . . and one day you will suddenly experience a breakthrough and find yourself at peace.[11]

Whereas Madame Wu appears to have kept largely to her Pure Land devotions, Madame Zhu was more interested in the more intellectually, if not necessarily more spiritually demanding, encounter dialogues of classical Chan like those Miyun Yuanwu and his followers made popular. In fact, she often engaged Qiyuan Xinggang in poetic "Dharma battles" such as the following:

Chaochen presented a hymn which went:

The palm of the master—I know it was one of compassion,
Suddenly shattering the doubt, erasing the last speck of dust
Brandishing the sword, sounding the zither: all is the Way.
In an instant, I topple it over and expose the pearl of Truth.

"What is it that you are toppling over in an instant?" asked the Master [Qiyuan]. When Chaochen hesitated in replying, the Master abruptly raised her fist and demanded: "What is it you have toppled over?" Chaochen could not answer. The Master said: "So they were empty words after all. You still need to put out the effort to investigate and study before you will have gotten it." Chaochen said: "Each and every matter I have tried to distinguish clearly, but the point of this technique is still insufficiently sharp." The Master then instructed her by means of the following gatha:

Intelligence and cleverness are worldly abilities.
Linji's Chan style eliminates every speck of dust.
Aspiring to the top of the pole, knowing where to land;
Instantly you will topple it over and match Heaven's truth.[12]

Wu Zhongmu's wife was also a lay disciple of Qiyuan Xinggang, who had given her the name of Chaofang. Once when Wu Zhongmu was quite ill, she asked Qiyuan Xinggang to deliver a Dharma talk on his wife's behalf. In this talk, Qiyuan Xinggang recounts how "once in the hustle and bustle surrounding the eve of the lunar New Year," Wu's wife underwent an unexpected change of heart and from that time began to cultivate the Way with diligence and devotion." In fact, Qiyuan Xinggang says, Chaofang may truly be considered "a hero among women." She uses the opportunity of this particular Dharma talk to draw analogies between the illnesses of the mind and those of the body:

What I hope is that your wife will take everything and just let it all go—the four great [elements] and the five skandhas, fame and reputation, wealth and nourishment, circumstances whether smooth or contrary, the worries of a painful and critically serious illness, and the anxieties of a head filled with ten thousand karmic conditions. Then with a clean and naked mind, she should rest herself in the middle of the emptiness and, with stability and firmness, do nothing but study her original face. If she studies in the morning and investigates in the evening, and does it resolutely every day, one morning she will suddenly and heroically wake up to the key condition of life and death; instantaneously, she will have advanced forward, tread upon, and fully grasped the environment of her original ground. Then both the illnesses of the mind and the illnesses of the body will naturally dissolve, and everything will become lucid and open.[13]

Yet another of Qiyuan Xinggang's lay women disciples was Lady of Virtue Zhao from Xiushui. She was the widow of Zhu Daqi, a well-regarded official who during the late Ming held various high offices, including that of vice-minister in the Ministry of Justice. Lady Zhao herself was held in extremely high regard by the empress. Perhaps even more significantly, she was the mother of Zhu Maoshi, who would one day write a glowing preface to Qiyuan Xinggang's discourse record collection. Zhao Shuren was also the great-aunt of Zhu Yizun, the noted poet and scholar whose rather unsympathetic poem about lazy and lascivious nuns was quoted in Chapter One. Zhu Yizun appears to have met Qiyuan Xinggang in 1649, when he was only twenty-one *sui* and the abbess was fifty-three *sui*.[14] When in 1705 he compiled his anthology of Ming poets, *Mingshi zong,* he would include a poem by Qiyuan Xinggang and, in his collection of poetry talks, would note: "My great-aunt Zhao Shuren regarded [Qiyuan Xinggang] as her teacher and would always consult her about any doubts that she had. . . . [Qiyuan Xinggang] was grave and dignified, simple and straightforward."[15] Tellingly, Zhu Yizun also provides a possible reason why, as a Buddhist nun, Qiyuan Xinggang was allotted a relatively generous space in several local gazetteers: "Regardless of her moral activity in the [realm] of the Empty Gate [i.e., Buddhism], it is fitting that, as a chaste woman, she be discussed and that a few of her lines be preserved as fresh admonitions for the [male] phoenix tower."[16] Clearly, it was Qiyuan Xinggang's Confucian virtues rather than her Buddhist convictions that won her Zhu Yizun's begrudging admiration. Nevertheless, it is interesting that the "few of her lines" that he chose to include in his anthology were from a series written toward the end of her life after she had gone into retreat:

A worn patched robe hangs lopsided from my shoulders;
When hunger comes, I will eat; when I get tired, I will sleep.
Sitting still on my cushion, I will completely forget the world;
As in the midst of all the dust, the years and months pass by.

It is perhaps worth remarking that despite Zhu's avowed intention to preserve Qiyuan Xinggang's poem, he also appears to have seen fit to change the last line, which in the version preserved in the *yulu* collection reads, "I let the days and nights pass by in front of my window." [17] Qiyuan Xinggang's original line, I would suggest, is much more vivid and immediate, showing not only a sense of agency ("I let") but also a clear awareness of the alternation of sun and moon, days and nights, outside her window. Zhu's line abstracts this experience and relegates her to the position of a world-denying ascetic who, in her rejection of dusty or secular concerns, ignores the passage of time. In fact, Qiyuan Xinggang, for all her transcendental concerns, was by no means oblivious to the world around her, whether the world of nature or the more difficult and painful suffering that so many were enduring around her. In two letters addressed to an aunt, we get a glimpse of this:

Recently the world has been in confusion and dispersion, and there is little one can do about it. In times like this, there is only the effort of meditation and investigation that is the most skillful [thing to do] since there is nothing else that one can do; one can still achieve a mind-set that is open, and there one can see clearly one's original face and achieve a great inner ease. When others are like the waves hitting up against the heavens, we can remain profound and imperturbable. I and my disciples have resolutely maintained our aspiration and practiced together. We have also suffered great disasters, and I have advocated sitting calmly. The numerous disorders of the household have turned to nothing. Let us wait until the external situation is a bit more peaceful; then I look forward to the day when you will come to visit this convent as I so wish.[18]

From Qiyuan Xinggang's writings, we can also see that she maintained frequent contact with fellow monks. Once, for example, when an eminent monk from Guangdong was preaching at the famous Heavenly Peace Monastery (Tianning si) in Changzhou in the neighboring province of Jiangsu, she herself traveled to the monastery to listen to his Dharma talks as well as to engage in dialogue with him.[19] Monks also came to see her at her the Lion-Subduing Chan Cloister. She mentions, for example, a visit by "Elder-Brother Zhanxu," who was a Dharma heir of Muyun Tongmen.[20] Yet another layman-turned-monk with whom Qiyuan Xinggang appears to have frequently conversed and corresponded was a man by the name of Zheng Gongxun, more familiarly known by his style name of Yundu. After the fall of the Ming, Zheng Yundu, who was a native of Meixi, became a formal lay disciple of Muyun Tongmen at the Gunan Monastery and later built a small hermitage south of the town that he called the Autumn Pavilion (Qiuting).[21] The following poem was written by Qiyuan Xinggang about this place:

The great earth completely effaced by this single thatched pavilion,
Railings of mist and clouds encircling it from dawn to dusk.
Niches of pine, walls of stone; there are no echoes that linger.
This autumn scene with its empty purity; who would hear them?[22]

Elsewhere, Qiyuan Xinggang mentions a visit Zheng Yundu made to
the Lion-Subduing Chan Cloister with another monk, most likely also a
disciple of Muyun Tongmen's, in order to request that she write a prefa-
tory inscription for a copy of the *Lotus Sutra (Fahua jing)* that had been
written out using ink mixed with blood—an act of devotional piety. Qiyuan
Xinggang at first refused to write this inscription, modestly claiming that
she was not up to the task, either spiritually or in terms of her writing
skills. But when the two men insisted, she used the opportunity to deliver
another rhetorical sabotage, turning the copying of the sutra into a kind
of *huatou:* "Where does the blood come from?" she asks. "Who is the
one who copied out this sutra? . . . [If you can answer this, then] you will
be able to break open the burning house and allow the true method to
reveal itself. . . . If the layman wants to truly experience this, then the most
fitting thing would be to consign [this copy of the sutra] to the flames
so that not a single character remains. Then you will be happy."[23] In yet
another letter addressed to Zheng Yundu, Qiyuan Xinggang mentions
having received a manuscript of something he had written. She praises it
highly but also reminds him that he must continue to apply himself with
great urgency to the matter of attaining a full understanding of the truth
without being "overwhelmed by the sea of prose and the river of poetry."
Only by avoiding this trap will he truly become "a great gentleman who
lives in the dusty [world] but is not of the dusty [world]."[24]

Interestingly, what is being described here is a woman Chan master
meeting and then defeating a male literatus on his own playing field—
that is, the realm of words and letters. As her disciple Yikui Chaochen
tells us, many "men of letters, scholars of the brush and knowers of the
world," as well as Buddhist monks, came not to sing her praises but to
engage Qiyuan Xinggang in philosophical debate. Ultimately, they were
forced to "sheathe their swords and put away their knives":

> Those who came with Dharma phrases and gatha lines, spewing them out
> glibly but without having understood or experienced them, were forced to
> return to being deaf and dumb until [she] exposed their ignorance and
> caused them to awaken to true knowledge. There were also those specious
> flatterers and artful tongues who resisted transformation but, when they
> met our Master, would respectfully take refuge, correct their errors, and

turn over a new leaf. There were also those who came from families who for generations had been officials and gentlemen who boasted of their noble birth; when they met the Master, then they would become humble, and changing their demeanor, they would kowtow and beg for teaching. Men of letters and those who were worldly-wise and greatly eloquent, when they met the Master, they would sheathe their arrows and put away their swords, becoming as if tongue-tied and stupid.

In emphasizing her teacher's uncompromising integrity in contrast to the glib superficiality of some of her visiting literati, those "specious flatterers and artful tongues," Yikui Chaochen was clearly placing her teacher among those who regarded the lay literati's fascination with Chan classical texts (such as appear to have been encouraged by Miyun Yuanwu himself) as a sign of the degeneration rather than the revival of genuine Chan practice.

In any case, Qiyuan Xinggang did not restrict herself to delivering sermons and holding interviews. She and her nuns also provided various other sorts of religious services to the local lay community. One important Buddhist festival was the celebration of the birthday of the Buddha on the eighth day of the fourth month, the central ritual of which involved the bathing of a statue of the Buddha. Both of these festivals brought in crowds of lay devotees and onlookers, and often the abbess would deliver special Dharma talks designed with her lay audience in mind. Funeral services were another important service offered by the convent. The major ritual in this regard was that of the Water and Land Mass *(shuilu zhai),* and in the fall of 1653, one year before her death, Qiyuan Xinggang traveled to Mount Yunqi near Hangzhou to learn for herself the rituals for the *shuilu* ceremony. Chan master Yunqi Zhuhong had taken it upon himself to "clean up" what he considered to be its many "errors and intrusions." [25] A visit to Yunqi may also have been necessary since Yunqi Zhuhong's *Shuilu yigui* was a very terse text, consisting primarily of litanies for recitation, and as Daniel Stevenson notes, "Apart from the most elemental cues of procedure, the details of ritual performance are left to oral instruction." [26] As someone who had tried in her own way to emulate Yunqi Zhuhong's strict monastic discipline, Qiyuan Xinggang was impressed to find that the monastic regulations set up by Yunqi Zhuhong were still in full force at Yunqi Monastery—which, one gathers, was by no means the case in other monasteries and convents. Again and again, we find her lamenting that those who come to study Chan practice are many, but "those who carry it out are few." One must be very careful, she admonishes herself and her nuns, not to "yammer on about emptiness or spread around baseless information simply to amuse oneself and others."[27]

It was Qiyuan Xinggang's reputation not only for spiritual achievement but also for strict discipline and frugality that inspired trust and, most importantly, the patronage of lay donors. Building and maintaining a convent or monastery required constant financial support, especially in the rapidly changing social and political climate of mid-seventeenth-century China, when fortunes (and loyalties) could rise and fall almost overnight. Fund-raising was a tricky problem. On the one hand, eminent monastic figures and more, particularly, their patrons among the literati, found begging very distasteful. As Timothy Brook notes, "The concern over begging may have reflected the gentry's desire that the institutional Buddhism they patronized not be confused with the popular, lower-class forms whose representatives could be seen going door to door with their begging bowls, earning a dubious reputation for Buddhism among the privileged in Chinese society."[28] A better alternative, and the one chosen by Qiyuan Xinggang, was to present a model of rectitude and authentic religious commitment that would inspire Dharma patrons to extend their support. Qiyuan Xinggang often spoke of her desire to personally emulate the strict discipline of the great Chan masters of the past, men like Danxia Tianran (739–824) and Zhaozhou Congsheng (778–897). This, of course, fit in well with the larger project of the revival of the Linji Chan lineage and the spirit of the Tang and Song masters. As Yikui Chaochen tells us:

> To this day, [the fact that we] have respectfully kept the pure regulations and do not depend on almsgivers is all due to the quality of the Master's arrangements. In time, [the monastery] became a hub of activity for Chan followers. Because the meditation halls were cramped and small and it was difficult to accommodate the assembly, the Master added two rooms to the West Dharma Hall, as well as a section of monk's living quarters. They were all completed within a couple of days, and the Master simply entrusted the matter to fate and did not anguish and worry over it.[29]

In other words, although surely Qiyuan Xinggang did receive support from lay donors, what Yikui Chaochen seems to emphasize is their relative independence or at least that, because of her frugality and faith, Qiyuan Xinggang did not have to resort to "begging" for support. In fact, the apparently unsolicited generosity of local donors was such that she was able to share some of the beneficent donations not only with other religious establishments in the area but with the poor and needy as well:[30]

As she traveled through Danghu and Yanguan, she would distribute all of the abundant donations she received to the Chan mountain monasteries so that they could repair their ancestral stupas or prepare vegetarian feasts for the monks. I and the others who accompanied her were impressed by this. When she arrived at Yunqi, she encountered sedan-chair carriers and boatmen begging along the way. Seeing them caused her great distress, and she personally distributed money as she went along. When she met with pious folk and poor gentry, she would secretly make sure that they were fully provided for. When she saw them leap and cry out for joy, she would take her leave.[31]

In the last years of her life, Qiyuan Xinggang appears to have traveled considerably, often to visit convents established by her own women disciples. By this time, her reputation was such that, if we can believe the accounts, even the shortest journey would bring out thousands of pious men and women, jostling and pushing for a chance to get a glimpse of her and receive her blessing:

[Qiyuan Xinggang's Dharma heir Yiyin] from Danghu had built a new Dharma hall and invited [her master] to celebrate with her. Before her boat had even docked on shore, a crowd of a thousand people, all pious folk bearing sticks of incense, were kneeling there to welcome her. Endless streams [of people] came begging her for teachings, and the streets and alleyways were so crowded that it was impossible to get through.[32]

In the spring of 1652 (two years before her death), Qiyuan Xinggang was invited by one of her Dharma brothers, Xigan Xingyuan (1609–1679)—who, like Qiyuan, was an official Dharma successor of Shiche Tongsheng—to oversee the cremation ceremonies for his deceased mother. In the description that Yikui Chaochen provides of this occasion, she even goes so far as to compare the excitement of Qiyuan Xinggang's arrival to that generated by the famous Miyun Yuanwu himself:

The district magistrate, [certain] spiritually inclined gentry, and male and female lay disciples all [took her to be a] living Buddha who had manifested in the world, and were delighted that they were able to look upon her compassionate face. From the city center to the outskirts of town, swarming like bees and clustering like ants, they would surround her and kneel before her, while those who stood by the side of the road [to catch a glimpse of her] must have numbered at least ten thousand. When the lighting of the [cremation] fire was completed, some of the gentry of the area requested

that she ascend the hall to give short interviews, while others begged to take
refuge and be given instruction. The shoulder-to-shoulder and axle-to-axle
crowds were such that it was nearly impossible to force one's way forward.
There were also those who prepared incense and special ceremonies as a
way of expressing their respect, and others who laid out vegetarian feasts
in her honor. [However, these] our Master steadfastly declined and did not
attend, [but rather,] like a floating cloud or a wild goose, she set her sails
[homeward to] Meixi. Those who had not been able to see her lamented
and raged, wept and scolded, and [followed her] on foot until the Lion-
Subduing Chan Cloister came into view, begging for teachings, just like a
child unwilling to leave its mother. Her fame was such that monastics and
lay people from all four directions claimed that this was an extraordinary
occurrence, the likes of which were rarely seen even in the distant past and
[more recently] had not been seen since the venerable [Miyun Yuanwu]
from Tiantong.

Qiyuan Xinggang herself tells us that Xigan Xingyuan's mother had
herself become a nun and had attained a reputation as a teacher before
she died, which may well explain the extent of the funeral ceremonies
conducted by her son. What is particularly noteworthy, however, is the
extent to which this indicates the mutual respect between Xigan Xingyuan
and Qiyuan Xinggang, male and female Dharma heirs. Clearly, not only
did Xigan Yuan feel that it was completely appropriate that Qiyuan Xinggang should officiate at his mother's funeral, but also Qiyuan Xinggang
herself felt that she was very much on terms of spiritual equality with
Xigan Yuan.

There is nothing more important in this world than [the matter of] life and
death. Even those who live for a long time in a monastery cannot escape
from this. There is only the elderly master who, steeped in the Dharma,
can wander free and easy among the four mountains. The wise mother who
gave him birth has long been a model [of virtue]; a hero of the Dharma,
she was also able to die [with dignity]. Her son and I share the same path
in life. One morning, the myriad things came to an end and, with a wave
of the hand, returned to wander in emptiness. The conduct of the Elderly
Master Shaojue [Xigan's mother's religious name] through her entire life
was such that she was able to completely transform herself.[33]

In the autumn of the year 1652, Qiyuan Xinggang's health began to
suffer, and sensing perhaps that she did not have long to live, she put the
management of the day-to-day affairs of the Lion-Subduing Chan Cloister
(which she and others still referred to by its old name, the Dong Con-

vent) into the hands of two of her senior nuns and embarked on a period of solitary retreat. A Dharma talk delivered around this time explains her motivations:

> This mountain monk has lived here at the Dong Convent, finding peace in poverty and joy in the Way. I have experienced all manner of circumstances: twisted and convoluted, favorable and unfavorable, as well [as those] difficult to regulate, difficult to harmonize. [But] I have willingly taken them all upon myself. For over twenty years, this mountain monk has labored with diligence and with determination, each and every one of my thoughts devoted to the propagation of the orthodox teaching (zhengzong), and with all my heart and mind [I] have [endeavored] to establish [the basis] for those [coming afterward] to study. My desire has been to practice with strong determination together with all of the elder and younger brothers [i.e., nuns] of the community. By looking upon others as I do myself, I have managed to tranquilly negotiate the dangers, even though my virtue is minimal and my ability deficient. Now, however, I am going to close the doors behind me and go into retreat and [also] take care of this illness. . . . In order for [one to be able to] do this, one should in solitude return to the site of liberation. To dwell secluded in a single room with the door closed is the same as living on a cloud-covered peak in the deep mountains and letting your nature go free and following [one's] karmic flow. Although we will not see each other face-to-face, when I am hidden away in the great radiance, I will be able to see you all personally, assembly, Dharma patrons, and devotees. This is none other than what is called the Buddha realm without limit, from which you are not separated by even a hair. Nor are you separated from the ten generations past and present from beginning to end. Keep this teaching in mind.[34]

Yikui Chaochen tells us that while Qiyuan Xinggang "living in seclusion, her face became light and ethereal like that of a divine immortal living in pure leisure between Heaven and Earth." Qiyuan Xinggang herself wrote a number of poems, such as the following two quatrains, which reflect her state of mind during this period:

> After teaching and preaching, running about for so many years,
> Now I've shut my door and retired to the hidden forest spring.
> Heaven and earth kicked open; now my feet can stop moving.
> Alone I sit before the winter window, the shimmering moon full.

> Spending all day in a foolish way; no need for any method.
> Here within there is neither existence nor nonexistence.

Solidly I sit until the road of the sage and fool become one;
Since time immemorial to the present day it has been thus.[35]

Two years later, in the summer of 1654, Qiyuan Xinggang wrote a
letter to her disciple Yigong Chaoke, who was then living in Nanxun at
the Prajñā Convent, and asked her to come to the Lion-Subduing Chan
Cloister to see her. When she arrived, she found her teacher preparing
for her imminent death. As was befitting a realized master, she predicted
that she would be leaving the world at the end of the eighth month and
asked her disciples to assist her in making preparation both for her own
death and for the future of the Lion-Subduing Chan Cloister.

Qiyuan Xinggang's announcement of her imminent death marked
the first stage of the ritual drama that traditionally surrounded the death
of a Chan master: "The first task of a truly enlightened master [is] . . .
to foretell, not only his forthcoming death, but the precise time of his
'transformation.'"[36] Thus the annals of Chan Buddhist history are filled
with the stories of great masters and patriarchs who have predicted their
death, a skill that may well be associated, Faure reminds us, with Daoist divinatory techniques that came to play a central role in Chan Buddhist death mythology. We also see traces of Daoist techniques in the
fact that, although clearly suffering from poor health, Qiyuan Xinggang
showed neither any sign of illness nor any change in the color of her complexion. Moreover, she refrained from eating grains and refused to take
any medicine, stating: "For this illness of mine, there is no need to take
any medicine." She told her worried disciples, "I well know that when
autumn comes to an end, then I must go." The ability to predict one's
death serves not only the ritual function of affirming that one is indeed a
realized master but also the more practical function of ensuring that one
has time to put one's affairs in order before one dies and to ensure the
smooth transfer of spiritual authority.

Chan lineages were based on the Confucian familial model; that is to
say, they were quasi-familial lineages based on father-son inheritance. This
becomes particularly evident in Chan funerals for eminent monks, which
involved the transmission of the most central "property," which, Alan
Cole suggests, is enlightenment itself. In other words, masters produce
disciples who carry on the family essence, thereby establishing a "house"
(zong) that "serves to maintain enlightenment in this hallowed world."
Even more significantly, "invisible Buddhist enlightenment is graphically
represented by a chain of masters who own it and are made visible" in the
form of statues and portraits that are formally installed in special rooms
or buildings and virtually worshipped by their spiritual descendants.[37]

From the accounts, it is clear that Qiyuan Xinggang's death and funeral adhered to the pattern expected of eminent Chan monks. In other words, it would appear that the template of "father-son" transferal of real and symbolic property from eminent monks to their male descendants was adopted, seemingly without any problems, by eminent nuns passing on their "inheritance" to their female descendants.

Qiyuan Xinggang's preparation for her departure from the world are described in considerable detail in her vita, an indication of the importance of this ritual transference of both property and authority. It is interesting to note that in making her preparations, Qiyuan Xinggang again sought the advice of her spiritual adviser, Muyun Tongmen, now an elderly monk living in retirement at the Gunan Monastery. Yikui Chaochen, however, is quick to assure her readers that "the Master was making her own decisions; she just wanted the venerable [Master] to be a witness to them."

One of the most crucial of these decisions was the question of who was to succeed her. Qiyuan Xinggang (after consultation with her lay patrons) decided that Yigong Chaoke, who, although not her first disciple, had entered the religious life at the age of eight *sui* and thus had been a nun the longest, was best suited to take over the leadership of the Lion-Subduing Chan Cloister. However, by this time the convent had become a large and flourishing establishment, and perhaps realizing that Yigong Chaoke did not have the energy and charisma with which she herself had been blessed, Qiyuan Xinggang also asked Yichuan Chaolang—by this time the abbess of the Prajña Convent in Nanxun—to return to the Lion-Subduing Chan Cloister to assist Yigong Chaoke and in particular to oversee the completion of the stupa garden, which would require the continuing financial patronage of lay donors. The funerary stupa in which their ashes would be preserved was an important matter of concern for many Chan masters. Even Hongren, traditionally regarded as the Fifth Patriarch of Chan Buddhism, is said to have carefully watched over the construction of his funerary stupa and even to have delayed his death so that it would be completed on a suitable date.[38] In fact, as we shall see, the placement and construction of Qiyuan Xinggang's funerary stupa continued to be a major issue in the lives of her Dharma heirs for some time after her death.

After she had designated a successor and clarified her final instructions, the next ritual step for the dying Chan master was to assume the lotus posture. That is what Qiyuan Xinggang did in the early hours of the twenty-sixth day of the eighth month, after having bathed and changed her robes. To quote Faure yet again:

[A Chan master's] death became a public event, and he was required to
die in a seated posture in order to show, not only that he was intent on
practicing until the end, and that he was facing death in the quiet com-
posure of *samādhi*, but also that he had become ritually identified with
the paradigmatic Buddha (the historical Buddha having died lying on his
bed). So powerful was this model of 'sitting *samādhi*' that it came to super-
sede all others."[39]

Seated in the lotus posture, presumably in a state of enlightened consciousness *(samādhi)*, the Chan master than carries out a final ritual act
and leaves a "death verse," which, as Faure notes, is in many ways equivalent to the verse marking the master's first enlightenment experience. In
other words, the two verses: the enlightenment verse and the death poem
"mark the beginning and end of the master's teaching."[40] Such death
poems early on became quite codified and as such must be regarded as
part and parcel of the ritual of dying rather than a spontaneous expression of the awakened mind. Qiyuan Xinggang's own death poem reflects
her understanding of this ritual significance:

Like the moon shining on a thousand rivers,
The disk of luminosity is pure and unsullied.
Now I will teach by sitting in the lotus position;
Sentient beings will look and see through it all.
If you ask what the last phrase is,
Clapping my hands, I will say it is this.

The traditional signs of extraordinary spiritual achievement do not,
however, come to an end when the Chan master dies. Her disciples were
provided with further proof of Qiyuan Xinggang's sanctity when they
noticed that "at the break of dawn, a warm vapor like steam exuded from
the crown of her head." This points to yet another popular tradition,
traceable to more esoteric sources, that a person's rebirth could be predicted by, among other signs, "finding what part of his body cooled last."
According to Holmes Welch, who found this belief to be very much alive
in the first half of the nineteenth century, if the last part of the body to
cool was the crown of the head, one could be sure that the person was
destined for a rebirth in the Pure Land, and if the last part to cool was the
feet, "the poor fellow was on his way to hell."[41]

After a Chan master died, it was up to his or her followers to carry on
with the required ritual performance, a performance that extended over
forty-nine days, the liminal period that marked the transition from death
to rebirth in the next life. This ritual is not described in great detail in

Qiyuan Xinggang's biography, although we are told that her casket was left undisturbed for three days, as was customary. During this time, yet another sign of her sanctity became evident: "her complexion remained as when she was alive." This is yet another fairly common detail found in the hagiographies of holy persons not only in the past but in recent times as well.[42] The ultimate proof would be if the tomb of a Chan master who died in this way were reopened after three years to find that the corpse was still as if alive, with pliant flesh and hair and nails that have grown—said to have been the case with many great Chan masters, including the traditional Sixth Patriarch of Chan Buddhism, Huineng, who died in 713 CE, and, closer to Qiyuan Xinggang's own time, the Buddhist master Hanshan Deqing. We have no indication that Qiyuan Xinggang's disciples actually went so far as to open up her casket later to check on the state of her corpse, but it is significant that they do appear to have refrained from cremation and placed her body into the funerary stupa intact. This may indicate that they expected it to become a "flesh-body," or self-mummified body, which, again, was a sign of extraordinary sanctity.[43]

At the time of her death, Qiyuan Xinggang was fifty-eight years old. She had been a nun for twenty-three years and left behind seven female Dharma heirs and countless disciples and devotees, both monastic and lay. Yikui Chaochen and the male Chan master Baichi Xingyuan, among others, were moved to write heartfelt poems of mourning. Yikui Chaochen's poem is written from the perspective of a disciple or even a daughter:

> She who spent years humbling, shaping, and polishing us
> Is now gone like a broken noon dream, and I am still in tears.
> Alas, it was far too soon for me to have been parted from her;
> Her personal things are now in ashes and know not sorrow.
>
> Since when have spring and fall passed without me serving her?
> The cries of the nightjars fill the branches left bare of blossoms.
> Brokenhearted, I sorrowfully listen to their three-note calls.
> Then silently shut the brushwood gate against the wind and rain.[44]

The poem composed by Baichi Xingyuan is fairly conventional in its use of imagery (although it is important to remember that Qiyuan Xinggang's death occurred in autumn, so that the images of yellow chrysanthemums and early frost work on both the symbolic and literal levels). However, it does seem to express not only respect but also genuine affection:

> A frosty wind roars through the leaves, the rooftops are chill;
> As suddenly the "Jetavana Forest" puts down her fishing rod.[45]

The yellow chrysanthemum in its grief nurses a thousand tears;
The verdant river in its anger rolls out ten thousand rapids.

Lonely and desolate, who will lead along the Dharma path?
Quiet and dignified, we contemplate her courage and wisdom:
In the light of eternal quietude, she seems to be nodding "yes."
We will meet again as before, without deceiving each other.[46]

Qiyuan Xinggang's *yulu* collection was compiled and edited by her
seven women Dharma successors: Yikui Chaochen, Yigong Chaoke,
Yichuan Chaolang, Yiyin Chaojian, Puwen Chaoyuan, Yiran Chaoshe,
and Guding Chaozhen. In addition, three well-known Buddhist laymen
contributed prefaces. The first preface was provided by Zhu Maoshi, who
as we have seen, was the son of Qiyuan Xinggang's disciple Lady of Virtue
Zhao. Zhu Maoshi was also heavily involved in the production of the Jiaxing canon and was the author of the (still useful) index to its contents
(mulu). As one of the group of lay Buddhists responsible for collecting
materials for the Jiaxing canon, he no doubt had something to say about
having Qiyuan Xinggang's discourse records included. The second preface was contributed by Wu Zhu; as we saw earlier, he and his wife were
loyal patrons of Qiyuan Xinggang. Wu Zhu's preface is dated 1648, indicating that the preparation of the *yulu* collection began before Qiyuan
Xinggang died and perhaps even under her supervision. The third preface was contributed by Wu Qingxiang, a Buddhist layman and a disciple
of Shiche Tongsheng, who was Qiyuan Xinggang's own Dharma master.
These three prefaces are all written in the sometimes rather hyperbolic
language that was characteristic of such compositions. They focus on
Qiyuan Xinggang's moral stature and religious achievements and on her
gifts as a teacher; all three draw on the usual comparisons with Moshan
and Miaozong. Wu Qingxiang further notes how unusual it is to encounter someone who embodies both the way of women *(fufa)* and granny
Chan *(laopo Chan)*; in other words, she managed to embody the ideals of
both a Confucian woman and a Chan master. At the same time, all three
preface writers emphasize Qiyuan Xinggang's role in the continuation
of the Linji lineage and her contribution to its flourishing. Thus, just as
Miaozong is referred to in relation to Dahui Zonggao, Qiyuan Xinggang
is always spoken of in the context of Miyun Yuanwu and Shiche Tongsheng. And finally, given that the *yulu* represents in fact a literary collection, they note Qiyuan Xinggang's eloquence and literary talents; Wu
Zhu sighs over her "golden narratives and jade phrases" *(jinzhang yuju)*.

CHAPTER FIVE

Passing on the Lamp

The Dharma Successors of Qiyuan Xinggang

Chan master Yikui Chaochen
(1625–1679). From *Cantong
Yikui Chaochen chanshi yulu,
Mingban Jiaxing dazangjing*
(Taipei: Xinwenfeng
chubanshe, 1987), 39:7.

Qiyuan Xinggang had seven officially designated Dharma heirs,
although many more disciples either lived at the Lion-Subduing
Chan Cloister or spent time with her on retreat. Of these seven, we know
the most about Yikui Chaochen (1625–1679), who was the author of the
biography of Qiyuan Xinggang that was quoted extensively in the previous
chapter, and who also left an extant *yulu* collection of her own. There is
also an extant *yulu* for Yigong Chaoke (1615–1661), one of the two nuns
charged with the leadership of the Lion-Subduing Chan Cloister after
Qiyuan Xinggang's death. Unfortunately, there are no extant *yulu* collections for the remaining five Dharma heirs, Yichuan Chaolang (d. 1656),
Yiyin Chaojian (d. before 1666), Puwen Chaoyuan, Yiran Chaoshe, and
Guding Chaozhen (the dates for the latter three all unknown). What this
means, of course, is that much more is known about Yikui Chaochen and
Yigong Chaoke than about the others.

Of these seven Dharma heirs, the eldest was Yichuan Chaolang, the
only daughter of Madame Li, and Qiyuan Xinggang's first disciple. From
the beginning, it would appear that she was very frail and suffered from ill
health, which may explain in part her reluctance to marry and her desire
to devote herself to religious pursuits. Her mother, as we have seen, had
a private cloister built for her, which later was expanded to become the

Lion-Subduing Chan Cloister. We are able to gather a few glimpses of her provided by those who knew her, such as the following poem by Yigong Chaoke entitled "A Gatha Presented to Elder Dharma [Sister] Yichuan Who Experienced an Awakening at the Lion-Subduing Chan Cloister":

> Riding the wind: a fierce tiger in the groves of the Lion-Subduing Chan
>   Cloister.
> Grasping the moon: all the resentments of the past years vanish.
> Tears and smiles both forgotten, her entire self experiences release:
> She lets go from the cliff's edge, calling only on the Honored One.[1]

After having her realization confirmed by Qiyuan Xinggang, Yichuan Chaolang became the abbess of the Prajñā Convent in Nanxun, where Yigong Chaoke was also living. Upon the death of Qiyuan Xinggang, as we saw, she and Yigong Chaoke were both summoned to take over the leadership of the Lion-Subduing Chan Cloister. Only two years later, however, Yichuan Chaolang also passed away, leaving Yigong Chaoke in sole charge. Although Yichuan Chaolang had never enjoyed robust health, it appears that her death came as a blow to Yigong Chaoke:

> Alas! There was none like my elder Dharma [sister], the nun of the Prajñā
> [Convent]. Her heart was just like that of a child [but] in her deportment
> surpassed that of the ancients. She had met the Way for ten years and
> with insight carried out the Way. Skillfulness can seem like awkwardness;
> wisdom can seems like stupidity; eloquence can seem like inarticulate-
> ness; steely resolve, like weakness. She treated others as she would herself,
> and exhausted all of the strategies of both humans and gods. You and I
> engaged in religious practice together, but now you have abandoned me
> and departed this world forever. Alas![2]

Sometime later, Yikui Chaochen was asked by Yichuan Chaolang's mother, Madame Li, to conduct a seven-day retreat at the Prajñā Convent. In a Dharma talk delivered on this occasion, Yikui Chaochen refers to its previous abbess and in particular to her considerable efforts at sustaining both the convent and the lineage:

> This Prajñā Convent has for over ten years been a lofty mirror of the lin-
> eage. No one expected that my departed elder Dharma [sister] would van-
> ish. She has passed into eternity, and today the Dharma path is lonely and
> desolate. . . . All of her life, with great determination, she exerted all of her
> efforts to steer the boat [of the Dharma] against the [worldly] current.[3]

For Yiyin Chaojian as well, little biographical information is available beyond that her secular surname was Ge. Given that Yikui Chaochen refers to her as "elder Dharma [sister]" we can assume that Yiyin Chaojian had entered the religious life before Yikui Chaochen. It is known that she was born sometime before 1625, and although she appears to have been afflicted with illness in her later years, she apparently had a long life; Yikui Chaochen's discourse record collection includes a poem written on the occasion of her Dharma sister's seventieth birthday.

After receiving Dharma transmission from Qiyuan Xinggang, Yiyin Chaojian became the abbess of a newly refurbished Protection of Goodness Convent (Shanhu an) in Danghu—as we saw in the last chapter, Qiyuan Xinggang traveled to Danghu to inaugurate the new Dharma hall Yiyin Chaojian had built for this convent. Baichi Xingyuan, in whose discourse records are several texts addressed to Yiyin Chaojian (whom he refers to as his Dharma niece, or *fazhi*),[4] appears to have attended these inauguration ceremonies as well, and a few years later we find Yiyin Chaojian inviting him back to the Protection of Goodness Convent to give a Dharma talk. In this talk, he comments on how the convent has grown and flourished since his previous visit. Elsewhere, we find Yiyin Chaojian, together with her woman disciple Haoyue, asking Baichi Xingyuan to ascend the Dharma hall and give a talk. This time it appears that she went with her disciple to visit him. In his talk, Baichi Xingyuan refers to Grindstone Liu, the indomitable woman disciple of Tang master Guishan. In yet another verse, a poem of encouragement or exhortation, he reminds Yiyin Chaojian how fortunate she is to have had Qiyuan Xinggang as her teacher:

She could not bear to associate with corruption within the Dharma gate;
Beard and whiskers willing to act like women from the inner chambers.
I love most the teaching of the elder matriarch of the Lion-Subduing
    Chan Cloister,
Who, it has been said, had been Miaozong in a previous incarnation.
The insight at the end of her stick resounded through heaven and earth;
The unselfishness beneath her blows caused ghosts and spirits to weep.
My niece is fortunate in being able to follow in her eminent footsteps,
And under her guidance needn't lament the spring of yesteryear's
    gardens.[5]

Yikui Chaochen also wrote a eulogy for Yiyin Chaojian, which provides the closest thing we have to a biographical profile, although in the end it tells us more about the strong bonds of friendship, admiration, and support among these abbesses than it does about Yiyin Chaojian herself. There is also an underlying note of melancholy, a distinct premonition—which would, in fact, prove to be correct—that this group of women would also in time disappear, leaving only faint traces of their once-vibrant existence:

> At this time, although our Dharma family is flourishing, to find a true person of the Way is as rare as finding a moon among all the stars. My elder Dharma [sister], whether active or in retirement, always acted in profound accordance with the family style of the ancient worthies. Her nature was upright, with a backbone of steel, and she had liberated herself from the burrows and caves of her contemporaries. For thirty years she shouldered the burden [of the life of an abbess], toiling and laboring on behalf of the Dharma and on behalf of others. I admire the Master, who from beginning to end never wavered, and instructed her students from morning until night without weariness. Although she was confined for a long time to her sickroom, her regulations were orderly, and her commands strict and meticulous. For this reason, the fact that this lineage remains intact is thanks to my elder Dharma [sister] providing us with mutual support. When the announcement of her death arrived suddenly, it was like a thorn stabbing into the heart, like a bird finding its wings clipped. Alas! The Dharma line of the Lion-Subduing Chan Cloister is gradually fading away.[6]

About Yigong Chaoke we know significantly more, since her extant discourse record collection includes a relatively detailed vita compiled by her disciple, Mingyuan Weiyi. Although the first part of this account (dated 1678) is missing, there is enough information to reconstruct the basic outlines of her life. We know, then, that Yigong Chaoke was a native of Meixi and entered the monastic life at the age of eight *sui*—it may well be that she had lost her parents or for some reason had been entrusted by her family into the care of nuns at a local convent. The convent where she first lived—we are not told where it was or what it was called—was burned to the ground during the fighting and turbulence of the transition period. After that, she moved into the Prajñā Convent in Nanxun, where, as we have seen, Yichuan Chaolang was serving as abbess. In fact, it was probably Yichuan Chaolang who encouraged her to visit Qiyuan Xinggang. In any case, we are told that the elder nun immediately recognized Yigong Chaoke's spiritual abilities and said to her, "You are "truly one [worthy of] striking the bell in the [meditation] hall."[7] Upon hearing this, Mingyuan tells us, Yigong Chaoke asked herself, "If I do not attain a real realization, how will I be able to personally approach this venerable nun, since the doubt within my breast has not yet been dissolved?" Yigong Chaoke did not, however, immediately become a disciple of Qiyuan Xinggang. In fact, what is perhaps most interesting about Yigong Chaoke's biography is that it shows a woman going from teacher to teacher—both Linji and Zaodong—all of whom appreciate her spiritual potential, but with none of whom she really makes any substantial progress. Only twenty-four *sui* at this point, Yigong Chaoke sought out the eminent Zaodong Chan master (and advocate of the dual Chan/Pure Land practice) Shiyu Mingfang (1593–1648), who assigned her the *huatou* "What were you before your father and mother were born?"

As was the case with Qiyuan Xinggang, we are told that Yigong Chaoke struggled with her *huatou* and went through periods of profound depression bordering on despair. She then went to Lingyan Monastery in Suzhou to study for a while with Jiqi Hongchu (1605–1672), a second-generation Dharma successor of Miyun Yuanwu. Jiqi Hongchu, who had several women Dharma heirs of his own, appears to have been quite impressed with Yigong Chaoke and is said to have remarked when she first entered his quarters for an interview: "What a heroically spirited nun!" *(haoge yingling na zi)*. Although Jiqi Hongchu claimed they had a spiritual connection and even gave her another religious name—Kuiyin—and composed a very complimentary gatha for her, she decided to return to the Prajñā Convent, where, Mingyuan recounts, she remarked to Yichuan Chaolang, "Several times I have been praised by enlightened masters, and yet I have been unable to liberate myself. I must definitely bring this to a conclusion or else I will not be able to [attain enlightenment] until my next life!"

Primed now for intensive practice, Yigong Chaoke found out that there was a monk from the Soul's Retreat (Lingyin) Monastery in Hangzhou who had come to Nanxun to recuperate from an illness. This monk—we are not told his name—was apparently famous for his ability to help practitioners "pull out the nails and wrench out the poles," that is, to break out of their spiritual double bind and remove the last obstacles to enlightenment. Yigong Chaoke was convinced that with his help she would be able to achieve that for which she had struggled for so many years. She persuaded Yichuan Chaolang to help her obtain the permission of the Dong family to invite this teacher to give a seven-day intensive meditation retreat at the Prajñā Convent.[8] It apparently was not usual for a male teacher to conduct such retreats at a convent, but Dong Hance agreed to allow the monk to do so, provided the convent was divided into two separate halls. When the retreat was in session, the monk would not enter the nun's hall except for occasional instruction. In this way, Yigong

Chaoke got her wish, and, according to Mingyuan, she made the best of this unusual opportunity:

> Yigong then made a great vow that she would not leave the hall until she had had an experience of enlightenment. Silently and with great intensity, [she practiced] day and night without a break. On the ninth day, as she was making a full prostration in front of the statue of the Buddha, suddenly she completely understood the [meaning of the koan about the] bamboo fly whisk and the bottom of the bucket fell out. She felt light and happy all over, and she spoke to the monk, saying: "Now there is no way you can pull anything over my eyes." The monk replied: "That may be, but you still need to turn yourself over beneath the staff of a great lineage master before you can [say you have] achieved [enlightenment].

It was not until a few years after this, when Yigong Chaoke was thirty-six *sui*, that she returned to Qiyuan Xinggang, who by this time had acquired a reputation as a truly eminent nun and great master. Mingyuan provides us with a rare account of an exchange between a female Chan master and her disciple:

> At that time the Dharma there was flourishing and visitors came and went unceasingly, and in the end Yigong's opportunity to enter the abbess's quarters for an interview with Qiyuan Xinggang was determined by the proctor [*weina*]. [But] Master [Xinggang] had long known that Yigong was a Dharma vessel, and their karmic connection was established at a single glance and [she knew] that she needed to be sternly pushed forward. One day Yigong was entering the [abbess's] room and was just about to lift the curtain and step over the threshold when Xinggang stopped her, saying: "That which is within cannot be released out; that which is without cannot be released in. Try and say something!" Yigong found that there was nothing she could say in reply, and so she returned to the hall. Giving up both eating and sleeping, [she had practiced the *huatou* until she felt that] in her mind the doubt had already reached its greatest extent. Matters seemed so completely clear and distinct, but when [Xinggang] spoke these words, she found herself blocked once again.

In the months that followed, Yigong Chaoke continued to practice under Qiyuan Xinggang, whom she now accepted as her formal Dharma master. She also appears to have spent many hours in discussion with Yikui Chaochen, the fellow disciple with whom she felt the most affinity (*zui xiangqi*) and who was at this time serving as Qiyuan Xinggang's personal attendant. Yigong Chaoke made steady progress, and before long, Qiyuan Xinggang rccognized her as a senior student. She was also asked to serve as head administrative officer of the convent, but after only a year of these duties, which she found to be extremely onerous, she requested and received permission to return to the Prajñā Convent to engage in a solitary retreat *(biguan)*, much as Qiyuan Xinggang had herself done many years earlier. In the seventh month of the year 1654, however, Yigong Chaoke was called out of her retreat by the dying Qiyuan Xinggang:

> [Qiyuan Xinggang said to her:] "I called you because we will not have another chance to see each other." [Yigong] said: "My only wish is that you live among time in this world in order to spread the Dharma and benefit sentient beings—what is this you are saying [about not seeing one another again]?" [Qiyuan Xinggang] replied: "Although I am not lying in my bed, the illness I have is already very advanced. By the time the frost settles, I will have left the world."

Qiyuan Xinggang then informed Yigong Chaoke that she had chosen her and Yichuan Chaolang to assume leadership of the Lion-Subduing Chan Cloister after her death, and that she was making Yigong Chaoke responsible primarily for building her funerary stupa in the southern garden of the Lion-Subduing Chan Cloister. A large part of the work of an abbot or abbess, as of any high-ranking administrator today, was fund-raising—whether for new monastery buildings, Buddha statues, or funerary stupas. Raising money depended on the goodwill of the lay donors, which was unpredictable and often involved the personal, familial, and religious relationships between the nuns and the donors. Qiyuan Xinggang, who, as we have seen, was a woman of considerable charisma and force, had over time attracted a number of well-off lay donors. It would appear, however, that Yigong Chaoke was of a more retiring nature—we saw how when she had first been given administrative duties as a senior nun, she quickly tired of them and asked to be allowed to go on solitary retreat. In any case we are told that after Qiyuan Xinggang's death "people's feelings changed" *(renqing jie bian)*, and Yigong Chaoke encountered many obstacles to the building of her teacher's stupa garden—a task that, in fact, she ended up leaving to others to complete. Nevertheless, as we can see in the following poem written in praise of Yigong Chaoke's labors by Yikui Chaochen, she managed to keep things going:

> The ancestral hall is tall and lofty, and as pure as autumn.
> "The myriad shapes so majestic," this phrase says it all.
> Spring arrives and naturally the flowers produce brocades;
> When sound and fragrance fill the world, who can grieve?

You have kept the lamp glowing as it did with our Master;
The Chan community flourishes and puts out new shoots.
The gates and halls are in order all thanks to your efforts;
It is truly the time to throw out the bait and cast the line.[9]

It was not long before Yigong Chaoke herself fell ill and returned briefly to the Prajñā Convent to recuperate. Sensing that her illness was actually quite critical and that her days were numbered, and convinced that the only person who could replace her after her death was Yikui Chaochen, she wrote a letter to the Dong family, requesting that Yikui Chaochen be the one asked to fill the abbess seat she would soon leave empty. Yigong Chaoke knew very well that Yikui Chaochen was as fond of quiet and contemplation as she herself had been, and when they met, she said to her, according to Mingyuan's account: "I know full well that you, my Dharma [brother], have always been fond of tranquility, which is why you've not wanted to come and live here with me [earlier]. It is just because matters have reached a critical point, and I need your support so that the Dharma gate will not be abandoned, that I must rely on you to take care of matters after my death."

It is important to note that Yigong Chaoke specifically requested that Yikui Chaochen help with the preservation of her writings: "I am leaving a two-fascicle draft of [my] discourse records [yulu] and songgu [poetic commentaries on old Chan cases]. The others may understand one or two things, but they are very young and will not be able to write my biography [xingzhuang]. So, may I trouble you to prepare a detailed outline for Mingyuan, in which you record all the details of my life?" This demonstrates that these women were very conscious not only of their legacy, both spiritual and literary, but also about how they were to be represented and remembered.

With the memory of the difficulties she herself had experienced when she took over the leadership of the convent after Qiyuan Xinggang's perhaps still fresh in her mind, Yigong Chaoke also made a point of gathering the community together and asking for their assurance that they would welcome Yikui Chaochen with open arms and to "treat her exactly as you would myself."

The account of Yigong Chaoke's death is true to form in that it describes her ability to predict the time of her death, the composition of a final death poem, and a conscious and peaceful passing. However, there are certain small details in this account, such as her last conversation with Yikui Chaochen and how her last, parting poem came to be written, that make it both personal and poignant. Yikui Chaochen's biographical account describes these last days as follows:

Yikui came to her, and they talked at great length for half a day without feeling even a hint of weariness. At that time, there was a basin full of profusely blooming grasses and epidendrum in front of them from which Yigong herself plucked out the weeds. Yikui said: "I see that you seem to have a bit of energy. Why don't you leave a gatha?" Yigong took up her writing brush and inkstone and wrote a few characters, but then laid the brush down and said with a sigh, "Lifting this pen is like lifting a huge pole." Her attendant, afraid that she was getting overly agitated, helped her over to the couch so that she could rest peacefully. [The next day] at early dawn, after the first sutra recital, she then turned to Yikui and said: "Yesterday, I composed a gatha but was unable to write it down. Today I will recite it so that you can write it down for me."

> For twelve years I have blown on a flute without holes;
> Friends who understand one are not often found.
> It is just because I have never left off with the music
> That today my worldly karma is completely fulfilled.
> Footloose and fancy-free, I clap my hands and return home.
> All my life I have been liberated, free and independent;
> What need to stir up everyone's sadness and grief?

She then pressed her hands together in front of her chest and thanked her, saying: "I will make my departure early tomorrow morning." Yigong died just before dawn on the following day. She was forty-seven *sui* and had been a nun for thirty-nine years.

After Yigong Chaoke's death, Yikui Chaochen moved Qiyuan Xinggang's stupa to her own hermitage and built one for Yigong Chaoke right beside it. In addition, together with Mingyuan Weiyi, she gathered together Yigong Chaoke's recorded talks and other writings. Mingyuan, in consultation with Yikui Chaochen, took responsibility for writing the official biography of her teacher, at the conclusion of which she explains that although she had long wanted to have it printed, she was ashamed of her own lack of literary skills and did not dare venture to present the life of her teacher in such away as to arouse people's contempt. However, one day an elderly visitor saw the manuscript and, clapping his hands in delight, exclaimed, "Here we have an exemplary woman. Why did you not have it printed and circulated earlier!" Mingyuan Weiyi concludes by telling her readers that, upon reflection, she realized that the visitor was right, and, assuming full responsibility for errors of fact or infelicities of style, she decided to have her master's discourse records published, along with the biographical account.

This distinguished visitor was probably Gao Yiyong, the literatus-official from Jiaxing, since his is the preface that opens the printed edition of Yigong Chaoke's discourse records. In this preface, Gao tells us that one day a relative of his took him to visit Yikui Chaochen's convent, where he saw the funerary stupas belonging to Qiyuan Xinggang and Yigong Chaoke, and where he also met Yigong's disciple Mingyuan Weiyi. The disciple took advantage of the visit of a well-known literatus to show him the draft of her teacher's writings and asked him to write a preface for it. Gao Yiyong asked Mingyuan to tell him about her teacher, which she was able to do "from memory." The preface that he then wrote, while no doubt based to some extent on what Mingyuan Weiyi him, betrays the fact that he had not known Yigong Chaoke personally. Thus, although he provides a moving description of her as a person and of her character and writing talents, one cannot help noting the extent to which Gao Yiyong transforms her into a figure more reminiscent of the image of the talented but ill-fated woman so beloved by male literati of the late imperial period:

> [Mingyuan Weiyi described her teacher to me:]
>> Airy and graceful, free and at ease, openhearted and extraordinary: such was her abundant measure of calm and ease. Solemn and serious, clear sounds distant and transcendent: such was her orderly and grave Sanskrit chanting. Affable and agreeable, with the purest of emotions: such was the pleasant manner with which she treated people. When it came to wielding the brush, she was elegant and meticulous; her brushwork was graceful and lovely, screened from the glare; even her occasional women's work [weaving] was completely imbued with her essential thoughts. Jade bits and fragrant grasses, all of them teeming with an elegance that immediately exhausts all praise. How could it be that, by simply sitting like a withered tree, one could accomplish this!
>
> The words of [Mingyuan] Weiyi were like this. At the time, the autumn cloudiness had just cleared up and the fragrance of cassia infused my robes. The white clouds floated in the heavens, and the bright moon [was reflected] in the waters. [As] I sat between the kingfisher green willows and the azure wutong trees, it was as if Yigong [Chaoke] were there, and if one called to her, she would be willing to come out. And so I took up the brush to write this preface.[10]

Yikui Chaochen, in her own postface to Yigong Chaoke's discourse records, laments her fellow nun's premature death and inability to fully develop her talents, both spiritual and literary. She also refers to Yigong's

rather ethereal and otherworldly character, but without the sentimental-
ization and near eroticization of Gao Yiyong's preface. Her emphasis is
on Yigong Chaoke's intelligence and secret inner life rather than on her
externally graceful elegance:

> The Confucian master Zhuxi said: "Alas, after my death, fame will be to me
> like a floating cloud." He also said: "When people do good, that is their
> own affair. What need is there to write about it?" How much more is the
> case in our teachings [of Buddhism], which cares little for wordy phrases
> or establishing a reputation for virtue! Once someone has departed, to
> take the words they have left behind and entrust them to pearwood [for
> carving], is this not also vanity, a case of [unnecessarily] adding a handle to
> a bowl? . . . It is just that my elder Dharma [brother] Yigong all her life was
> intelligent above all others, and ethereal, unconventional above the rest of
> the crowd. After having obtained the mind transmission of our departed
> Master, she would stroll among the springs and boulders, secretly cultivat-
> ing herself, and it was many years before she was willing to display the
> mysterious clouds of compassion and the permeating and enriching rain
> of the teaching. No one expected that she would suddenly pass away [and
> melt away] like a mud oxen thrown into the sea.[11]

Despite all of the efforts of Mingyuan Weiyi and Yikui Chaochen to preserve the latter's writings, in the end only one fascicle of her discourse
record remains extant. Of the texts included in this record, the most
notable are the elegies Yigong Chaoke composed for her teacher, Qiyuan
Xinggang, and a Dharma talk she gave on the occasion of the first anniversary of Qiyuan Xinggang's death. The latter is of particular interest
because it describes a ritual conducted in front of a portrait of Qiyuan
Xinggang, perhaps even the portrait described in Chapter Four. We also
find another series of *yuanliu song*, which, as noted earlier, was a new religious literary genre commemorating (and testifying to) one's Dharma
lineage. Like Qiyuan Xinggang before her, Yigong Chaoke's *yuanliu song*
begins with Nanyue Huairang and continues down to Shiche Tongsheng,
the thirty-fifth generation. However, she does not stop there but, rather,
continues on to add the name of her own master, Qiyuan Xinggang. In
the biographical account that precedes the customary commemorative
poem, she recounts, almost verbatim, the story of Qiyuan Xinggang's
final intensive push to realization and her enlightenment experience
right after having had her head shaved.

It is clear then that, for all her protestations of humility, Yigong
Chaoke saw herself as the next in line. However, as far as we know, Mingyuan never ascended to the heights of her teacher, nor does she appear

to have left behind either a discourse record collection of her own or a *yuanliu song* with her own name inscribed forever into the Linji lineage of Miyun Yuanwu.

With the successive deaths of her teacher and two of her closest Dharma companions, Yikui Chaochen appears to have been at a loss.

> Waking from my dream, full of sorrow I listen to the morning bell;
> No point in strumming "Tears of Blood Dye the Red Maples."
> I think back on how together we sang the songs of the Unborn;
> How could I have known the wind would blow in a different tune?[12]

Yikui Chaochen would not be allowed to grieve for long, however, as she would soon be sought out by the lay patrons of the Lion-Subduing Chan Cloister to fill the vacuum left by these deaths. She was not overly eager to assume these responsibilities, especially since by this time she had a flourishing convent of her own. But she certainly would have been more than qualified to follow in her teacher's footsteps. In fact, the literatus-layman Wang Ting (who, as we have seen, was a very enthusiastic lay Buddhist and also wrote an inscription for the Lion-Subduing Chan Cloister) goes so far as to claim:

> Of the seven women to whom Qiyuan Xinggang transmitted the Dharma . . .
> Yikui Chaochen was the most outstanding; she was known for being even wiser than her teacher.[13]

Up to this point, Yikui Chaochen's poetry and biographical writings have been frequently used here to reconstruct the lives of Qiyuan Xinggang and two of Yikui Chaochen's elder Dharma sisters. It is now time to turn our attention to Yikui Chaochen herself. She is a very interesting woman, for whom there fortunately exists a detailed vita *(xingshi)* redacted by Puming, her senior disciple and one of her Dharma successors, as well as a brief autobiographical profile that she herself wrote "for the edification" of her students. Both of these are included in her discourse record collection, which apparently enjoyed a fairly wide circulation. Although she does not get an entry of her own in Yuan Guozi's 1682 Jiaxing gazetteer, her name does appear in the biographical notice he provides for Qiyuan Xinggang, in which he writes, in agreement with Wang Ting's assessment of her ability: "Among those who, [as numerous as] clouds, followed [Qiyuan Xinggang], there was one nun, Yikui Chaochen, who was her top student. Both of them left discourse records that circulated in the world."[14]

Yikui Chaochen, née Sun, was born in Pinghu, Jiaxing Prefecture, on the first day of the sixth month of the year 1625. Her great-grandfather Sun Zhi (posthumous name Jianxiao, *jinshi* 1535, d. 1586) had held various high official posts, including minister of justice and minister of works. Her father, Sun Maoshi, held an official position in the Directorate of Education, although it would appear that, after the fall of the Ming, he returned home to Pinghu to live in retirement with his family. Unlike Qiyuan Xinggang, who was an only child, Yikui Chaochen had many siblings. One of her brothers, Sun Zhongrui (most often referred to by his style name, "Sun Zilin"), was known for his interest in the Three Teachings (Sanjiao) and played a pivotal role in Yikui Chaochen's life. She was the youngest of three sisters and, quite likely, the most doted upon. Even as a child, her disciple Puming informs us, "she was very bright and lively, and talented at women's work. Even without the benefit of a teacher, she mastered the principles of calligraphy and of painting."[15] There is little mention in her vita of youthful religious piety. Rather, Yikui Chaochen appears to have been destined for a life as wife, a mother, and, if lucky, a companionate partner to a similarly handsome and talented young scholar. She married a first-degree holder by the name of Sheng Zida, with whom she appears to have been quite happy, even as she successfully fulfilled all of the traditional requirements of both behavior and character that were traditionally demanded of a good wife. As Puming tells us, "With complete competence she carried out the wifely way; she served her father- and mother-in-law with filiality and got along peacefully with her brothers and sisters." In fact, it would seem that she would never have even thought about religious renunciation had her young husband not fallen ill and died. This was not an unusual circumstance, especially during these tumultuous and difficult times.[16] What was somewhat different in Yikui Chaochen's case was that, during his last days, Sheng Zida spent much of his time with a Linji Chan monk named Linquan Jihui, who accompanied Chan master Poshan Haiming—one of the twelve Dharma heirs of Miyun Yuanwu—to Jiaxing in the early 1620s and had remained there after Poshan Haiming returned to Sichuan in 1634.[17] Linquan Jihui is said to have led the quiet life of a hermit for over thirty years and during that time acquired a reputation for his religious practice:[18]

It so happened that the eminent monk Linquan and Sheng had a special [karmic] affinity with each other. When Sheng saw that his illness was very grave, he begged [Linquan] to come and give him religious instruction. Yikui Chaochen listened to [the teachings] secretly [from behind the door], and her spiritual inclinations grew even stronger.

Yikui Chaochen became a widow in the late autumn of 1647 and apparently had no children. Inspired no doubt by the teachings that she had listened to from behind the door (an interesting twist on the manner in which many talented young women are described as having acquired an education—i.e., by secretly eavesdropping on their brothers' lessons), after her husband's death she put away all of her cosmetics and silks, gave up eating meat, and, retreating to her rooms, devoted herself single-mindedly to the chanting of sutras and Buddha recitation. According to her vita, Yikui Chaochen wrote on her wall in large characters, "The myriad dharmas are all empty; with focused mind recite the Buddha's name." This phrase reflects the combination of Pure Land and Chan practice, the first line being part of a famous koan: "The myriad dharmas all return to one; then where does the One return to?" In this she appears to have been following the teaching of Poshan Haiming. Although known to have adhered closely to the "blows and shouts" espoused by Miyun Yuanwu, Poshan Haiming also taught *huatou* meditation. He especially advocated a single-minded focus on the "who" of "Who is it that is reciting the name of the Buddha?"

In what we see emerging as a recurring motif in the biographical accounts of these seventeenth-century nuns, Yikui Chaochen found herself in need of further instruction and guidance. The first person she turned to was her brother Sun Zilin. He was Yikui Chaochen's primary spiritual mentor and, to the end of her life, her most devoted supporter. He never aspired to a higher degree and, after 1644, devoted himself to a frugal and even ascetic life of study, self-cultivation, and charitable activities.[19] He was primarily interested in the Three Teachings and in the study of the *Book of Changes (Yijing)*. He was familiar with *huatou* meditation as well and apparently himself engaged in an intensive seven-day solitary retreat in order to show his sister how it was done. He then assumed the role of teacher, urging her: "Hurry up and apply yourself. When you have completely [realized yourself], then I will not be able pull anything over on you. But you must investigate the *huatou* until you have understood it completely."

Despite her brother's example, Yikui Chaochen still found herself unable to make any headway. In fact, her brother's success appears to have made her seeming failure even more frustrating:

When she saw how carefree and at ease the layman [Zilin] seemed to be, she became more and more insecure and depressed. At that time she was strict and ascetic like Venerable Lady Tang,[20] and she resolutely continued in her practice; even when the weather was hot and humid, she would sit dccp into the night, completely ignoring the mosquitoes buzzing around her and biting her.

Although Yikui Chaochen's primary practice had become that of *huatou* investigation, she also joined her mother, Madame Gao, and other family members in sutra chanting. In fact, according to her vita, they were often joined in this by people from outside the family as well:

> Together with her mother and several people of like mind, morning and night they would recite sutras in front of the Buddha, the sound of which could be heard outside of the house and which inspired several tens of people from near and far to come and engage in extended fasts and take refuge in the teachings. It was very much like the family of Layman Pang [of the Tang dynasty].

We see from this description that the primary practice among her family members was still sutra recitation. But like Yigong Chaoke and Yichuan Chaolang before her, Yikui appears to have been interested more in (immediate) realization than simply in devotional practices designed to bring a better rebirth. It was at this point that she decided to pay a visit to Qiyuan Xinggang, who had just recently assumed the position of abbess at the nearby Lion-Subduing Chan Cloister.

Yikui Chaochen had actually heard a lot about Qiyuan Xinggang, for both her parents and her brother Zilin had already been to visit the abbess several times. A number of poems in Qiyuan Xinggang's collection are addressed to both father and son, and Madame Gao appears to have become a lay disciple as well. Later, in her biographical account of her teacher, Yikui Chaochen would reminisce that because her brother "was extremely well versed in the Three Teachings and because he had realized the emptiness of the world, he had a special karmic affinity with [Qiyuan Xinggang]. There was a period when he was assisting her with some problems [having to do with the convent], and sometimes he would accompany her on her walks. Secretly observing [Qiyuan Xinggang's] demeanor, he would sigh that he could never live up to her standards." However, since Yikui Chaochen, a proper young widow, "never went out of the inner quarters, she had not yet had the opportunity to pay her a visit." It was not until the spring of 1651 that Yikui Chaochen and her mother, taking with them a gatha written for Qiyuan Xinggang by Sun Zilin, went to the Lion-Subduing Chan Cloister. It would seem that a connection was made immediately, and Qiyuan Xinggang advised Yikui Chaochen to continue working on her *huatou* under her brother's supervision.

The shared—and eclectic—religious aspirations of the Sun family—
are perhaps most vividly expressed in the following episode recounted in
Yikui Chaochen's vita:

> One day, when everyone, including Layman Zilin, was seated together on
> their meditation cushions, each spoke of their greatest aspirations. [Yikui]
> said: "My aspiration is to emulate the Venerable Master Qiyuan Xinggang.
> Layman Zilin said: "I want all my kith and kin to be saved and to enter into
> the Way. I would rather be a chicken or a dog on the isles of Penglai than
> to be a duke or a lord in this dusty world."[21]

Several months later, Yikui and her mother returned once again to the
Lion-Subduing Chan Cloister, where the two of them participated in two
intensive seven-day meditation retreats. It was at the end of this retreat
that Yikui appears to have had her first breakthrough:

> After [Yikui] had sat for two seven-day sessions in succession, she suddenly
> went into a state of samadhi that lasted for the time it took for four sticks of
> incense to burn down to ashes. In a twinkling of an eye, the great earth was
> immersed in peace, and she completely realized her original face. When
> Layman [Zilin] heard this, he was very happy and, laughing, said: "A dull-
> witted fellow you are to have tarried until this morning before finally grab-
> bing hold of the nostrils! How could you have been so obtuse!"

It was not long after this that Yikui Chaochen gave away all of her possessions "without leaving a single thing for herself" and took the tonsure
with Qiyuan Xinggang.[22] After this, according to Puming, her spiritual
progress was extraordinarily swift: "Possessed of a wisdom from a previous
life, whenever she entered [Qiyuan Xinggang's] quarters for an interview, she completely grasped challenges posed [by her], and within two
years, she had received Dharma transmission."

Yikui Chaochen remained at the Lion-Subduing Chan Cloister for a
short time but then returned home to be with her family. Several years
later, her mother passed away and, not long after that, Qiyuan Xinggang.
For Yikui Chaochen, it was as if she had lost two mothers. Her quasi-filial
devotion to the latter is vividly illustrated by her cutting off a piece of
her flesh (gegu) to make a medicinal broth in the hopes it would restore
Qiyuan Xinggang to health.[23] Her double loss motivated her to commit
herself with renewed determination to her religious practice. In "A Brief
Account of My Life for the Edification of My Disciples," Yikui relates what
happened next:

When I was thirty, my mother died in the sixth month, and in the ninth month my Master also passed way. At that time, my elder Dharma [sister] Yigong assumed the leadership of the Lion-Subduing Chan Cloister, while I mourned by the master's tomb. After the [prescribed mourning] period was over, I thought about building a thatched hermitage for myself but was unable to do so since I had no source of support. Fortunately, my brother Zilin shared my aspirations; he had made a head start in his Chan practice and fully understood the [truth that] the Three Teachings all returned to a single source. And so he built a hermitage to which he gave the name of Joining-the-Three Convent (Cantong an) . . . [and] he asked Master Hong-jue to inscribe [the characters for "Cantong"] on a plaque.

Sun Zilin belonged to those late-Ming circles of literati who advocated "the unity of the Three Teachings."[24] The name "Cantong" brings to mind the title of one of the most famous of all Daoist alchemical texts, the *Zhouyi cantong qi* (Token for Joining the Three According to the *Book of Changes*). In the case of this text, "the Three" refers to the *Book of Changes*, Lao-Zhuang philosophy, and Daoist alchemy, but Sun Zilin appears to have used the term to refer to commonalities among Buddhism, Daoism, and Confucianism.[25] Wang Ting, a good friend of Sun Zilin's (and the author of the inscription for Qiyuan Xinggang's stupa inscription), gives the following explanation in a temple inscription *(ji ming)* he wrote for the Joining-the-Three Convent in 1675:

> Zilin, having received his education from Confucianism and his initial real-ization from Buddhism and having mastered Daoism as well, believed in the common source of the Three Teachings; and so he chose the name of "Joining-the-Three." The character *"tong"* means "one." If you look at things from the perspective of their not being one, then within Buddhism, the doctrinal and the Chan schools represent two [different kinds]. And the Chan school is again divided into five [lineages], and these five again divided into ten and a hundred, to the point that they struggle and con-test with each other. Thus within unity there is difference. If one looks at things from the perspective of their unity, then the ten thousand dharmas all return to it; ordinary people's discussions, words and phrases, donated gifts, and occupations are not mutually opposed to the Buddha nature. How much more should this be the case with Confucianism and Daoism? Therefore within difference there is commonality. To investigate differ-ence and realize unity, means to scrutinize [*kui*] the tens and hundreds and see one; thus [Yikui Chaochen's] style name and the name of her convent appear to be complementary. In this way one can dissolve the dis-

putes [that mark] the latter days of the Dharma even as one dispels any suspicions of heterodoxy. The aspiration of Zilin was a great one, without which Yikui Chaochen could not have accomplished all of this![26]

In this same 1677 inscription, Wang Ting provides a description of the Joining-the-Three Convent: "It was surrounded by clear waters, behind it were shady [stands of] slender bamboo, and in the middle there were over ten buildings, all with winding corridors and curving rooms." He also notes that although the convent had begun as a private family cloister, it was not long before "Yikui declared it a public [convent]." This transformation from private to public also mirrored, in Wang's eyes at least, the transformation of Yikui Chaochen from a woman whom he knew primarily as the daughter of the Sun family and sister of his friend Sun Zilin to a Chan master. "Why did she make [the convent public]?" asks Wang rhetorically. "Because the Yikui Chaochen that took upon herself the great Dharma in order to universally transform everyone under heaven was not the [same woman] that the Sun family had had as a daughter, and her convent's worship of the Buddha, Dharma, and sangha was not something of which a single family could [claim to] be the owner." In fact, Wang Ting writes, just as the convent had "the lineage air" *(you zongfeng),* so its inhabitants lacked all outward signs of femininity *(wu nü xiang).* This was, no doubt, meant as a compliment, but it points once again to the widely held perception of the defeminization of Buddhist nuns.

Even after changing its status from a family cloister to an actual convent, the Joining-the-Three Convent appears to have been primarily designed as a small hermitage for Yikui Chaochen and a few female companions, a comfortable retreat from the hustle and bustle of the world, as she herself describes it:

> The cassia railings of its secluded chambers, the winding halls of its tiny rooms, and, beyond the kiosks by the ponds, the pavilions by the water, flowering plants, and slender bamboo. In the year *bingjia* (1656) the buildings were finished and everything was ready; and in the second month of the winter, I was invited to take up residence there. At that time, there were only six or seven people living in the hermitage; and I was able to fully enjoy the pleasure of [living in] the woods. The white clouds sealed the gates, and it was quiet and tranquil with no one around. Six years passed like a single day.

During these years, it would appear that Yikui Chaochen sought spiritual guidance from other Buddhist masters, including Muchen Daomin himself. She also maintained religious and literary friendships with numer-

ous other monks, nuns, and lay men and women. The nun to whom
Yikui Chaochen appears to have been particularly close, however, was her
"Dharma aunt" Weiji Xingzhi (d. 1672). Weiji Xingzhi was the daughter of
a distinguished family from Yaojiang (Zhejiang Province). Her father was
a lay Buddhist, and as a young girl she would often accompany him to visit
Master Miyun Yuanwu. It appears that even then she already knew she did
not want to marry; her family, probably due to its Buddhist inclinations,
readily agreed to her taking the tonsure under yet another of Miyun
Yuanwu's Dharma heirs, Shiqi Tongyun (1594–1663). After undergoing
several years of rigorous training, Weiji Xingzhi received Dharma transmission from Shiqi Tongyun and, in 1646, became abbess of the Heroic
Sage Convent (Xiongsheng an) in Hangzhou, where Yikui Chaochen frequently went to visit her. Weiji Xingzhi appears to have been a formidable
teacher, known for her strict discipline as well as for her eloquent poems
and forceful sermons, many of which were collected and circulated after
her death in the form of a discourse record collection, which unfortunately is no longer extant.

In the winter of 1670, Yikui Chaochen was invited to the Heroic Sage
Convent to lead a meditation retreat. After it was over, Puming tells us,
Weiji Xingzhi's senior student (and eventual Dharma heir) Jingnuo Chaoyue commented on how well it went, attributing this to the friendship
between Weiji Xingzhi and Yikui Chaochen, which was "like milk and
water" (shuiru jiaohe).[27] Both women may also have been aware that Weiji
Xingzhi's health was not good and that they might not see one another
again, which is why when the retreat was over, they "wiped away their tears
and parted" (huidi er bie). Indeed, two years later Weiji Xingzhi was dead.
Yikui Chaochen wrote the following poem of mourning:

> In my longing for the Way, I often sought her out over these twelve years,
> And, with the seasons, came to know her face from many different
>   angles.
> Fortunate to have obtained a pearl watched over by the Black Dragon;
> My greatest goal has been to attune myself with the strings of the Lion.
> Now suddenly out of the blue, the precious peak has half-toppled over;
> And it as if the boat of compassion has overturned in the Dharma sea.
> Although the melody played by the iron flute without holes has faded,
> Fortunately the Chan lamp is there to be handed down through the
>   ages.[28]

Yikui Chaochen also maintained close connections with other nuns
in the area. "She was also very friendly and loving with her elder and
younger Dharma [sisters] from the same lineage and, from beginning to

end, they were as one," writes Puming. One of these friends was an abbess
by the name of Dongyun, about whom I have been unable to find any
further information. In one of two poems addressed to this nun, Yikui
Chaochen plays on the meaning of *"dongyun"* (cloud-swathed cave). It is
also worth noting that, in the title, Yikui Chaochen refers to the abbess
Dongyun as her *chan you,* or Chan companion—and the poem certainly
conveys this sense of deep personal affinity:

> The ancient hall stands tall and proud, made to look new;
> Locked inside the cloud-swathed cave is a kindred soul.
> Burning incense, sitting silently, we attune to one another;
> The words of a tongueless person are the most novel of all.[29]

The second poem, written on the occasion of Dongyun's fiftieth birthday,
refers, as does the one above, to the abbess's work of rebuilding her convent, engaging in teaching, and maintaining the lineage so that "sons and
grandsons to come will be able to find their way to the source."

> You've forgotten the dusty world and realized your own inner ease;
> In middle age, your longing for the Way is as it was in the beginning.
> Examining errors, acknowledging mistakes: the spring dream knows.
> And in the fragrance of the lotus, enlightenment is truly explained.
> Of a hundred years, half have already vanished into the distant past;
> Carefully attending to things, each and every matter has gone well.
> Our grandfathers' fields and gardens have been tilled and are now ripe;
> Sons and grandsons to come will be able find their way to the source.[30]

Yikui Chaochen also had a number of such lay Chan companions. In an
editorial note to a letter written by the early-Qing female poet Shen Hui
(*zi* Lanfang) to her friend the female poet and calligrapher Gui Shufen
(*zi* Jiying), the editors divide Shen's various women friends into four categories: poetry friends *(shiyou),* painting friends *(danqing you),* calligraphy
friends *(shufa you),* and Chan-discussing friends *(tanchan you).*[31] As it turns
out, Shen Hui's *tanchan you* was none other than Yikui Chaochen.[32] In the
second stanza of a lyric poem entitled "Delighting at the New Building of
the Great Compassion Tower at Joining-the-Three Convent: To the Tune
of 'Raofo ge,'" Gui Shufen writes:

> The one who is ill has the most time on her hands.
> At dusk I call for Lianlian to dust off the old inkstone
> Or peruse my books till the humming makes me dizzy.
> Having waited until winter's end and the coming of spring,

I've often come to this Chan cloister.
This time as I climb up to the hall,
And slowly stroll through this monastery for women,
My pent-up emotions enjoy a measure of release,
As in the green shade,
I listen to the warbling of the yellow orioles.[33]

Women visiting temples and monasteries was a common motif in late imperial official literature and in fictional literature. More often than not, it was regarded as a practice to be strongly discouraged, since it was thought to place them in a situation of undefended (sexual) vulnerability. Gui Shufen's poem gives us a very different perspective, that of the pleasures as well as the emotional release that a literate gentry woman might derive from visiting a convent, and Yikui Chaochen's convent was known for being situated in a particularly peaceful and picturesque location. When visiting a convent, they might engage in conversation with women monastics, the same sort of pleasure as that experienced by male literati who visited with refined monks in their elegant monastic surroundings.

It was during this time as well, toward the end of 1661, that Yikui Chaochen's father, Sun Maoshi, passed away. Her response to her father's death was far more measured than it had been when her mother died. Although impeccably filial from beginning to end, she herself admitted that it came as somewhat of a relief to her: "In the past, I was always thinking about my old father. Now I can single-mindedly devote myself to the Way." [34] This, of course, was not to be, for it was around this time that Yichuan Chaolang and then Yigong Chaoke also died, and Yikui Chaochen was called upon to take up their unfinished tasks at the Lion-Subduing Chan Cloister, one of the most pressing of which was the completion of Qiyuan Xinggang's stupa. Initially, she tried to resolve this problem by simply moving her teacher's stupa to the Joining-the-Three Convent and building a stupa for Yigong Chaoke right next to it. In any case, it seems clear that Yikui Chaochen had no intention of taking up permanent residence at the Lion-Subduing Chan Cloister, and in fact she said as much to the Dong family when she finally acceded to their urgent request that she come to the convent. She expressed her ambivalent combination of duty and reluctance in the Dharma talk she delivered at the Lion-Subduing Chan Cloister upon assuming her position as its abbess:

After leaving nine years ago to return to my home in the forest, how could I have wanted to come back again to serve as abbess? . . . [But] nowadays when the Way has been wounded, and the time of the sages is far away, then the demons are strong and the Dharma is weak. It is for this reason that I have devoted my entire life to the emulation of the ancient styles and norms and have made no attempt to lord it over my contemporaries. And so I have found it best to cover my head with my Buddhist robes, close the gate, and pretend to be a fool. I had no idea that the lay patrons and Dharma protectors . . . would be so profoundly worried that the reputation of the Patriarch's family would sink and, splitting into factions, end up dividing into the way of the Dharma and heterodox ways. How could I sit and watch that happen?[35]

Elsewhere, she continues to explain how it is she returned to the Lion-Subduing Chan Cloister. It is clear that she never planned to remain longer than the time required to complete her tasks:

At the repeated urging of the lay donor from Xunxi, Dong [Hance], in the first month of the year renyin [1662] I reluctantly agreed to his request and went back [to visit]. When I saw that our late Master's stupa garden was located in an out-of-the-way place in the wilds where it was difficult for people to watch over it, I felt sad and anxious in body and mind. And so I returned to live at the Lion-Subduing Chan Cloister for six years. However, my sole concern was to deal with the matter of the stupa, and I remain untouched by my environment and uninvolved in worldly affairs. By the first month of the year bingwu [1666] I had begun the work of moving the stupa to a location to the left of the Joining-the-Three Convent; I had also built a completely new tomb and reliquary for my elder Dharma [brother] Yigong right beside our Master's stupa. By the time of the Clear and Bright Festival in the year dinghui [1668] the work of stupa construction was completed, and in the eighth month I retired from the Lion-Subduing Chan Cloister [and returned] to the Joining-the-Three Convent.[36]

True to her word, six years later, Yikui Chaochen left the Lion-Subduing Chan Cloister in the hands of some of the senior nuns and returned to live at her relatively smaller, and no doubt much more tranquil, cloister. The following years, however, were devoted not to teaching and quiet contemplation but rather to expansion of her own convent. As Yikui Chaochen herself proudly recounts:

That winter, we put up three buildings, and in the spring of the year wushen [1668] we began to build an entrance gate. In the year jiyu [1669] we built a bathhouse on the eastern side, and in the year gengxu [1670], on the birthday of the Buddha, we [began] construction of the great hall. When I left the household life, I had given away every bit of the marriage dowry [which had been given to me by my own] Sun family, as well as my share of the goods from [my husband's] Sheng family; this is something everyone, whether monastic or lay, knows well. I have spent twenty-six years toiling for this Dharma family, ten years of which have been devoted to the task of building, as gradually this convent has come into being. All of this has come from the trusting hearts of donors from all ten directions. It is for this reason that night and day I exhort and admonish you, my disciples: if we do not disregard our bodily [desires] and make our minds as if dead [to the world], how will we be able to ensure that [this convent] will continue for a long time without falling into decay? If you want to repay your Dharma ancestors, you must respectfully adhere to the pure regulations, and sincerely fulfill your vows. In this way, our simple and austere "family style" will last forever. Only by following these words will we be able to live together as a community and ensure that it be sustained for generation after generation. You must not betray that which has been the primary aspiration of my entire life![37]

Wang Ting's 1677 temple inscription provides a similar cataloguing of all of the additions and improvements that Yikui Chaochen made to the convent after her return from the Lion-Subduing Chan Cloister. In fact, it became so large and magnificent, he says, that "although it was just a convent, in appearance it had the air of a major monastery."[38] All of this required money, of course, and as we have seen, Yikui Chaochen had none of her own. Wang Ting notes that her frugal brother, Sun Zilin, was again of great help to her in this regard. But it is also apparent that by this time she had established a considerable reputation for herself and had attracted not only a great many disciples who desired to live in this convent but also a significant number of lay donors. Wang Ting confirms this:

It was because of her vow [to be of benefit to others] that Yikui Chaochen carried out this extraordinary work, and it inspired famous nuns from the ten directions, and virtuous [lay] families opened their hearts and offered donations, and in this way they worked together in a complementary way. How marvelous! This is how this convent [has contributed to] the flourishing of Chan in my district of [Jiaxing]. . . . I have observed that it has been over twenty years since Yikui Chaochen attained enlightenment; she does not harbor even a single thought of fame, reputation, or wealth, and in guiding and instructing her many students, she always puts the precepts and rules foremost and [regards] her mission as being one of teaching others and ensuring that they all return home to the ultimate truth. The

Chan style of Linji has been able to flourish, and the name of this Joining-the-Three [Convent] for women has become respected. People come
from far and near to receive it, and the worthies of the next generations
will cherish it.[39]

It would appear then, that Yikui Chaochen was, more than any of
Qiyuan Xinggang's other Dharma heirs, the one who most fully carried
on the spirit of her teacher. It is clear, for example, that she shared Qiyuan
Xinggang's profound concern for authenticity, integrity, and discipline
in a time when such seemed to be sorely lacking in Chan Buddhist circles.
As Puming tells us:

> She often observed how, in these latter days of the Dharma, there were
> many who produced writings that robbed emptiness and lost truth, who
> practiced [Chan] techniques and methods for the sake of private gain, and
> who took [spiritual] understanding to be something common and ordi-
> nary, [Yikui Chaochen] instructed her disciples to regard true principles
> and authentic conduct to be the most important thing and not to spend
> their efforts on literary elegance and glib speech.

In one of her Dharma talks, Yikui Chaochen reminds her nuns how fortunate they are to have such good conditions for spiritual practice—clean
accommodations, plenty of food, quiet and tranquility, and, although she
does not say this in so many words, a teacher who is genuinely concerned
for their well-being and wants them to attain enlightenment in this very
lifetime. In particular, she urges them to resolutely devote themselves to
the determined investigation of their *huatou*. Again, the teachings are
not original; one finds in them lines and images that can be found nearly
verbatim in the Dharma talks of countless male Chan masters. But again,
at the risk of belaboring the point, in this case their being presented as
being words of advice delivered by a woman Chan master to her female
disciples shows that, for some women at least, being a Buddhist nun was
serious business—unlike the impression provided by so many popular
accounts.

As was true of her teacher, Yikui Chaochen's reputation was such that
she was able to attract a wide range of lay donors, as she herself indicates
in a Dharma talk delivered on the occasion of the consecration of a statue
of the Buddha:

> I have been fortunate to receive donations from Dharma protectors who
> are officials of both county and prefecture, from donors both gentry and

commoner from city and district; and from different convents, elder and younger Dharma [sisters] have also contributed Dharma donations to the Inexhaustible Treasury (i.e., monastic coffers) and planted the divine sprouts in the mind-field that lies beyond time. With joined hands we have supported each other and brought into being this holy image on this day.[40]

And like the Lion-Subduing Chan Cloister under the leadership of Qiyuan Xinggang, the Joining-the-Three Convent became a locus for traveling monastics and others who, in a time of increasing political turmoil and social disruption, flocked to her door not only for spiritual instruction but for basic food and shelter as well. According to Puming, Yikui Chaochen did what she could but found it to be exhausting work. The Joining-the-Three Convent was no longer the quiet and tranquil retreat it had been when Sun Zilin had first had it built for her:

> From the four directions more and more people would show up [at the convent]. In years when the harvests were bad, it would be filled with traveling monks and [life in the convent] became more and more austere every day, since there were four to five hundred people to feed. The master labored and toiled to provide everyone with what they needed, but because she was ashamed to ask for donor subscriptions, she often found herself in a quandary about what to do, and her energy began to flag.

We have seen before that the first sign of the imminent death of a hardworking abbess was that her apparently endless energy began to fail. And this was the case with Yikui Chaochen, who, to judge from her portrait, was not particularly sturdy or strong. Her death and subsequent funeral were described in considerable detail by her disciples. We are told that the first sign of her passing was that she found it difficult to swallow her food, although she had no pain in her body. She then refused all medications and gradually stopped eating rice and other grains and began to subsist on nothing but water, a kind of ritual suicide that since early times was also a part of the dying ritual of a Chan master. She then went to great lengths, much as her teacher Qiyuan Xinggang had done before her, to assure that everything was in order within the convent before she died. In the end, as in the beginning, the primary person she relied on was her brother Sun Zilin:

> On the seventeenth day, she requested her aging [brother] Layman Zilin to come to her bedside so that she might discuss with him what was to

be done with the monastery after her death. Their conversation did not touch on personal matters at all. Layman [Zilin] then wrote out [Yunqi Zhuhong's] *Rules and Agreements for Communal Living at Yunqi*[41] and showed it to the Master, who said: "We can have these carved on wooden boards: one to be hung on the monastery gate, one to be hung in the Dharma hall, and one to be hung in the refectory."

What is perhaps most striking about this entire description is the central role played by Yikui's brother Sun Zilin, by this time a very elderly gentleman himself, in assuring her that the entire transition would be carried out properly. Since the Joining-the-Three Convent had been built and funded primarily, although by no means entirely, by Sun Zilin, the two siblings together made the decisions as to who would succeed her. As in the case of Qiyuan Xinggang, the responsibilities, both practical and spiritual, were divided among several students. To Puming, her first and senior disciple, fell the primary responsibility for the spiritual leadership of the convent. To Fayuan Mingling, another woman Dharma successor about whom we know very little, was presented the wish-fulfilling scepter that Qiyuan Xinggang had herself held in her hands: "This [scepter] was handed down from Master Huanyou to Master [Shiche], who then passed it down to our former teacher [Qiyuan Xinggang]; today it is passed on to you. It is not something ordinary and commonplace, and you must always take precious care of it." Mingyuan Weiyi was then presented with the master's fly whisk, also a symbol of teaching, with the words: "[This is] to use whenever you speak a few phrases relating to matters of the Dharma." And then finally, an iron scepter was presented to yet another of her women Dharma successors, Xingyuan Mingshen, with the words: "Your mind should be like iron in your vigil over and care for the community."[42]

As we saw earlier, the next step in the ritual of dying required Yikui to leave a "death verse." As Faure points out, a few Chan masters of the past objected to this ritualization and even tried to avoid having to leave this final poem. However, Faure notes, such behavior was actually quite atypical because "it risked being seen by the disappointed disciples as a mere admission of failure on the part of the master and could have dealt a potentially fatal blow to his school."[43] The result of this was that the only way to get around this ritual was to leave a verse expressing one's reluctance to do so. This is precisely what Yikui Chaochen appears to have done at first:

The venerable Layman [Zilin] said: "Do you have a [final] gatha?" "No, I don't," replied the master. The elder Layman said, "A wordless phrase is already a phrase made up of words." [Yikui Chaochen] said, "Our lineage [teaches] nondependence on words and letters; the Honored One preached the Dharma for forty-nine years without ever uttering a single word. If I were to [produce] words and phrases, this would be slandering the Dharma. Now each of you can take something from my wordless words.

The last step in the ritual then takes place, as Yikui Chaochen to the very end exhibited a lucid mind and complete control regarding not only the manner but also the time of her final transition (she put it off by a day to make sure that everything was ready). When everything appeared to be in order, she passed away, we are told, exactly at the time she had predicted. She did, however, relent and leave behind a death poem:

> All her life, this "fellow" has been as tough as nails;
> Once she dug her heels in, she could not be moved.
> At twenty-four, she first found out about this matter;
> Ten years she bitterly struggled, for forty forgot herself.
> The nine bonds[44] of this suffering world were untied
> When she saw how to cut through its ways like water.
> She's long wanted to leave, and now her karma agrees;
> Seven springs in a single day, iron nails turned to dust.
> The four great elements dispersed by wind and fire.
> Leaves fall, it is clearly autumn: time to return to the root.
> Ha, ha, ha!
> Footloose and fancy-free—that's me![45]

Yikui Chaochen's discourse records were compiled primarily by two of her Dharma heirs, Puming and Mingling. One of the prefaces, in which she is, predictably, referred to as a modern-day Miaozong and Miaodao, was written in 1680 by Shi Bo. A friend of her brother's, Shi Bo had devoted himself to his scholarship after the fall of the Ming dynasty and enjoyed a high reputation in the Jiangnan area for his erudition and gifts as a teacher; students would come to him from all parts of China.[46] He was also an aficionado of Buddhism and referred to himself as a follower of Muyun Tongmen, the monk from the Southern Antiquity Monastery who was Qiyuan Xinggang's spiritual adviser in Jiaxing. Included in the front matter of the discourse record collection is a portrait of Yikui Chaochen, accompanied by an inscription penned by Chan master Muchen Daomin. Yikui Chaochen's portrait shows a woman whose physical type differed greatly from that of Qiyuan Xinggang: her face long rather than square, her build slender rather than solid. She holds the scepter passed on to her by Qiyuan Xinggang, but at an angle rather than upright and, one might say, almost gingerly. In fact, one might even say that this is a portrait of an intellectual rather than a pragmatist.

What happened to the Joining-the-Three Convent, the Lion-Subduing Chan Cloister, and the other convents associated with Qiyuan Xinggang and her immediate Dharma successors is unclear. In 1687, twenty years after Yikui Chaochen's departure from the Lion-Subduing Chan Cloister and more than thirty years after the death of Qiyuan Xinggang, we find Wang Ting, who had long been a supporter of the convent, writing another fund-raising appeal. He begins his appeal with a description of his childhood memories of the convent at its peak, a truly splendid and impressive place and, indeed, the "finest convent anywhere." He contrasts this childhood vision with how he found it more recently, completely overgrown with weeds, its walls falling down, its windows broken and torn, and its Buddha statue lying destroyed and exposed to the elements. He notes that its regular patrons, the Dong family, have been away and unaware of what has happened to the convent—and indeed, by this time their fortunes and prestige have declined considerably. But, he writes, there were still some people around, including members of the Li family and the elderly Wang Ting himself (whose wife, Madame Jiang—also the daughter of a prominent Jiaxing family—by this time had built herself a cloister behind the Lion-Subduing Chan Cloister), who were committed to raising the funds necessary to restore the convent to at least some of its former glory. They were also determined to find a suitably eminent abbess to oversee its revival. The woman Chan master they found was Jueke Benxin, a Dharma heir of Muchen Daomin. Born in Tongxiang, Jueke Benxin was the granddaughter of Governor-General Qian Chengjiang. Left widowed at the age of twenty-five, in 1651 she entered the religious life under the guidance of Muchen Daomin.[47] For several decades, Benxin Jueke had been the abbess of the flourishing Luminous Cause Convent (Mingyin an), which was also located in Jiaxing and housed over a hundred nuns. We are told that she was somewhat reluctant to leave the Mingyin Convent and assume leadership of the Lion-Subduing Chan Cloister; in fact, it appears that after Yikui Chaochen had returned to her own Joining-the-Three convent, Jueke Benxin had been invited to assume the abbacy of this convent but had refused. Only when she heard about the terrible state of disrepair and decline that the once-famous convent had fallen into did she finally agreed to come. With the help of local literati donors and the nuns still living at the convent, she did her best to raise funds for the renovation. This time, however, economic conditions where much more difficult, and, we are told, Jueke Benxin had to appeal to donors from townships and counties outside of Meixi as well. Gradually, however, the Lion-Subduing Chan Cloister began to make a slow comeback, and once again lay donors and visiting monastics began to flock to its halls. In 1682, however, Jueke Benxin fell ill and decided to return to the Mingyin Convent, leaving the Lion-Subduing Chan Cloister in the hands of Yuanduan Yufu, a Dharma heir of Shanshao Benzhi (1620–1686), who, like Jueke Benxin, was a Dharma successor of Muchen Daomin.

We do not know much about Yuanduan Yufu, except that she was from a well-established family of Jiading and had taken the tonsure at a small convent in Changzhou at the age of twelve *sui*. She later studied with Shanshao Benzhi and, after having received his transmission, became the abbess of the Luminous Cause Convent in Hangzhou. Because Yuanduan Yufu left no discourse records and only a handful of poems, we do not know much about her as an abbess, nor do we know how long she was able to keep the Lion-Subduing Chan Cloister afloat.[48] There is no further mention of the convent until 1874, when we find Wang Ting's 1687 appeal reprinted in the Meixi gazetteer.[49]

Long before this time, however, these convents, if they still existed at all, had probably already begun their transformation into sites of nostalgic memory. Sometime around the turn of the seventeenth century, Dong Wei, a descendant of the original patrons of both the Lion-Subduing Chan Cloister and the Prajñā Convent, recorded an excursion he took with a friend to the latter. Dong Wei's account, with its profoundly elegiac tone, gives some indication of the fate of these seventeenth-century convents:

> Fish large and small in the narrow brook that surrounded the village; cold pools everywhere filled with sands of gold. At the side of the brook: ancient trees just beginning to shed their leaves, and three or four straw-roofed huts. We then followed the river until we reached the Prajñā Convent. Inside the convent it was tranquil and still, the hubbub of town notable for its absence. Suddenly I felt as if this body of mine had entered into a secluded valley, and all around me, I already felt as if I were very far from the dusty world. Tall and stately, the lofty halls seemed to soar, and the vermilion railings on all four sides circled and wound about. Ten jeweled banners fluttered in the pine breezes, and a hallway of clouds circled over Mount Jinsu. I recalled how, in the past, my ancestors would come to this place, [and] following one on the heels of the other, the guests would arrive; how very busy it was! Bamboo leaves, brimming goblets, the silver flutes playing, fallen leaves blanketing the ground, the drifting vapors of

tea. . . . Fifteen years ago, and it is all like a dream. Dignified and impos-
ing, the months and years slide by like a weaver's shuttle. Musing over
things of the past, I turn my head, and although I would like to cleanse
the sorrow from my heart, I have no goblet of wine. But fortunately I have
a good companion with me, with whom I can engage in lofty conversation
that brings a smile. As evening falls, hand and hand we leave the gates of
the convent, and all that can be seen is the setting sun hovering over the
scattered willows.[50]

CHAPTER SIX

From Hengzhou to Hangzhou

Jizong Xingche

Qiyuan Xinggang and her seven Dharma successors were all born and raised in the Zhejiang-Jiangsu area, the heartland of seventeenth-century Buddhist and literary culture. Two of the women Chan masters whose *yulu* are preserved in the Jiaxing canon, however, were originally from outside of this area, although both ended up traveling to the southeast and spending a significant time there as abbesses of various nunneries. One of these women was Chan master Jizong Xingche (b. 1606), who was from Hengzhou, in present-day Hunan Province, the other—whom we will meet in Chapter Seven—was the late-seventeenth-century Chan master Ziyong Chengru, who was from the Beijing area.

Jizong Xingche, as we can see from her date of birth, was about nine years younger than Qiyuan Xinggang and somewhat older than most of Qiyuan Xinggang's women Dharma successors (several of whom Jizong Xingche knew personally). She is officially listed as a Dharma successor of Wanru Tongwei (1594–1657), one of the twelve senior students of Miyun Yuanwu. She received most of her early training, however, from Linji Chan master Shanci Tongji (1608–1645), and it is from him that she would most likely have received Dharma transmission, had he not suffered an untimely death in 1645. Originally from Sichuan, Shanci Tongji was a Dharma successor of Tianyin Yuanxiu, who was, along with Miyun Yuanwu, one of the three Dharma heirs of Huanyou Zhengchuan (1549–1614). Shanci Tongji was teaching on Mount Heng in Hunan when Jizong Xingche became his student.

As is true of all of the nuns in this study, the biographical details of Jizong's life must be pieced together from various sources, although most of what can be gleaned comes from the prefaces and other materials contained in her five-fascicle *yulu*, printed in 1656. It makes sense to begin with the brief vita *(xingshi)* that Jizong Xingche herself provided much

later in her life when of a group of laymen asked her to address the congregation of the Universal Salvation Convent (Pudu an) in the seaport
city of Ningbo in Zhejiang, where she arrived as an honored visitor. She
begins by telling us that her father's name was Liu Shanchang, and her
mother's surname was Gao. Her account of her early life is marked by several hagiographic conventions—details that, if not in fact inserted afterward by her disciples when they were compiling her discourse records,
would indicate the extent to which by that time Jizong Xingche had fully
assumed the traditional religious role of venerable Chan master. Thus
she describes the prognostic dream her father had before she was con-
ceived, and the miraculous birdsong and light that filled the room on the
night she was born. And she notes as well:

> Even at a young age, I disliked eating nonvegetarian food; just one taste of
> meat and I would spit it out. When I became a little older, I took pleasure
> in reading Confucian texts and Buddhist sutras. I felt revulsion for the dust
> and confusion of the world, and I thought deeply about the matters of life
> and death and begged my father to let me sacrifice myself and enter the
> religious life, but he refused. Later, I was engaged to marry a man named
> Chen, but after only a few years, he perished on his way to take up a gov-
> ernment post.[1]

The themes here are hagiographically familiar: an early piety, the
unsuccessful attempt at avoiding marriage, and a (perhaps fortunate)
early widowhood. One of the prefaces to Jizong Xingche's *yulu* provides
a few more supplementary details regarding her life before she became
a nun. We are told, for example, that she came from an eminent scholar-
official family, noting that her maternal grandfather had served as a vice-
censor-in-chief in southern Jiangxi and at one point made a journey south
to Caoxi to pay his respects to the "flesh-body" of the monk Hanshan
Deqing. This was of particular significance to the author of this preface,
Tan Zhenmo (*jinshi* 1624), a well-known literatus-official from Jiaxing
who held a number of high-ranking posts in the last years of the Ming but
is perhaps best known for his long association with the late-Ming master
Hanshan Deqing.[2] In his preface, Tan also tells us that Jizong's pater-
nal grandfather had served as a department magistrate in Suzhou and,
while there, had visited with a number of Chan Buddhist masters and
achieved a measure of spiritual insight. He recounts the story—an anec-
dote that Jizong refers to as well in one of later addresses to her congregation—about how former minister of works Gao Xuanqi from Suzhou
was assigned to an official position in Hengyang, the hometown of Jizong

Xingche's grandfather, where he served for seven years, and acquired
such a reputation that, upon his departure, a shrine with an inscribed
stela was erected in his honor. Tan goes on to relate how, on the very day
that Gao took up official residence in Hengyang, Jizong Xingche's grandfather, who was ninety years old at the time and living in Suzhou, heard
the sound of a bell and, seating himself in the lotus position, peacefully
passed away with a smile on his lips. For preface writer Tan, these accounts
provided further confirmation not only of Jizong Xingche's distinguished
background and regional connections with the Zhejiang-Jiangsu area but
also of her familial and karmic predisposition toward Buddhism.[3]

Another of the prefaces to Jizong Xingche's *yulu* was composed by
the well-known Buddhist layman—and Jiaxing native—Yan Dacan (1590–
1671).[4] In this preface, Yan Dacan mentions Jizong Xingche's short-lived
marriage to the man named Chen:

> While serving in an official post in western Guangdong, Chen lost his life
> in the turmoil of the times. The Master wrote a letter laying out her griev-
> ances and desire for retribution, but then, determined to cleanse herself
> of her feelings of resentment, she abandoned family life in order to study
> the Way.[5]

It is not clear how exactly Chen lost his life, although we do know that
the Guangzhou area was, like the Jiangnan region, one of the centers of
Ming loyalist activity in the seventeenth century. He may have even been
a member of the well-known Restoration Society (Fushe)—as we shall
see, there is yet another preface appended to Jizong Xingche's discourse
records that is signed by a large group of male literati, most of whom
were Ming loyalists and several of whom joined the society in 1629. It is
not clear what Jizong Xingche wished to achieve by writing her letter of
grievance, but it may have been official acknowledgment of his death on
behalf of the tottering Ming court. In any case, all we know is that despite
her early religious inclinations, it was at least in part the untimely death
of her husband that motivated her to enter a life of religious practice. As
with Qiyuan Xinggang, her first move was not to take the tonsure and
enter a convent. Rather, she simply took up residence in a small hermitage where she could devote herself to religious practice in the time she
had free from her domestic duties, including caring for her in-laws and
her children. Wang Duanshu, in an editorial note to the poem by Jizong
Xingche that she includes in her 1667 anthology of women's poetry, states
that Jizong Xingche had three sons and a daughter, although I have not
found mention of this anywhere else.[6] As Jizong Xingche herself tells us,

I then built a hermitage in which I installed a [Buddha] image and began
to engage in the cultivation of a merit field. At dawn and dusk, I would take
time from my other duties to sit in quiet meditation; I took such delight in
adhering to the precepts and [religious] discipline, that I became determined to leave the householder's life and, in the days that followed, began
to seek out teachers of knowledge and wisdom.

Whether or not we are prepared to take her at her word, what we do see
in Jizong Xingche's account is an apparent discrepancy between male
accounts of religious women, with their emphasis on the self-sacrifice and
suffering, and those written by women themselves, where there is just as
much emphasis on the delight and sense of inner freedom gleaned from
their solitary meditative practices. Jizong Xingche's comments confirm
what Kang-i Sun Chang observes of Ming-Qing elite women, for whom
"life's greatest challenge was to find leisure time for reading and writing
amidst a daily routine over-full of domestic duties" and, as a corollary,
"widowhood made it possible for many Ming-Qing women to escape from
the routines of everyday life and to nourish a life of solitude that was conducive to literary imagination."[7] As Grace Fong and others have noted,
illness was another means by which elite women were able to carve out a
space for themselves.[8] In fact, the term *qinghuan* (pure joy), which Kang-i
Sun Chang tells us many women writers used to describe the feeling of
self-contained solitude afforded by occasional illness, is almost the same
as that used by religious women, and especially nuns, to describe their joy,
not in the sick room, but in the cloister.

Jizong Xingche—as seems to have been the case with many seventeenth-century abbesses—was not content to simply engage in Buddha
recitation as would befit a pious woman, and in particular a pious and
loyal widow, of her times. Rather, the taste of joy and freedom impelled
her not only to make a more radical break with the domestic sphere but
also to actively seek out instruction from qualified teachers. Again like
Qiyuan Xinggang, Jizong Xingche first sought out someone nearby, a
Master Haitian in this case. Master Haitian was important not for who
she was—indeed, I have been unable to find any information on her (or
him?) at all—but for the text that Jizong Xingche found sitting on her
table, a copy of the *Nanyue Transmission of the Lamp Records (Nanyue chuandeng lu)*. This collection of accounts of past masters in the Linji lineage
had been recently compiled by Chan master Shanci Tongji, who was then
living in a modest hermitage on Yanxia Peak on nearby Mount Heng.[9]
After avidly reading this collection, Jizong Xingche immediately sought
Shanci Tongji out. Her first interview, according to her own account,
went as follows:

The Master asked me, "What spiritual achievement have you attained at home?" "I have engaged in Buddha recitation [*nianfo*]," I replied. "Has Buddha recitation got you anywhere?" he asked. "I have come to you precisely in order to seek your guidance," I answered, bowing respectfully. Then he said: "You should investigate the following [*huatou*]: 'When not a single breath arises, then where will you settle yourself?'"

What is interesting here is the implication that simple Buddha recitation, the practice deemed most suitable for most laypeople, and in particular for women, was in Jizong Xingche's case simply not enough. Clearly, her motivation was to "get somewhere" in this life—the immediate enlightenment that the intense practice of *huatou* meditation was supposed to precipitate—and not simply to aspire to rebirth as a man in the next. After her meeting with Shanci Tongji, then, Jizong Xingche applied herself to her *huatou* alone in her small family hermitage. Her practice did not (and, for the purposes of the story, *could* not) come easily. Occasionally, Shanci Tongji recommended that she study other religious texts, such as Yunqi Zhuhong's *Progress on the Chan Path (Changuan cejin)*, a selection of accounts of Chan masters.[10] She tells us that the account she found most inspiring was one in which an aspirant is exhorted not to "simply forget form and deaden the mind, for that is a [spiritual] illness that is most profound and difficult to cure," which was Dahui Zonggao's primary concern as well.

Jizong Xingche's immersion in these texts, however, appears to have led her (as it did countless other lay Buddhists) to an overly intellectual understanding of enlightenment, which Shanci Tongji found necessary to counteract, in true Linji Chan fashion, with a few blows from his staff. However, in the end, it was a text that precipitated what she felt to be her first breakthrough:

Whether walking or sitting, for a full seven days and nights I did not even close my eyes once. Then, one day I read in one of the *yulu* of the old [masters] about how "a hundred years and thirty-six thousand days come and go" [and] in the end it was this fellow's words that led me to realize that the roots of karma are all illusory and unreal transformations.[11] The everyday and the ordinary, I realized, are nothing more [than Buddha nature]. I then composed the following gatha:

There is that which is neither born nor perishes;
That is formless and neither sacred nor mundane.
Morning and evening come and go in succession;
Why sit shivering on the cold cliff writing poems?

Shanci Tongji was, however, not as impressed with this gatha as she had hoped he would be. It was a good poem, he acknowledged, but it was the product of intelligence and literary talent. They were not, he told her, "words that reflect your personal witnessing, your personal enlightenment. If someone with enlightened eyes were to look at it, he wouldn't even think them worth a smile." This rejection spurred her on, as she tells us:

> After this, whether walking or sitting, I tirelessly investigated [the *huatou*] for forty-nine days and nights until suddenly I found myself in a state of consciousness lasting three or four hours in which I was not aware of having either a body or a mind. Then, by chance, I heard a peal of thunder, and with the speed of [a bird] released from his cage, at that moment my doubts vanished like a silver mountain and iron walls collapsing into smithereens. I then composed the following gatha:
>
>> At the end of eighty thousand gates is a single pass,
>> A pass that was once completely concealed from view;
>> A peal of thunder and suddenly the main gate opens;
>> The "family" passes the entire day at ease in the halls.
>
> This time when I presented my gatha to Master Shanci, he accepted it.

After this initial experience, Jizong Xingche continued to refine and deepen her insight. Interestingly, she admits that Shanci Tongji and other teachers continued to find it necessary to warn her against the spiritual dangers not of emotionality or distraction—thought to be the primary obstacles faced by women on the religious path—but rather of her own intelligence. In the discourse records of one of Shanci Tongji's Dharma successors, Chan master Erzhan Zun—who presumably had been a senior student when Jizong Xingche first came to study with Shanci Tongji and thus knew her well—we find what appears be a reply to a letter by Jizong Xingche. In his letter, Erzhan Zun remarks on her obvious literary talents but warns her of their dangers as well:

> If you wish to understand the great matter of life and be a good vessel of the Dharma gate, you must first cut off all empty words and apply yourself to [your practice] with integrity and strict rigorousness, never deviating from this until death. Enlightenment is like a flip of the palm, [after which] no one will be able to cheat and mislead you. But if all you have is a wide and extensive memory, [your words will be] nothing more than chatter with which you deceive both others and yourself. [If you continue in this manner,] you will most certainly lose sight of the true reason for hav-

ing left the household life, and if you fall into this sort of error, I am afraid it will be difficult to extricate yourself from it.[12]

Shanci Tongji in his exhortations to his woman disciple emphasizes yet again the absolute necessity of unremitting (and manly) resolve and determination in order to achieve one's spiritual goal. "When you climb a mountain," he reminds Jizong Xingche, "you must climb to the highest peak; when you enter the sea, you must go down to the very bottom. If you don't go down to the very bottom of the sea, then you will never know how vast and wide it is. If you don't climb up to the summit of the mountain, you will never know how vast and wide the universe is." [13]

And yet, Shanci Tongji was by no means oblivious to gender distinctions. In yet another text addressed to Jizong Xingche, for example, he brings up Miaozong and also mentions the Flower-Scattering Goddess, who in the *Vimalakirti Sutra* dramatically shows Sariputra the gender-bound limits of his understanding of emptiness. Shanci Tongji, however, also sees fit to remind Jizong Xingche of the necessity of going beyond gender:

These sorts of teachings are like grabbing hold of the pearl of the divine dragon; round and alive, it turns on its own, whether horizontally or vertically; it [encounters] no obstacle, nor does it leave any traces. For this reason, if you search for the female form, in the end you will not be able to find it. On each and every head it will become realized; on each and every object it will become manifest. Those who live a householder's life can achieve this; those who become nuns can also do this. How can there be any distinction between purity and contamination! [14]

It was only after studying with Shanci Tongji for a number of years that Jizong Xingche actually left home and, at the age of 33 *sui,* took both the tonsure and the ordination, settling down to live near her teacher in a small hermitage on nearby Mount Heng. In her account, she elaborates on several of their Dharma encounters. She also quotes several of the gathas that she composed in the context of these ritual interviews. These gathas certainly demonstrate her mastery of Chan texts as well as a certain literary flair, if not originality, for which she later became quite well known:

The fragrant wind that blows in from the south—when will it end?
The halls and pavilions are a bit chilly, only you yourself will know.
In the fine weather, the butterflies flit about following the scent;
And at dawn the roosters herald the sun as it rises from east to west.

From this moment I have penetrated the true meaning of things;
Even the myriad beings of the underworld break into laughter.

In response to this particular gatha, we are told, Shanci Tongji asked
her, "What is the place where you know yourself?" Her reply: "A sliver
of moon hangs in the heavens, its glow destroys a ten-thousand-layered
mountain." His question: "If the mountain is already destroyed, where
then will you be able to rest your feet?" Her reply: "I'll turn a somer-
sault and vault into the heavens, and pull heaven along by the nose ring."
Then, she tells us, Shanci Tongji "tossed the draft of the gatha back at me,
and I left the room."

Jizong Xingche had not been a nun for very long when Shanci Tongji
left Mount Heng and accepted an invitation to teach at the Southern
Source Monastery (Nanyuan si) in Changsha, in northern Hunan. One
gets the feeling that he did so with a bit of reluctance, and Jizong Xingche
was unhappy to see him go: "I felt that it was too soon to be separated
from my teacher," she writes. "I too wanted to leave the mountain [to
join him]." Before she was able to do so, however, she received word that
Shanci Tongji had unexpectedly passed away. The lands used to grow
crops in the mountainous areas of Hunan had been ravaged by the war-
fare and turmoil of the last years of the Ming, and Shanci Tongji and his
disciples were forced to live on wild greens—a meal of which ultimately
caused his illness and early demise. It would appear from her account
that, after his sudden death in Changsha, she was one of the disciples
entrusted with making sure his remains were returned to Mount Heng
and that all of the funerary ceremonies, including the building of a relic
stupa and the compilation of his *yulu,* were carried out properly. This is in
itself rather remarkable, given that, although a senior student of Shanci
Tongji's, she had not actually received his Dharma transmission, as had
a number of his male students. All of this took some time, and it was not
until 1650 that, Jizong Xingche writes, "I paid obeisance and, taking leave
of my teacher's funerary stupa, descended Mount Heng and made my
way to Wuchang." One may speculate that if Shanci Tongji had not unexpectedly passed away, Jizong Xingche would have received his Dharma
transmission and remained on Mount Heng—as we shall see, she was
very attached to her home province and later returned to live out her last
years in the mountains that she loved and whose tranquil pleasures and
scenic beauties she often celebrated in her poetry.

She must have felt that her religious education was not yet finished,
and thus began a new chapter in her life as a Buddhist nun, one that
involved traveling many miles, meeting many people, and giving teachings in various convents and temples. Her first stop on her way south was

Wuchang, an important city even then, located in eastern Hebei on the south bank of the Yangzi River. Her journey began inauspiciously: the place where she had taken lodging in Wuchang and all of her personal belongings went up in flames (perhaps due to fighting between Manchu and Han forces, although she does not say this). However, a group of local gentry and clergy invited her to take up temporary residence at the Bodhi Convent (Puti an) in Wuchang's sister city, Hankou, where she stayed for several months before resuming her journey. This would be only the first of many times that she was hosted by local gentry groups. In fact, as we shall see, one of the noteworthy characteristics of Jizong Xingche's life and works is the extent to which she was able to garner support from the literati. Included among many of her patrons were a significant number of literati known for both their loyalist sympathies and their Buddhist proclivities.

The precise itinerary and chronology of Jizong Xingche's travels in the Jiangnan area is not easy to establish, but her travels were considerable enough to warrant mention (and admiration) by her contemporaries. As Yan Dacan notes in his preface:

> After the death of Master Shanci [Tongji], with nothing but her walking staff, she sailed down the River Xiang, crossed Lake Dongting, and fearlessly roamed among the Tiantai Mountains in the south and the Wutai Mountains in the north.[15]

Jizong Xingche herself, in a letter written many years later to the brothers she left behind in Hengzhou, explicitly refers to the extent of her travels:

> The several decades since I left home have sped by more quickly than a blink of the eye, and you can imagine all of the changes the world has undergone since then. Gazing far away in the direction of home, I really can't imagine what it might be like anymore. With nothing more than a tattered robe and a wooden walking stick, wherever I found myself I made do, and in this way I completely traversed the rivers of Chu and the mountains of Wu. This is what is meant by [the saying] "I share the same root with heaven and earth; I share the same substance with the myriad things."[16] My feet, from toe to heel have [taken me] in this direction and then that; what does it matter that my body is covered with mud and my patched robe drags along the ground?[17]

Jizong Xingche's travels were not, of course, merely for the purpose of sightseeing, but rather were an integral part of the traditional Chan training, which required visiting a number of different teachers and deepening one's understanding. However, they were also a way of affirming and perhaps even publicizing her own place in the lineage of Linji Chan. Thus her primary destinations are the masters and monasteries of the Jiangnan area that were associated with the Linji lineage of Shanci Tongji. This conviction of the importance of lineage (and after she received official Dharma transmission, her own place in that lineage) is something she shared with Linji Chan nuns like Qiyuan Xinggang. This is demonstrated also by the fact that, like Qiyuan Xinggang and Yigong Chaoke, Jizong Xingche composed a series of *yuanliu song,* the literary genre that reflected the new concern with self-definition as lineage holders. In addition, the warm welcome and strong support of local gentry that she would receive in the Jiangnan area were based in great part, although not entirely, on her authority as a certified Dharma successor in the lineage of Miyun Yuanwu.

One of the first Linji Chan masters Jizong Xingche visited was Muyun Tongmen, who, as we have seen, served as Qiyuan Xinggang's primary religious adviser when he was living at the Southern Antiquity Monastery (Gunan si) in Jiangsu Province. When Jizong Xingche visited with him, however, he was serving as abbot of the Egret Grove Monastery (Helin si) in Zhejiang Province. She then traveled on to Jiashan in Jiaxing Prefecture, where she met with Chan master Ruo'an Tongwen (1604–1655), a Dharma brother of Shanci Tongji (and the author of his funerary inscription). Jizong Xingche's own account of their meeting illustrates once again the particular pride she seems to have taken in her travels and the freedom, both religious and physical, that they represented:

> Master Ruo'an asked me if I was the Jizong, the disciple of Master Shanci from Nanyue [i.e., Mount Heng]. "Yes, I am," I replied. "What do you mean by abandoning your home and wandering about aimlessly?" he asked. "Leaping and vaulting through past and present, the brilliance shattering both heaven and earth," I replied." Then he said, "You have indeed abandoned your home to wander aimlessly." "I have overcome [surrendered] the body and stand alone outside the great void; from my nostrils emerge the upper lips of the pagoda," I replied. Then he said. "I have thirty blows that have not yet touched you," at which I shook out my sleeves and left the room.

Jizong Xingche tells us that she accompanied Ruo'an Tongwen to Mount Qing in Hangzhou, where, for three months, she "studied with him from dawn to dusk and received his guidance." She then left to go to Mount Longchi in Jiangsu, where she paid a visit to the relic stupa of her Dharma grandfather, Master Huanyou Zhuandeng (1549–1614). It was there that she met yet another of Shanci Tongji's Dharma brothers, Wanru Tong-wei (1594–1657), the master from whom she would ultimately receive Dharma transmission. She apparently made a real connection with the elderly monk, and her *yulu* contains several accounts of interviews that she had with him in his abbot's quarters, such as this example:

> On another day when I went to his quarters, Master Wanru said, "See if you can give me a single line even as you completely get rid of all words." I whistled and pointed downward with my finger. "Is there anything else?" he asked. "The great void is weary of giving birth," I replied, and went out.

Wanru Tongwei appears to have been quite impressed with his new disciple, as evidenced by the following text, "Instructions to Senior Nun Jizong." Preserved in his discourse record collection, it is worth translating in full:

> Feet planted on true ground [seek to be] neither companion of the myriad of dharmas nor neighbor of the thousand sages. Once you have established yourself, you will be solitary and lofty; naturally empty at the center and accommodating on the outside [*zhongxu waishun*], you will [be able to] provide testimony to no-mind [*wuxin*]! If every day you just keep tranquil and calm, when you need to confront a crisis and deal with tangible matters, then like swirling wind and rolling thunder, in a blink of an eye, you will have come a thousand *li*, ten thousand *li,* and naturally gone to the head of the line [*churen yitoude*]!
>
> Have you not considered [women such as] the nun Moshan, Person of the Way Kongshi, and the Thirteenth-Daughter Zheng, all of who them had complete insight into the Dharma source, which is why their responses to circumstances [*yinji*] were spontaneous and on target, without falling into either heterodoxy or sterility [*pianku*]? Now, Person of the Way Jizong, although born to wealth and status, was not fettered and trapped by them. Because of this [she was able to] devote herself to single-minded investigation and study, which led to an [experience] of insight. She then left Chu and came to Wu to study with this old monk here at Longchi. She has repeatedly come to me with her questions and, persistently availing herself of these opportunities [*dangji burang*], has maintained her integrity and her meticulous effort. And so I have written the following gatha for her:
>
>> As for the bloodline of Caoqi—there is really not much to it all![18]
>> When the right time comes, then the waves will once again rise.
>> I charge this Person of the Way with cultivating herself deeply,
>> So she may help those of her kind to escape the suffering world.[19]

This text provides a good illustration, such as we saw in Chapter Two, of how male teachers found ways, both textually and practically, to integrate their female disciples into the larger, and largely male, Chan tradition. In the opening paragraph, for example, Wanru Tongwei is in fact using as a template a letter composed by the famous Song-dynasty master Yuanwu Foguo (1063–1135) to one of his senior male disciples.[20] Wanru Tongwei uses (with slight modifications) many of the same phrases and images in this original letter. However, given that Wanru Tongwei's instructions are directed to a senior female student, in the second half of the text he draws on the familiar exemplars of female religious achievement to both praise and exhort her to further application and effort. What is very clear is that Wanru Tongwei sees in Jizong Xingche the qualities of leadership, and in his gatha he urges her to cultivate herself (or, in an alternative translation, to apply the fruits of her own cultivation)[21] so that she may both carry on the (patriarchal) lineage of Caoxi (i.e., that of Linji Chan) and serve as a (matriarchal) teacher and guide to others "of her kind" *(tonglei)*, that is, to other women.

After Jizong Xingche's extended visit to the southeast and her periods of study with Wanru Tongwei and other eminent monks of her lineage, she appears to have originally planned to return to Hunan and resume her former life of solitary contemplation on the slopes of Mount Heng. Wanru Tongwei, however, had his own plans for her:

> The next day I went to take leave of Master Wanru and return to Nanyue [Mount Heng]. But Master Wanru said: "It is very difficult for those who have [mistakenly] left the road to study the way. So put an end to your thoughts of returning to the mountains. When this old monk is gone, your work will be to liberate those who have missed the path." He then presented me with the lineage records and the fly whisk. I vigorously declined, since I wanted to return home. But Master Wanru said, "It is best if you remain in the Jiangnan area."

Wanru Tongwei clearly regarded Jizong Xingche not only as a worthy Dharma heir (remember, he only named three such successors) but also as someone whose qualifications as a religious teacher would be wasted in a life of solitary retreat. Like Qiyuan Xinggang and Yikui Chaochen, Jizong Xingche is represented (and in this case, represents herself) as a reluctant abbess: someone who would have preferred to pursue a life of contemplation rather than activity. This may, of course, be part of the rhetorical requirements of this genre: an expressed reluctance to enter the public arena could only strengthen the image of a virtuous woman.

But this reluctance may also have been in part quite genuine; the life of an abbess (or abbot) was not a particularly enviable one, even for those with natural administrative abilities. And, as we shall see, Jizong Xingche was deeply attached to Mount Heng and would often write of her longing to return. This desire she was finally able to fulfill at the end of her life, but not until after she served as abbess of several convents.

The newly certified Chan master Jizong Xingche began her abbatial career at the Universal Salvation Convent (Pudu an) in the city of Xinghua in Jiangsu. Then, in 1654, at the age of forty-eight *sui*, she was invited to head the Wisdom Lamp Convent (Huideng an) in Suzhou. As was often the case when a monk or nun was asked to become the head of a newly established or newly refurbished monastery or convent, the invitation to assume the position was extended by the local gentry and donors. Interestingly, the official invitation extended to Jizong Xingche, the text of which is included in her *yulu*, is "signed" by more than thirty men. The list of names reads like a who's who of Suzhou literati. Interestingly, many of these men belonged to the Restoration Society (Fushe), the political-literary association founded by Zhang Pu (1602–1641).[22] Among these names are several men who later also wrote prefaces. One of them was Ye Shaoyong (style name "Jiruo," but also known as Layman Miaogao); his name also appears at the top of the list of donors who extended Jizong Xingche the invitation to become abbess of the Wisdom Lamp Convent. A native of the Suzhou area, Ye Shaoyong was a *jinshi* degree holder and held various high offices during the late Ming period. One of those offices took him to eastern Guangdong, where he went to pay his respects at the stupa of Huineng, known traditionally as the Sixth Patriarch of Chan Buddhism. It was during this visit that he apparently underwent a conversion of sorts, and after the fall of the Ming he retired from official life and became a full-time lay Buddhist, studying under Chaozong Tongren (?–1648), one of the twelve Dharma successors of Miyun Yuanwu.

The list of literati donors illustrates Timothy Brook's contention that during the late Ming much of the energy of the gentry was taken up by patronage of Buddhist monasteries and temples. Brook, however, argues that, for these male literati, there was far greater symbolic capital to be gained by investing in the larger public monasteries *(si)* than in the smaller private establishments *(an)*.[23] He does not mention the patronage of nunneries as being even a source of small change in this regard. While male patronage of nunneries such as Jizong Xingche's Wisdom Lamp Convent may have been exceptions that prove the rule, it is important to include them in our larger understanding of lay Buddhism of this period.

As was true with Qiyuan Xinggang, Jizong Xingche appears to have soon acquired a reputation for eloquent and effective preaching as well as her powerful use of "blows and shouts"—she was a Linji Chan master, after all. As Yan Dacan writes in his preface:

> The gentry officials all looked up to [Jizong Xingche] with admiration; the four classes (monks, nuns, laymen, and laywomen) flocked to her in droves; and there were none who did not wish to extend her an invitation to preach the Dharma. Her blows and shouts were delivered with the power and swiftness of lightning; her preaching of the Dharma was of benefit to sentient beings.[24]

It is not clear if Jizong Xingche ever actually met Qiyuan Xinggang. However, it is quite likely that she did, especially considering that she spent time at the Goodness Protection Convent (Shanhu an) in Danghu when both Yiyin Chaoke and Yigong Chaojian were in residence there. We do not know how long she stayed at the Protection of Goodness Convent, but it does appear that it was not just a brief visit. In her *yulu* are two accounts of Dharma talks she is said to have delivered at this convent: one requested by "Abbess Yigong" and the other by "Chan master Yiyin." In both cases the requests were made not only by these two nuns but also by local "Dharma protectors and gentry" *(hufa shenjin)* and donors *(tanhu).*[25] In the first of these talks, Jizong Xingche, in response to a query from one of the senior nuns, raises the story of an encounter between Miaozong and Dahui Zonggao. In this encounter Dahui Zonggao asks Miaozong about the meaning of the famous story of Deshan, who was able to enjoy fried sesame cakes in the village without ever leaving his quarters. She responds, "Only when the monk lets Miaozong go will Miaozong dare give a reply." Dahui then says, "I have let you go; now see if you can say something." This time Miaozong says, "Miaozong has also let the monk go." Dahui Zonggao is surprised and delighted by her response and finally Miaozong gives a shout and leaves the room, presumably victorious. Although Jizong Xingche does not even mention the name of Miaozong, I would suggest that in making use of this particular story in this particular context, she is playing a double role as it were. In other words, in using the story as a teaching device, she is playing the role of Dahui Zonggao. But clearly she is also intimating that she herself, like Miaozong, has been able to win her own Dharma battles with her teachers and that the women practitioners she is addressing should be able to do the same. To repeat a point I have made earlier, there is a difference between male and female Chan masters' use of Miaozong and other such women as a "precedent" for their female disciples. The difference is simple but significant. Women Chan masters can both point to and identify with Miaozong, whereas male Chan masters normally identify primarily, if not solely, with the role of Dahui Zonggao and point to Miaozong as an example of an extraordinary female disciple, "a great gentleman." The same can be said of Jizong Xingche's use of the phrase "The Great Way is not divided into male and female" in the second of these two Dharma talks.[26] It is worth considering that such a statement when uttered by a woman Chan master, even if still largely rhetorical, may have carried a different weight than when proclaimed by a male teacher.

That Jizong Xingche moved in some of the same circles as Qiyuan Xinggang and her women disciples did is also indicated by the appearance of many of the same names in all of these women's discourse records. In Jizong Xingche's collection for example, we find a letter addressed to Gao Yiyong, the Jiaxing scholar-official who in 1658 wrote a preface to Yigong Chaoke's discourse records. Like many of her counterparts, Jizong Xingche appears to have felt impelled to warn literati of the dangers of the purely literary. Thus, while she praises Gao for having distanced himself from the lure of fame and fortune, she indicates that he is still overly attached to his "five cartloads of books." And she adds, "When you are able stop searching the stage for marionettes [i.e., seeking for truth in externals], you will finally come to recognize the master within yourself."[27] Jizong Xingche's critique of local literati is made even more explicitly in a letter to a certain Huang Chaoyun:

> I have lived in Suzhou for many years now and have often observed, of laymen-officials who investigate and study this Way, that if they are not gazing at the ground like withered trees, then they are making a big to-do about their knowledge and understanding. Those who truly investigate and sincerely study are not enough to count on the fingers of one hand.[28]

Another familiar name that appears in Jizong Xingche's discourse records is that of Shi Bo, who, as we have seen, wrote a preface for the Yikui Chaochen's *yulu* and was a friend of her brother Sun Zilin. In the poem addressed to Shi Bo, Jizong Xingche affirms the inherent compatibility of her own more orthodox Linji Chan Buddhist practice and Shi Bo's more eclectic perspectives: "Righteousness [in whatever form] can be linked by a single [thread], and principle does not have any biases [*yi neng guan, li wu pian*]."[29] In a poem written to a literatus by the name of Chen Fangsan, we see again this combination of respect for the compatibility of Confucian and Buddhist worldviews, and a warning about getting stuck in the purely intellectual:

I fully realize that the Old Man I call my teacher [the Buddha],
And the nostrils of your Confucius have always been the same.
Sweeping away words and phrases, superfluous leaves and branches,
Realization and knowledge of the good [*liangzhi*] are ultimately both
     empty.
You aim for wordlessness, but in so doing [, you] let everything leak out.
I do not hide myself away, and in so doing[, I] manifest the true wind.
All you need to do is chew away and get at the flavor within;
The study of the Way [*Daoxue*] is linked together by a single thread.[30]

Although it does appear that male literati were Jizong Xingche's
primary correspondents, she also attracted a following among gentry
women.[31] But it is worth pointing out that Jizong addresses most of the
women, except nuns of course, as "wife of so-and-so"—perhaps an indication of the extent to which, as an honorary male, she identified with
male literati. However, it is important to note as well that, as with Qiyuan
Xinggang (and Dahui Zonggao before her), the message she conveyed to
gentry laywomen was not that they should leave home to become nuns,
but rather that they should engage in intensive *huatou* practice within
the home. Even more importantly, she insists that their goal should be
"genuine" enlightenment in this very lifetime, and she criticizes those
who would have women believe otherwise. As she instructs a certain Lady
Xiang, the wife of a Hanlin scholar:

> [The old masters of the past said,] "In practicing Chan, one must seek
> enlightenment; if there is no enlightenment, there will be no way by which
> one may escape the great sea of birth and death. Nowadays [so-called]
> followers of the Way mistakenly swindle by means of mouth and ear those
> who dwell in the inner chambers when they tell them that they do not need
> to be enlightened in order to be liberated from life and death; glib and
> loquacious, they vilify the great wisdom of insight and even go so far as to
> completely obscure its sacredness. This demonstrates a lack of gratitude
> toward the sages of the past. How can it not be lamented![32]

From many of the Dharma talks in Jizong Xingche's *yulu* that were
addressed "to the congregation," we can see that the standards to which
she held her nuns were high indeed. As with Qiyuan Xinggang, it is clear
that Jizong Xingche felt she had a particular responsibility to counter
the perception, often well founded, of moral laxity and lack of discipline
within Chan Buddhist establishments. Not only was she clearly anxious to
prove by her own impeccable behavior that she was worthy of the Dharma
transmission that Wanru had given her, but also, as a Chan master, she was

meticulously careful about not indiscriminately bestowing such transmissions herself. In his preface to her *yulu,* the Buddhist layman Yan Dacan makes explicit mention of this:

> Although among the followers both in their homes and in her community there were many in whom insight was awakened, the Master did not indiscriminately give her stamp of approval. On one occasion, she said: "Those in the school of nonduality who adhere strictly to the precepts and discipline are very few; those who in the entire Buddha universe who have truly attained enlightenment are even fewer." Therefore the Master's discipline was as coldly stern as a mouthful of snow, and her leadership of the community as solemn as mouthful of twigs. [In this, she demonstrated] not even the slightest bit of hypocrisy or excess—unlike those workmanlike teachers among her contemporaries who recklessly bestow Dharma seals and ignorantly impart instructions to unworthy people who lack the requisite goodness. °33

This concern for discipline, or at least for a perception of discipline, is evident in all of the recorded Dharma talks in which Jizong Xingche addresses her community of nuns. It is a discipline that she especially emphasized on holidays in which those who had not left the world took particular pleasure. An interesting example of this is the following Dharma talk delivered by Jizong Xingche on the occasion of the Dragon Boat Festival, celebrated on the fifth day of the fifth month. On this day, the custom was (and still is) to conduct races between gaily decorated dragon boats, with drummers at the stern to urge on the rowers. But this festival fell in a month that was considered to be particularly prone to pestilence and danger, and there were other customs, designed to keep illness at bay, associated with this festival. They included such traditions as hanging calamus (also called water-sword because of its shape) and mugwort *(moxa)*—both believed to ward off illness—from doorways and adding realgar to the food and drink consumed on this holiday (realgar in wine, for example, was thought to help cleanse the poison accumulated in the human body over time). Jizong Xingche's Dharma talk plays on all of these customs but infuses them with a strictly Chan significance. The first part of this text reads:

> The dragon boats dance along the river;
> The flags flutter in last nights' breezes.
> The clamor is of the drums of yesteryear.
> The seasons of the year do not spare us;
> The flow of time does not surrender to us.

Those who've yet to realize their mind
Should ponder the sufferings of life and death
And quickly, quickly grasp their calamus swords,
And, backs straight, ride their mugwort tigers.
Rout out the six bandits from their lairs and caves;
Purge the grief and suffering of the three poisons![34]

There are also poems and other instructional remarks addressed to
individual nuns. Although the non-gender-specific nature of many religious names makes it sometimes hard to tell whether the addressee is
a man or a woman, it is safe to suppose that unless there is some other
indication of gender, it is usually a woman. Often the content of the texts
provides a hint, as in the following short poem addressed to Person of
the Way Yizhen:

In this world, among fellow soldiers, how many practice together?
I especially admire how you've managed to realize your freedom.
Having shut completely the gate of passion, you are as cool as water;
Having fully understood the sea of bitterness, you float like a cloud.
No longer harboring sorrow, no longer piling up the dust of the world;
Your heroism has made you companion to the Buddha and patriarchs.
Once you have broken through the external form of male and female,
Where in the great universe will you not find yourself totally at ease?[35]

In this poem, the rhetoric of heroism is striking. The term *tong dui* could
be simply translated as "those in the same group"—that is, of the same
gender—but the word *dui* is most often used to refer to members of a
common military unit. We see in this poem also the emphasis on (manly)
heroic spirit *(yingqi)* and, most importantly, on the need not only to cut
off the roots of emotion and desire but also to transcend the gendered
duality of male and female form in order to be a companion (not a bride,
as would be the case in the Christian context) to the Buddha and the
patriarchs and to enjoy unrestricted freedom. It is with this image of the
"liberated" woman that Jizong Xingche herself most clearly identified.
And given her many travels, it is also clear that the psychological ease, if
not always physical comfort, with which she traveled was part of her conception of this spiritual liberation.

Travel, whether in the form of short boat trips, mountain excursions,
or long overland journeys, was a very central part of Jizong's experience
and is reflected in much of her writings. From the time she left Hengshan
and headed to the Jiangnan area, she was engaged in almost continuous
travel of one kind or another. It was not always easy, for she was living

in times of political chaos and bloodshed, with much of the south and certainly the Hunan area plagued by bandits and famine as well as the scourges of battle that accompanied the protracted demise of the Ming dynasty. She provides a hint of these difficulties—which may be read both literally and metaphorically—in the following poem, entitled "A Chant in Midjourney" (Tuzhong yin):

> Looking ahead at rivers and plains, the road of the world is circuitous,
> Twisting and turning through valleys among the ignorant and foolish.
> Wind smelling of blood on wide slopes, as the foxes form into troops.
> Sun weak on the cold cliffs, as the tigers are defeated at strategic points.
> So lonely and desolate, it is naturally difficult to find a travel companion;
> Stretching on and on, who can understand?—few are those who feel
>   this way.
> The hoary heavens weep; on whom can I depend to accompany my way?
> Just the wooden staff that I carry with me through mountains and peaks.[36]

But travel could also be exhilarating in and of itself, as we can see from the following short poem entitled simply "Writing My Feelings:"

> The road through rugged terrain, first proceeding then halting;
> Momentarily, I note how worldly affairs are like rivers flowing east.
> Eyes reaching to the far corners of heaven empty out past and present;
> Feet step along there among the clouds, going or staying as they please.
> Often I sit together with the Master of the Spring and of the Boulders;
> And sometimes I travel along together with the Daoist of the Pine Flower.
> And occasionally I come up with a phrase, as, whistling, I ride the void:
> Better even than exchanging poems with the fisherman and wood-
>   cutter![37]

As we have seen, originally the primary reason for her travels was to visit the eminent masters (or if they were no longer living, their funerary stupas) associated with the Linji Chan lineage of her own teacher, Shanci Tongji. After receiving official Dharma transmission from Wanru, she continued to receive even more invitations, usually from local gentry, to deliver Dharma talks at various convents and monasteries both large and small in the Jiangsu and Zhejiang area. For all her sense of responsibility as a Chan master, however, it would appear that she derived as much, if not more, pleasure from a single unplanned night's lodging in a hospitable convent along the way, if the following poem entitled "Passing by the Universal Salvation Convent in Gaogiao, I Request a Night's Lodging," is any indication:

I trampled across the hoary moss and paid a visit to the old traces;
The new blossoms are lovely, the willow reflected in the river surface.
The mountains seem to glow, and the chilly mists of dusk encircle me.
I hang up my staff; what harm in lingering to hear the morning bells? [38]

We find these expressions of pleasure in the quiet life away from the hub-
bub of the convent and monastery scattered throughout the writings of
Jizong Xingche. We also find in many of her poems, including those written to see off fellow monastics returning to Hunan, a deep undercurrent
of homesickness and nostalgia. The following verse (the third of three)
from one such poem would seem to indicate that she was beginning to
feel that her mission in the Jiangnan had been accomplished, and that it
was time for her to return home:

A half hook of shiny moon, as bright as the sun on a clear day;
With my iron staff I follow the clouds; the exhilaration returns.
Cups floating on a thousand rivers spread the ancestors' way;
Poems like bouquets of jade sound in harmony with the *Li Sao*.
Recalling loved ones, I write a few tunes about returning home,
Nakedly honest, like the huge sea turtle who has escaped the net. [39]
My home-going plans—who knows when they will be realized?
Listen to the sounds of autumn beneath the thousand-year-old pines. [40]

We know very little about the last years of Jizong Xingche's life—or
the exact date of her death. It does appear, however, that she managed
to find her way back to Mount Heng and that she spent her final years
living in seclusion on the Vase of Purity Cliff (Jingping yan), not too far
from where her first teacher, Shanci Tongji, used to live. The following
are a few selected verses from a series of twenty-five poems. Although they
are undated, they may have been written during these last years and are
entitled "Living in Seclusion in the Southern Peaks (Nanyue)."

SEVEN
A jumble of boulders amid thousands of mountaintops;
A thatched hut leaning precariously against jade peaks.
Yellow orioles sing in the kingfisher-green willows;
White egrets punctuate the sweet-smelling woodlands.
The winding path cuts narrowly through the clouds;
The bramblewood gate is deep among the fallen leaves.
Moving from one vantage point to another and another
Until all the mountain scenes have been captured in verse.

EIGHT
On worldly roads, in wind and dust I've grown old;
Time to return home: wild greens to eat aplenty.
If you are frugal, even in poverty you will have enough;
If you are detached, even disasters in the end are light.
Learning comes from not despising the beginnings;
Wisdom relies on the purity of being free of affairs.
Let the bookish scholars and holders of high positions
Exert themselves to exhaustion for the rest of their lives.

ELEVEN
To dwell in noble solitude has been the dream of a lifetime,
So from now on I will live my life here on this mountain.
I have seen through the illusions of this dusty world
And am no longer embroiled in this floating existence.
The stone stalactites can be sucked on when needed;
The wisteria flowers can be pulled down as the mood dictates.
Heaven and earth—an emptiness that is so great and so vast.
Who understands the leisure to be found in all of this?

TWENTY
The azure sky in the window gleams pure and clear;
I open the door to let in the blue-green of the hills.
From out of the rosy mists, the lone crane returns,
Circling the rocks, then soaring up into the clouds.
A low bed of moss can be used as a meditation mat;
The scattered leaves on the eaves can serve as a robe.
The setting sun has disappeared far into the west;
The weary birds instinctively know their way home.[41]

We do not know anything either about Jizong Xingche's Dharma successors, although a certain Renhua Fa is said to have received her Dharma transmission.[42] Jizong Xingche—or at least her poetry—was not completely forgotten, however. Thus, in the Hengyang prefectural gazetteer of 1822, we find her name in the section on eminent Buddhist figures associated with Mount Heng; she is placed in the same company as the Song-dynasty Dahui Zonggao and the late-Ming master Hanshan Deqing. The only biographical details that seem relevant to the compiler of this gazetteer are that her secular name was Old Woman Chen (Chen *pozi*), that she was abbess of the Wisdom Lamp Chan Cloister in Suzhou, and, most important, that in the end she returned to live on

Vase of Purity Cliff on Mount Heng. He also includes what he describes as a Dharma talk, but one that is not found in her discourse records, which may indicate that there was more to this collection than remains extant today.

Jizong Xingche's name appears again in the *Nanyue zhi,* a mountain gazetteer devoted solely to matters relating to the Nanyue Mountains. In fascicle 16, the section devoted to "Buddhist monastics," she appears simply as "Jizong," and her entry is placed alongside that of the famous Buddhist hermit-monk Wuxue, who spent most of his life on Mount Heng and whom Jizong Xingche had met when she first began her studies with Shanci Tongji. The compiler of this particular gazetteer repeats verbatim much of the information found in the prefectural gazetteer, including all but a few lines of the sample of her writing. He omits, however, the reference to Old Woman Chen, and because he provides no other indication of gender, Jizong Xingche becomes virtually indistinguishable from the other eminent monks (all males) listed in this section. Her name appears again in the same gazetteer, in fascicle 8, which is also dedicated to Buddhists (here referred to as *fangwai*), but with a focus on their poetry. This time she appears not as Jizong but as Xingche, although yet again there is absolutely no indication of her gender; instead she is referred to simply as Shi Xingche (without the usual character *ni* [nun] that is usually appended to the names of female monastics) and as such is indistinguishable from the dozen other poets (all of whom are known to be male) whose poems are included in this section. The poem selected by this editor (who appears to have not realized that "Jizong" and "Xingche" referred to the same person, and that that person was a woman) is entitled "The Nine Immortal Daoist Monastery," one of the ten poems that Jizong wrote on famous sites of Mount Heng and is included in her *yulu.*

It is not clear when and how Jizong Xingche's *yulu* was finally compiled and printed. However, in a preface to the *yulu,* the Taizhou literatus Wang Xiangshuo recounts that in the autumn of 1656, on her way back from Wulin, Jizong Xingche stopped to visit Yan Dacan in Jiaxing. The two appear to have hit it off well, and it was on this occasion that she gave the drafts of her *yulu* to Yan Dacan to have them printed; another local literatus, Wang Xiangshuo, who appears to have visited Yan at the time, was instructed to assist him. The language of this account places Jizong Xingche in the role of a woman who wishes to ensure that her *yulu* are not only published but also widely circulated and is taking an active role is making sure this happens. "The Master [i.e., Jizong Xingche] took out the drafts and handed them over to an engraver so that they could be widely circulated," and, Wang Xiangshuo tells us, "I received the Master's command to be the assistant editor." Yan Dacan says that his first reading of Jizong Xingche's drafts was "like eating a pear from the Ai garden: one's mouth felt fresh, and one's heart enlivened."[43] As for Wang Xiangshuo, he wrote:

> When I read [this collection], I knew that it truly manifested the one [orthodox] transmission, sweeping away forever all of the weeds and briars. [Her] great methods and great expedients surely embodied the complete realization, a truth that was realized beyond words and phrases. And in this way, I came to have even greater trust in the saying "The Great Way is not divided into male and female."[44]

The woman poet Wang Duanshu, who included three of Jizong Xingche's poems in her 1667 anthology of women's poetry, appears to have agreed with the assessment of these two male readers. "When I read her discourse records," she writes, "I cannot help feeling spiritually transported [*bujin shenwang*]."[45]

CHAPTER SEVEN

From Wise Mother to Chan Master

Baochi Jizong

Baochi Jizong and Zukui Jifu (whom we will meet in Chapter Eight)
were both Dharma heirs of Jiqi Hongchu (1605–1672)—the same
Jiqi Hongchu who, when Yigong Chaoke visited him at his monastery on
Mount Lingyan in Suzhou, declared her to be a true "Dharma vessel."
Jiqi Hongchu was a Jiangsu native who received Dharma transmission
from Miyun Yuanwu's Dharma heir Hanyue Fazang (1573–1635), and
after serving as the abbot of more than ten large monasteries in Zhejiang,
Jiangsu, and Hunan, he settled down on Mount Lingyan in 1645. Jiqi
Hongchu's great popularity among the Jiangnan literati was due as much
to his undisguised loyalist sympathies as to his religious attainments or
spiritual charisma, and he was praised for "taking loyalty and filial piety
to be Buddhist practice" *(yi zhongxiao zuo Foshi).*[1] He counted among his
friends many of the famous loyalists of the day, perhaps the most well
known of whom was Xu Fang (1622–1694). The son of loyalist martyr Xu
Qian (1597–1645), Xu Fang retreated to live in resolute retirement in the
countryside outside of Mount Lingyan after his father's death.[2] Xu Fang's
profound admiration for Jiqi Hongchu can be seen in numerous of his
writings. In the editorial notes to a poem, for example, Xu Fang writes:

> The monk Lingyan and I have had a close and mutual relationship for
> many years now. Once I commented to a friend [about this relationship],
> saying: "Within the four seas, [the master of] Lingyan is someone to be
> admired and looked up to. Venerable scholars from all over say that he
> is among the very few great teachers that there have been since the Song
> dynasty. . . . I, however, consider him to be the only great teacher there has
> been since the Song dynasty![3]

Given his equally fervent allegiance to the Ming dynasty and to the
Linji lineage, it is not surprising that Jiqi Hongchu identified strongly

with the Song-dynasty Chan master Dahui Zonggao, who was also known for his strong patriotic fervor. Zhang Youyu (*zi* Dayuan, 1589–1669, *jinshi* 1622), a Buddhist layman who had held various high offices during the Ming before retiring in 1644 to Mount Lingyan to study with Jiqi Hongchu, is also very explicit about the parallels: "After the disappearance of Dahui [Zonggao] there were five hundred years of cacophony and chaos, until the Venerable Lingyan emerged and returned [the Chan school] to its correct beginnings."[4]

Like Dahui Zonggao, Jiqi Hongchu had female disciples, including at least three women Dharma heirs: Chan masters Renfeng Jiyin, Baochi Jizong, and Zukui Jifu. Renfeng Jiyin's discourse records appear to be no longer extant.[5] However, the discourse records of both Baochi Jizong and Zukui Jifu can be found in the Jiaxing canon. In fact, of all of the seventeenth-century women Chan masters in this study, these two women have together left the greatest collection of extant writings. For Baochi Jizong we have a two-fascicle discourse record collection, and for Zukui Jifu we have not one but two collections of five fascicles each, as well as a third collection of religious verse that she wrote in collaboration with Baochi Jizong. Indeed, as we shall see, he actively encouraged not only their work as women Chan masters but also the collection and publication of their religious writings. Indeed, it might be said although these two women certainly do not appear to have lacked personal charisma, administrative skills, or moral discipline, they were known primarily for their profound mastery of the classical Chan textual tradition, as well as their own, often poetic, responses and re-creations of that tradition. This impression may, of course, be due simply to our knowing so very little about their actual lives. Unlike the *yulu* of the nuns we have looked at so far, theirs contain no biographies *(xingzhuang)*, and even the prefaces to these collections contain only a minimal amount of biographical information, if any. Thus, although it is possible to reconstruct sketchy biographical profiles of these two women, it does appear—and this is particularly true of Zukui Jifu—that both they and their followers were more interested in promoting and preserving their expressions of spiritual insight and literary eloquence than in presenting the women as exemplary abbesses. This is a point that will be developed at greater length in the next chapter, which is dedicated to a discussion of the writings of Zukui Jifu. The present chapter contains a brief discussion of the Dharma heir for which we have the least information, Renfeng Jiyin, followed by a more extensive discussion of what we know of Baochi Jizong, who became a Chan master in later life, after having already acquired a reputation as a loyal daughter and wife and the wise mother of a successful son.

Renfeng Jiyin was born into a distinguished family of writers and scholars from Kunshan in Jiangsu Province; her great-uncle was the poet and eminent Hanlin scholar Gu Tingchen (1473–1540, *jinshi* 1505). Wang Duanshu includes one of Renfeng Jiyin's poems in her 1667 anthology of women's writing, *Mingyuan shiwei* (Classic Poetry by Famous Women) and in a brief biographical note mentions that, as a child, Renfeng Jiyin showed a distaste for (gendered) worldly things such as clothes and jewelry and that, when she reached marriageable age, she asked to be allowed to enter a convent instead. Her mother agreed and gave her what she needed, although we do not know if she went so far as to build a special cloister for her daughter as had Yichuan Chaolang's mother, Madame Li. Renfeng Jiyin does not appear to have led a particularly cloistered life; nor does she appear to have suffered from ill health. We are told that she traveled to various Buddhist monasteries and temples and visited a number of different teachers before finally becoming a formal disciple of Jiqi Hongchu. After receiving the Dharma transmission, she took up residence at the Numinous Peak Convent (Lingshi an) on Mount Yufeng in Kunshan, where she appears to have lived out the rest of her life.

The poem that Wang Duanshu includes in her anthology of women's poetry is entitled "Gatha on Ascending the [Dharma] Hall":

> In the pine grove the moon is chill, and frost threatens from afar.
> Plums on the peak emit their perfume; the spirit of spring returns.
> But this spirit is not something that derives from heaven or earth;
> How could heroes possibly rely on the changing of the four seasons?[6]

In this poem we see the familiar "heroic spirit" that was so admired during this period. Renfeng Jiyin could easily have been giving expression to a loyalist sentiment, although the poem is a hymn supposedly composed extemporaneously in the Dharma hall. It probably refers as well to the heroic spirit required of Chan aspirants. In the editorial note appended to this poem, Wang Duanshu, who was more of a loyalist than a Buddhist, expresses great admiration for Renfeng Jiyin's religious achievements:

> The Master came from a famous family and yet at a young age was able to renounce all its comforts and concentrate on Buddhist texts [*neidian*]. After a period of fifteen summers and winters, she received the Dharma [transmission] of the monk of Lingyan, a direct lineage descendant and a great vessel of Buddhism. I sigh with amazement! One can tell, by this single gatha, how extraordinary she is.[7]

The only other references to Renfeng Jiyin that I have been able to locate is an account of a visit her Dharma sister Zukui Jifu made to the Numinous Peak Convent, and a poem Zukui Jifu wrote on the occasion of Renfeng Jiyin's fiftieth birthday. In the following lines from the birthday poem, we can see, beneath the hyperbolic language, an admiration for a fellow Chan master's teaching methods:

> Just one of [her] roars can be heard both near and far;
> Foxes and hares hide their traces, and skulls shatter!
> And she uses her claws and teeth; everyone is startled;
> Kill! Revive! Front and behind, nothing is left unrevealed.
> The verdant shadows in front of her hall are fully complete,
> Exhaling pure and fragrant breezes that circle the world!
> Together we cultivated our lives, together we blossomed;
> A hundred thousand humans and gods can always rely on her![8]

About Baochi Jizong—to whom we will devote the rest of this chapter—a little more is known, although much of her biographical information must be stitched together from various sources. One of her sons, Xu Jiayan, would later become so famous that she would be known in various non-Buddhist sources primarily as "the mother of Jiayan," with no mention of her subsequent religious career.

Baochi Jizong, née Jin Shuxiu, was born in Haiyan, located in Jiaxing Prefecture. We have no dates for her birth, but given that her son Jiayan was born in 1631, it must have been sometime in the first decade of the seventeenth century. She was the granddaughter of a well-known literatus, Jin Jiucheng (*zi* Boshao, fl. 1576), and her father, Jin Shouming, was a fairly high-ranking official who appears to have perished in the political chaos of the transition period. Jin Shuxiu's mother is referred to in the sources as Yao Ruren, or Child Nurturess, the seventh-highest of nine honorary titles awarded to the mothers and wives of both civil and military officials. Jin Shuxiu early on acquired a reputation for being an exemplary filial daughter; when her widowed mother fell ill, we are told, she performed the act of thigh slicing *(gegu)* several times, although ultimately her mother did not survive. After her mother's death, she used her own money to purchase a piece of land where both her parents could be properly buried. By this time, she appears to have been the only remaining child; her artistically talented brother, Jin Shanrong, had died unexpectedly (again possibly as a consequence of the political turmoil of the times), leaving a seventeen-year-old widow, Lady Zhong, and two daughters, whom, we are told, Jin Shuxiu helped care for as if they were her own.[9]

Jin Shuxiu was married to Xu Zhaosen, the son of a well-known loyalist family from nearby Xiushui. Xu's grandfather was the famous official Xu Bida (*jinshi* 1592), and his father was the Ming loyalist martyr Xu Shichun (1585–1641, jinshi 1618), who perished—along with his two concubines, his second son Xu Zhaoliang, and eighteen other family mem-

bers—while defending the city of Suizhou in Hubei Province against the
attack of rebel Zhang Xianzhong (1605–1647). After his father's death,
Xu Zhaosen appears to have devoted his life primarily to the preservation
of his father's memory. Jin Shuxiu, who by this time had been married to
Xu for more than ten years, added her own "hairpins and earrings" to the
funds needed for the sons to petition successfully for honorary posthumous titles for their martyred father.[10] This last bit of information appears
only in the 1682 Jiaxing gazetteer, which perhaps is not surprising, given
its subversive connotations. Her biographical notices in later gazetteers
become shorter as well, as she is gradually stripped of any identifying
roles apart from those of filial daughter-in-law and wise mother. Although
what does remain of the 1682 account is identical in wording, gone from
the 1878 reiteration is any reference to her being the granddaughter of
Jin Jiucheng and to her being a precocious young woman who delighted
in study and had a decided talent for painting and calligraphy. Gone too
is the reference to the collection of texts that she composed together with
Chan master Zukui Jifu. In this regard, she is an example of the way the
thousands of other women whose names appear in these gazetteers have
so often been stripped down and flattened out to fit their prescribed roles
as filial wives and wise mothers.

During her own time, Jin Shuxiu, although primarily lauded for her
virtue, was, like many of her gentry women counterparts, also praised for
her talents, especially in calligraphy, painting, and poetry. She would even
earn a brief biographical notice in the *Guochao huazheng xulu* (Sequel
Records of Qing-Dynasty Painting), a collection of biographies of eminent artists compiled by Xiushui native Zhang Geng (1685–1760) and
published in 1739. Zhang tells us that Jin Shuxiu was especially known for
her Yuan-dynasty style landscapes, which she executed in "a skillful and
lofty manner" *(judu xuanchang)*, and with a "gentlemanly air" *(zhangfu
qi)*.[11] Zhang also notes that Jin Shuxiu "did not take the art of painting
lightly, which is why there are so few [of her paintings] in circulation."[12]
Anxious perhaps to reinforce her respectability, Zhang Geng does not
include the information, found in another source, that that "the gentry
women of the Three Wu area all vied to purchase [her paintings]."[13]

Wanyan Yun Zhu includes two of Jin Shuxiu's poems in her 1836
anthology. One of these poems was written to be inscribed on a landscape
painting, possibly one of Jin Shuxiu's own:

Clouds and mist merge in purity;
Water and sky share a single hue.
A line of geese in the autumn light,
The trees sparse, the hills stand out.

A marvelous view of wooded springs,
Fashioned by heaven, styled by earth.
"What man could it have been?"
Steer the boat to the banks of the river.
Legs stretched out, nonchalantly whistling,
Feeling free, expansive, entirely at ease,
Here amid such secluded pleasures
That only refined people would appreciate.
Were the untutored and dull to wander here,
How could they possibly notice these things? [14]

This poem is redolent with the idealized eremitic images found in much literati poetry of this period.[15] That it may, if only indirectly, indicate a lament or even a critique of difficult times is suggested by the seventh line of this poem, which corresponds to the opening line of a poem from the *Classic of Poetry* translated by James Legge as "What man was that? His mind is full of dangerous devices."[16] The reference in the original poem is to an intruder with dubious intentions. In Jin Shuxiu's poem it can perhaps be read as referring to the opacity and tortured complexity of human motivations relative to the perfection and spontaneity of the natural world "fashioned by heaven, styled by earth." The vaguely Buddhist-Daoist language of this poem—"Clouds and mist merge in purity; / Water and sky share a single hue"—can also be found in much literati verse from this period. The poem is not, however, particularly melancholic or even nostalgic, although the last lines do reveal a distinct desire to separate oneself from the vulgar crowd. The poetic speaker is not longing for escape but is already feeling "free, expansive, entirely at ease." And, of course, given the stretched-out legs and cheerful whistling, the speaker is definitely not female. In this poem, the speaker, if not Jin Shuxiu herself, has left behind both the hurly-burly world of "the untutored and dull" and the secluded and often constrained and duty-bound world of the traditionally female.

By the time she reached middle age, Jin Shuxiu had become a widow.[17] The gazetteer accounts tell us that after the death of her husband, she abandoned both her painting and her calligraphy (and presumably her poetry writing as well) and devoted herself to looking after her family. She also spent her time engaged in extended vegetarian fasts and other religious devotions and applying herself to the embroidery of Buddhist images, which was a popular devotional practice among gentry women.[18] Officially, then, Jin Shuxiu's primary claim to fame appears to have been her status as wife and mother. In fact, if all one knew about her was what one could glean from the gazetteer accounts, one could not be faulted in assuming that she spent the rest of her days in quiet domesticity, engaged in her devotions and embroidery and watching with satisfaction her son's rise to eminence and fame. Xu Jiayan would become one of the group of Jiangnan literati who in 1679 sat for the special Outstanding Scholars of Vast Learning examination; subsequently he went to Beijing as one of the members of the commission established to compile the official history of the Ming dynasty.[19] Her son's prestige explains why later on Jin Shuxiu appears in Wanyan Yun Zhu's important anthology of women's poetry, *Correct Beginnings: Women's Poetry of Our August Dynasty (Guochao guixiu zhengshi xuji)* as well as in several prefectural gazetteers, simply as Madame Jin.[20] There is only one clue, found in Wanyan Yun Zhu's brief biographical notice, that she may have had other interests, not to mention an entirely different life: the editorial note that her primary literary collection was entitled *Collection of Harmoniously Resonant Eulogies on Ancient Cases (Songgu hexiang ji)*.

It is the preface to this collection, the unique nature of which will be discussed in the next chapter, that provides us with a few more bits of information about Jin Shuxiu's religious career. For one thing, we are told that even before her husband's demise, whenever she had some free time, Jin Shuxiu would go to the Marvelous Clarity Convent (Miaozhan an), where she would, "morning and night, study together with Abbess [Zukui Jifu] with great determination and resolve."[21] One day, we are told, Jin Shuxiu came across a copy of "Lingyan's records," which most likely refers to the *yulu* collection of Jiqi Hongchu. After reading it, she felt, in the words of the preface writer, "like a cold valley that suddenly experiences the spring warmth." Then, just as Jizong Xingche was compelled to seek out Shanci Tongji after reading a text that he had compiled, so did Jin Shuxiu decide to go to Mount Lingyan to meet Jiqi Hongchu personally. The eminent monk apparently had a favorable impression of Jin Shuxiu, "immediately seeing in her [the qualities] of a 'great gentleman,'" qualities that, as we have seen, Zhang Geng also noted in her painting.

It is important to note that Jin Shuxiu's interest in Chan, and her visits to the Marvelous Clarity Convent and then to Mount Lingyan, preceded the death of her husband. When he died, however (probably sometime in the mid-1650s), she went to Mount Lingyan again, this time to take the tonsure and the ordination with Jiqi Hongchu—and to assume her new name, "Baochi Jizong." She appears to have taken up residence near the monastery in order to fully participate in the religious training and group meditation retreats. In this respect, her experience was rather different from, for example, that of Qiyuan Xinggang, who practiced mostly on her own.

The accounts of Baochi Jizong's "Dharma encounters" with Jiqi Hong-chu found in her own *yulu* paint a picture of a woman who is anything but a demure and retiringly pious widow. In one of these accounts, for instance, we find Jiqi Hongchu questioning the fruits of her intensive religious cultivation: "It has been raining now for a long time, and the hills and creeks are all full; why have the ears of the robed monk not been able to grasp hold of even the slightest thing?" Baochi Jizong's response is not to defend herself but to "accuse" her teacher of having been preoccupied with other things: "The Old Monk has become accustomed to just thinking about his own retirement!" (By this time, Jiqi Hongchu was living in semiretirement.) Jiqi Hongchu then grabs his bamboo fly whisk, the symbol of his authority, and cries, "What about this!" Baochi Jizong replies by accusing her teacher of simply imitating stories of masters who engaged in these sorts of nonverbal theatrics: "Is that not the mistaken [sort of] question and reply [engaged in by] So-and So?" Jiqi Hongchu then turns her original comment back to her saying, "It really seems as if you have never thought on a daily basis about retirement." Baochi Jizong responds with the Chan shout "He!" to which Jiqi Hongchu retorts, "Idle!" Baochi Jizong, however, has the last word: "Today I have allowed the Old Monk to stick out his head!"

We do not know how long Baochi Jizong studied with Jiqi Hong-chu, but eventually he declared her a Dharma heir, and she then left to become abbess of the Marvelous Clarity Convent, where she had spent so many days as a laywoman. Jifu Zukui by this time had been named abbess of the Udambara Flower Convent (Lingrui an), which appears, judging from the references in her early poems, to have been located in Hunan Province, on the banks of Lake Dongting.

Judging from the letters and poems included in Baochi Jizong's *yulu*, it would appear that the break between her life as a gentry widow and her new role as Chan Buddhist master was not necessarily as radical as one might imagine. It is clear, for example, that, just as she had once gone to the Marvelous Clarity Convent in search of a "discussing-Chan companion," laywomen turned to her for advice and friendship after she became a Buddhist nun. A poignant instance of this can be found in a poem addressed to a certain Madame Zhang, whom she obviously knew from her days as a wife and mother:

This empty show in a blink of an eye reverts to clouds and mist;
Straw mat and hemp robes—I have learned to let go of my burdens.
When ill, I do not worry, but rather seek the marvelous medicine;
Once one has realized emptiness, then one can move all the gods!

The pearl-offering Dragon Girl was suited to become a Buddha.
The comb-sticking Wife of Pang was fond of studying Chan.
A melody of the Unborn is something we can speak of together,
Taking advantage of the currents, I dispatch a letter with the goose.[22]

This poem is interesting for its allusions to two female figures in Chan
lore. The first is the well-known story of the eight-year-old daughter of the
Dragon King; in the *Lotus Sutra,* she startles the disbelieving Sariputra by
presenting the Buddha with the jewel of enlightenment (and transform-
ing herself into a man), thus convincing the doubtful monk Sariputra of
her enlightened status. In a number of seventeenth-century texts, we find
her used to describe Buddhist laywomen who often took it upon themselves to present offerings (of food, robes, etc.) to the monastic community. The second allusion is to the wife of the Tang-dynasty lay poet
known as Layman Pang (d. 808); although she is always acknowledged
as having been a woman of insight, she usually takes second place to her
much more famous daughter, Lingzhao. The story summarized here can
be found in the *Discourse Records of Layman Pang (Pang jushi yulu).* One day
Mrs. Pang went into the monastery on Deer Gate Mountain, intending to
make an offering at a ritual feast. However, she was stopped at the door by
the proctor, who asked her what merit she hoped to gain by making this
offering.[23] She then took her comb, stuck it into her coiled bun of hair,
and said: "The merit has already been transferred." This line could also
be read as "I am done with performing works of merit for others," and
perhaps it would not be too far-fetched to interpret this as an indication
that Mrs. Pang was tired of other-serving virtue (the making of offerings)
and ready for something different, perhaps a bit like Jin Shuxiu herself.
And finally, the speaker in this poem instead of lamenting her illness—a
common trope in much poetry by women—prefers to engage her companions in "the language of no-birth," a clear allusion to one of Layman
Pang's most well-known poems. (Zukui herself wrote a poem on "Reading the *Discourse Records of Layman Pang,*" and one can assume that Baochi
was also very familiar with this text.)

There is a man unwilling to take a wife;
There is a woman unwilling to marry.
Father and son enjoy the joy of togetherness
And talk with each other about no-birth.[24]

A second poem, this one addressed to a certain Madame Hou (Hou
furen) from Luoyang, refers not only to the unsettled times and to Baochi

Jizong's transition from one kind of life to another, but also to her not unhappy acceptance of her new life as a Buddhist nun:

> Recalling the changes of the past, sighing over our parting;
> Ten years without any news to bridge our separate worlds.
> Golden cups on a sandalwood altar—have you been well?
> A stone hut and a meditation mat—just the right thing for me.
> The spring warmth has yet to melt the snow on my temples;
> Only after the dream breaks am I able to make sense of them.
> Often in them I've felt you there, providing encouragement,
> But, looking back toward the Central Plains, is anyone there?[25]

This is one of the few poems included in Baochi Jizong's *yulu* that speak explicitly of the trauma of the Ming-Qing transition, and in so doing it slips into the elegiac mode found in many literati writings of the period.

Perhaps because Baochi Jizong did not enter the religious life until later in life, or perhaps simply because we only have two fascicles of extant writings, it does seem that the circles she moved in were much more limited than they were for abbesses like Qiyuan Xinggang or Jizong Xingche. She also appears to have been less interested in institution building or even in leaving a legacy of her own as abbess. Unlike these other nuns, Baochi Jizong appears to have had far fewer exchanges or connections with local literati—perhaps because she was not so concerned with fundraising and donations. When names do appear in her poems, letters, or Dharma talks, they usually are those of laywomen friends, women disciples, or fellow monastics such as Zukui Jifu. Nor does her religious life appear to have been one of strenuous and solitary practice—her early training was carried out together with her fellow nun Zukui Jifu and in the context of Jiqi Hongchu's religious community on Mount Lingyan. In other words, her engagement with Buddhism—as represented by her *yulu*, of course—can be said to have been of a largely personal and literary nature. In this she resembles many male literati of the period, who sought in Buddhism not so much ultimate enlightenment as the possibility of an "alternative space" in which to live out the turmoil of the times.

Examples of the intensely literary quality of Baochi Jizong's self-representation as a Buddhist nun, and of the ways in which the personal, religious, and literary were inextricably intertwined in these representations, are the references in Baochi Jizong's *yulu* to the Lion-Subduing Chan Cloister, or, as she refers to it more familiarly, the Dong Convent. As we have seen, Yigong Chaoke had studied with Jiqi Hongchu before becoming a formal disciple of Qiyuan Xinggang, so this may explain the connections. That Baochi Jizong knew Qiyuan Xinggang is evidenced by the fact that she composed a colophon for Qiang Xinggang's portrait, perhaps even the same one discussed in Chapter Three or one very much like it. Baochi Jizong's colophon reads as follows:

> Robes in order, solemnly upright;
> Perfumed with discipline she glows.
> Generous in her treatment of others,
> Strict in the discipline of herself.
> The ten thousand dharmas complete,
> And not a single truth left out.
> The Master that I know,
> Is like this, and that is it.[26]

Elsewhere, in the record of a purported conversation between Baochi Jizong and Zukui Jifu, Baochi Jizong refers to an exchange between Qiyuan Xinggang and a student, which she says she herself witnessed during a visit to the latter's convent in Meixi:

> Once when I was at the Dong Convent, a student asked the monk [heshang, i.e., Qiyuan Xinggang]: "What is your original face?" The monk replied, saying, "[Estimating] from the left eye, it is half a catty; from the right eye, it is eight liang [ounces]." At that, the student leaped up into the air and went out. What do you think of her words? Rui [i.e., Zukui Jifu] said: "It would appear to be on target, and yet it also appears to be not quite on target" [siji sishi jiweishi]. The Master [Baochi Jizong] said: "I beg my senior 'brother' to supply a phrase of her own." Rui said: "Turn the skin on your face inside out and see." The Master said: "Our Way has been completely manifested."[27]

What is interesting about this text is that it shows three contemporary women Chan masters playing—and "playing" seems to be the right word here—with each other's ritual verbal performances. Even more interesting, however, is the account in Baochi Jizong's yulu of a visit from the prioress of Dong Convent—who well may have been Yigong Chaoke. The exchange that is recorded as having taken place between Baochi Jizong and this nun illustrates the extent to which these women are represented as enacting literary/religious roles not only as teachers but also as fellow students:

> The Master [Baochi Jizong] said: "We have not seen each other for three years! How are things going with all of your duties [benfen shi ruhe]?" The

prioress replied, "We meet in an open and spacious manner [*qinluo tang-tang*]." The Master said: "Is it still the same old burrow?" [The nun] said: "Could it be that in the time [since we last met] a new and fresh Buddha Dharma has [emerged]?" The Master said: "Yes, there has." [The nun] said: "I would like to hear it!" The Master said: "The emotions are cold and bland like the autumn waters; the path to the gate secluded and solitary—nothing but white clouds."[28]

Here Baochi Jizong is making clever use (as well as providing an alternative interpretation) of a poetic commentary composed by the Song-dynasty Linji Chan monk Juefan Huihong (1071–1128). Juefan Huihong was known above all for his championing of "lettered Chan" *(wenzi Chan)* and, as it happens, his friendship with Dahui Zonggao.[29] He was a prolific author who composed in many different literary genres and was particularly well known for his poetry—in fact he even wrote a book on how to write poetry, as well as a work of poetic criticism.[30] However, Baochi Jizong's allusion to Juefan Huihong represents—and whether or not this was a conscious decision on her part is debatable—just the tip of a much larger polemical iceberg. A brief detour will show why this was so.

Chan masters Baochi Jizong and Zukui Jifu were Dharma granddaughters of Hanyue Fazang, the independent-minded Dharma heir of Miyun Yuanwu whose disagreements with his teacher led to some of the most heated polemical infighting of the early seventeenth century. The story of the disagreements between these two men (and their respective supporters and critics) is a convoluted one and has recently been explored in extraordinary depth by Jiang Wu in his study *Enlightenment in Dispute: The Reinvention of Chan Buddhism in Seventeenth-Century China.* By the time we get to Hanyue Fazang's own Dharma successors, including Jiqi Hongchu, the nastiness of these disputes appears to have toned down somewhat. In any case, in these women's *yulu* we rarely see any explicit engagement in polemical debate, although they often decry the wasted energy and ink: "Using their scholarly erudition just to attack others," writes Zukui Jifu, "[and] forming factions, they fight over robe and bowl."[31] However, although both Zukui Jifu and Baochi Jizong continue to express their appreciation for Miyun Yuanwu, their writings do reflect some of the different perspectives and emphases that characterize Hanyue Fazang's interpretation of Chan doctrine and practice.[32]

For one thing, there is far less mention in these women's Dharma talks of "blows and shouts" (although it is by no means absent) than we find in the *yulu* of, for example, Qiyuan Xinggang. In fact, Zukui Jifu writes in a eulogy composed for her teacher, Jiqi Hongchu: "Without using Linji's shouts, without wielding Deshan's blows, he thoroughly clears away all the 'brambles and briars' and completely dissipates all manner of clever tricks."[33] This reflects, I would suggest, Hanyue Fazang's strong disagreement with Miyun Yuanwu's single-minded emphasis on precisely such "blows and shouts," which were an important component of the latter's "re-creation" of what he considered to be the central and most important practice of Linji Chan. Hanyue Fazang also disputed Miyun Yuanwu's claim that the Linji school represented the only true and orthodox expression of the central Chan principle of "the direct pointing at the mind" and that, especially in these "latter days of the Law," all of the other Chan schools (and their distinctive principles and practices) were secondary, if not completely irrelevant.

Hanyue Fazang, on the other hand, although certainly drawn to the principle and personalities of the Linji school, also argued for the continued importance of the so-called five traditional houses of Chan Buddhism (which apart from the Linji and Zaodong schools, had by this time largely faded into the realm of the textual). In his *Wuzong yuan* (The Origins of the Five Schools), Hanyue Fazang argued that each of these schools, along with their corresponding great masters, represented a distinctive and potentially useful principle. For example, apart from the three mysteries and the three essentials of Linji (which he considered to be as central as the "blows and shouts"), there were also Yunmen's "three propositions," Weiyang's "perfect signs," Fayan's "interpenetration of the attributes of being," and Zaodong's "five ranks." As it happens—and here we see the significance of Baochi Jizong's allusion—Hanyue Fazang reached back for confirmation to the writings of the Juefan Huihong, who had also advocated a revival of an appreciation of the Five Schools. In fact—and this was also something that incensed Miyun Yuanwu—Hanyue Fazang went so far as to claim that while Yuanwu had indeed confirmed his enlightenment by giving him his Dharma transmission, in fact he had received the true seal of approval (meaning that he had understood the principles that they represented) much earlier from not one but three great masters, Juefan Huihong, Gaofeng Yuanmiao, and Linji Yixuan himself.[34]

Hanyue Fazang's naming of not only the Tang master Linji Yixuan but also the Song master Juefan Huihong and the Yuan master Gaofeng Yuanmiao as his teachers and models would seem to also imply a renewed valuation of the use of words, as opposed to the exclusive use of nonverbal methods (that is, blows and shouts), in Chan teaching and practice.[35] It is important to note, however, that Hanyue Fazang was as rhetorically opposed to "dependence on words and letters" as was Miyun Yuanwu, and inveighed as forcefully against lettered Chan as he did against blows and shouts—not surprising, given that as Dale Wright puts it, "the critique of language [is] clearly fundamental to [Chan] discourse."[36] Nevertheless, unlike Miyun Yuan, who was a man of rustic origins and limited education, Hanyue Fazang was known, even as a youth, for his extensive mastery of the Confucian classics and, after turning to Buddhism, had thoroughly immersed himself in the textual world of the great masters of the Tang, Song, and Yuan. In fact, his first "enlightenment" experience came after reading the *yulu* of the Gaofeng Yuanmiao, whom, as we have seen, he later claimed as one of his three Dharma fathers. In other words, what Hanyue Fazang clearly objected to was the superficial and exclusive use of any single method or principle, whether verbal or nonverbal. For him, those who adhere to lettered Chan "drown themselves in words and phrases" *(moni yu yuyan)*, while those who engage in blows and shouts "drown themselves in wordlessness *(moni yu wuyan)*." According to Hanyue Fazang, one engaged in the words of past masters at the profoundest level, using them as pointers to the deeper truth that lay behind them. By so doing, dead words would come alive and, as such, serve not as obstacles to awakening, but rather, as Dale Wright puts it, as "the functioning of the Way itself."[37]

This approach to the texts of the past is reflected in the words of Sengjian Xiaoqing (1629–1690), a Dharma heir of Jiqi Hongchu and himself known for his strong literary bent. In the preface he composed in 1677 for Baochi Jizong's discourse records, Sengjian Xiaoqing writes: "The marvelous way does not depend on language, and yet it does not separate itself from language. To seek for it by clinging to language is like clinging to a flower and thinking that one has captured spring; but if one seeks for spring by dispensing with flowers, one will not find it either."[38] Needless to say, this is a perspective that can easily lend itself to a rationalization of one's literary attachments. In any case, it would seem that even if Baochi Jizong regarded herself, and was regarded by others, primarily as a Chan master, and her talks and writings as a form of skillful means designed to precipitate a deeper insight, there is no question that she was a classic example of lettered Chan.

In the colophon that Zukui Jifu wrote for Baochi Jizong, she compares Baochi Jizong not to Moshan Liaoran but to Wuzhuo Miaozong, yet another example of the extent to which many of these seventeenth-century women Chan masters identified with their twelfth-century predecessor:

She doesn't dwell in the cave of delusions;
But neither does she sit in the pit of liberation.
She does not entreat all the sages on the outside;
Nor does she turn her back on the spirit within her.

Like the great elephant fording the river, she goes beyond the hare;
Like the gold-winged roc, she can swallow the sea in a single gulp.
Earnest, serious, and full of grit: with whom can she be compared?
To the one-of-a-kind Miaozong, who also received the seal of Vulture
      Peak.
Sweeping away mist and clouds, the purity of the universe is revealed,
As, together with the wooden man, we all enjoy a spring of great peace.[39]

In the three-part colophon Baochi Jizong composed for her own portrait, she does not compare or identify with Moshan or any other female exemplar, although she does seem to imply that she understands the inner teaching of Bodhidharma as much as did his male successor Huike. Rather, in these colophons—the second and third of which I have translated below—she expresses a poetic (and presumably existential) reluctance to admit to any kind of fixed identity, much less a fixed representation represented by a painting:

To say that this is really [the abbess of] Marvelous Clarity
Is just like seeing the reflection but losing the head![40]
But to say that this does not seem to be like Marvelous Clarity
Is like ignoring the waves when looking for water.
If only you get rid of both identity and difference,
There will be another way to penetrate the principle.
Nirvana is not something glorious;
Samsara is not something shameful.
Boil the unicorn and roast the phoenix;
Looking backward, everything is different.[41]
Making their living by snatching away the hungry man's food
And driving away the plowman's ox—
I laugh at how the ancient sages have mistreated people!
Just look at this [abbess of] Marvelous Clarity [Convent]
Who, although she doesn't have a thing going for her,
Is content with her lot—sleeping, eating, and nothing more.
If you want to understand the "bone" Chan of Vulture Peak,[42]
Bodhidharma will smash out all of your front teeth!

Not yet captured by vermilions and blues,
Hard to manage with mulberry paper and ink,
But visit her in person and there is nothing concealed;
The autumn moon illuminates the great void.[43]

Toward the end of her life, Baochi Jizong left the Marvelous Clarity Convent in the hands of Zukui Jifu, who, although she had been a nun for far longer, was at least a decade younger. Baochi Jizong then retired to the Southern Search Chan Cloister (Nanxun chanyuan) in Haiyan. In a Dharma talk she gave at the Marvelous Clarity Convent on the occasion of her departure, she indicated her intention of living a quieter life: "And where will this mountain monk settle? In a leaf of a boat under the river moon, return to the cloud-covered ravines. In my hundred-patched robes of hemp, I will lie behind the bamboo gate."[44] And in the sermon she delivered upon taking up her duties at the Southern Search Convent, she says, "[This may be] a small convent by the corner of the city wall hidden by the green shade. But if one has completely dropped body and mind, every place is home."[45] We do not know to what extent these words represented wishful thinking, and whether or not Baochi Jizong's last years were in fact peaceful ones. Nor do we have a precise date for her death, although it probably occurred sometime in the last years of the 1660s. In Zukui Jifu's *yulu*, which were printed in 1670, we find several Dharma talks said to have been delivered first at Baochi Jizong's funeral and then subsequently at her death anniversary: "When she was alive, she was like a crane, its wings reaching up to touch the heavens; now she is gone, like a cloud passing through the human world."[46]

Baochi Jizong may have disappeared like a cloud, but she did leave two collections of writings that still exist today. Her discourse records appear to have been compiled after her death; in 1672 the nun Shizhao took the initiative to approach the monk Sengjian Xiaoqian to write a preface for them. The second collection of writings, *Collection of Harmoniously Resonant Eulogies on Ancient Cases,* turns out to have been composed and compiled together with Zukui Jifu, and is discussed in greater detail in the next chapter.

As for Baochi Jizong's son, Xu Jiayan, after his wife's death, he, like his mother, turned increasingly to Buddhism. After retiring from his official duties in Beijing, he returned to the Jiaxing area and became a lay follower of the Linji monk Hongxu Huiyue, from whom he apparently received his certification of enlightenment *(yinke).* Nowhere in his extant collection of published writings, however, is there any mention of the fact that his mother spent the latter part of her life as a Chan master.[47]

CHAPTER EIGHT

Reviving the Worlds
of Literary Chan
Zukui Jifu

O f all of the woman Chan masters discussed in this study, Zukui Jifu would seem to show the most profound, original, and certainly wide-ranging engagement with the classical Chan textual tradition. This per-ception is no doubt due, at least in part, to our having considerably more of her Dharma talks and writings than we have of any of the others. Aside from the collection of *songgu* that she wrote together with Baochi Jizong, Zukui Jifu's extant collections include a discourse records collection in five fascicles, and a second five-fascicle collection of writings, composed primarily of poems.

Chan Master Zukui [Ji]fu of Udambara Flower's Records from Marvelous Clarity Convent (Lingrui Zukui Fu chanshi Miaozhan lu) contains texts associ-ated with her tenure as abbess of the Marvelous Clarity Convent, a posi-tion she assumed after Baochi Jizong had retired to the Southern Search Convent. It was the first of her collections to be published, apparently during her own lifetime, and includes two brief prefaces. The first of these is by the literatus and Buddhist layman Li Mo (1600–1679), who was a disciple of Jiqi Hongchu.[1] The second preface, dated 1670, was written by a monk from Kunshan by the name of Xingji.[2] Neither of these prefaces offers much in the way of biographical information about Zukui Jifu as a person. Not surprisingly, we find both of them placing her solidly within the familiar lineage of eminent Chan women, including Moshan Liaoran and Miaozong. In fact, in his preface, the monk Xingji goes back all the way to the coming of Bodhidharma to China to make the point that one of the few to fully grasp the profound teachings of Buddhism at this early stage was Bodhidharma's sole woman disciple, Zongchi. Li Mo, however, goes a step further and says that all of these women, includ-ing Zukui Jifu, are "heroes like Lady Jinsan, who, unfurling her brocade banners, laid out a strategy, clarifying what was to go in front and what behind, and encouraging those to her left and to her right."[3]

Li Mo's use of Lady Jinsan (?–602) for comparison is intriguing, since this woman was not from the Jiangnan area, nor was she even Chinese. Also known as Lady Xian, she was a woman of the Li ethnic minority from southwest Guangdong Province who gained fame for her military leadership and prowess.[4] As we have seen, eminent nuns (and indeed, eminent women of all sorts) are ubiquitously referred to as "great gentleman," but this explicit comparison to a historical woman warrior is quite unusual. Li Mo continues with his rhetoric of heroism, albeit returning to the use of Chan metaphors, by describing Zukui Jifu as an extraordinary woman who has "seized the head and grabbed the tail of the tiger."[5]

The preface to Zukui Jifu's second collection of writings, *Chan Master of Udambara Flower [convent]'s Cliffside Flower Collection (Lingrui chanshi Yanhua ji)* was composed by Jiqi Hongchu's lay disciple Zhang Youyu who also composed the preface to *Collection of Harmoniously Resonant Eulogies on Ancient Cases*. From Zhang's preface, we learn that the *Cliffside Flower Collection* contains materials written and compiled during the period of Zukui Jifu's tenure as abbess of the Udambara Flower Convent.[6] However, it was not published until after Zukui Jifu had assumed the position of abbess at the Wondrous Profundity Convent, and her discourse records had already been printed and "circulated in the world" *(xingshi)*. In trying to explain why Zukui Jifu's collection is unique, Zhang Youyu goes to considerable lengths to distinguish between ordinary words, however clever or even beautiful, from words that emerge from a deeper insight: "Even if one has the nostrils of a robed monastic, if one does not have the diamond eye [of wisdom], how will one be able to distinguish and discriminate between dragons and snakes?" he writes. "People of today stop short of the source [of the teachings]; they are concerned only with flowing the waves and skimming the surface." Zukui Jifu, however, is an exception to this. In fact, Zhang claims that she has gone beyond even her early predecessor Zongchi, who was said to have grasped only the "flesh" of Bodhidharma's message. In fact, Zhang writes, she can be said to have not only "established the ground rules for nuns [but also] cut through the flesh to the bone of the Chan lineage [*Chanzong zhi gusui*]."[7]

These are highly flattering words, of course, and must be taken as such. However, and this is the important point, in all three of these prefaces, the emphasis is primarily on her exemplary talents as a Chan teacher, preacher, and writer; there is little or no explicit mention of her moral discipline, virtuous piety, or administrative abilities as an abbess. Interestingly enough Zukui Jifu herself also makes little mention of her accomplishments as an abbess—or at least not to the extent that we saw with Qiyuan Xinggang and Yikui Chaochen. It would seem, then, that it was her mastery of the textual tradition (and presumably the spiritual experience that her own textual productions were thought to both express and evoke) that best defined her in her own eyes and those of others.

In her brief but illuminating introductory colophon to the *Cliffside Flower Collection,* Zukui Jifu tells us both how this collection came into being and how she chose the title for it:

> [Once] when sitting the summer retreat at Dongting, the days were long and I had little to do, and so I took out a [collection of] "expedient words" by [the great masters] of the past and read them over and over until I had completely internalized them; then suddenly I had the inspiration *(shenhui)* to compose my own verses to them. . . . Over the years and months they gradually turned into a pile of paper and ink. A scholar then requested that they be carved [in order to be printed], but I still did not have a name for them. Then I remembered that the monk Xuedou [Zhong]xian, when he was living on Kingfisher Peak, spoke of how the original source of all the buddhas is like the rain that moistens the flowers on the cliff, and so I selected this as a name for the collection and called it the *Cliffside Flower Collection,* so as not to forget the significance of this original source.[8]

The Song-dynasty Chan master Xuedou Zhongxian (980–1052), to whom Zukui Jifu refers, is perhaps best known for his compilation of the one hundred koans that later became the basis for the famous *Blue Cliff Record (Biyan lu)* annotated by Yuanwu Keqin (1063–1135). The title of her own collection, she tells us, was inspired by one of the commentaries to case 6 of the *Blue Cliff Record* that tells the story of Subhuti, who, while sitting in silent meditation in a cave on the side of a cliff, found himself suddenly covered with flowers that had been showered down by Indra and the other gods in recognition of his skill in expounding the great wisdom. When Subhuti, who had been sitting silently and not preaching, reminded Indra that he had not said a single word about wisdom, Indra replied, "You have never spoken and I have never heard. No speaking, no hearing—this is true wisdom."[9] By her choice of title, then, Zukui Jifu clearly intimates that her own words should also be taken as "wordless," in that, rather than being self-referential, they speak with the thunderous silence of the Dharma itself.

The *Blue Cliff Record* was very popular even in Yuanwu Keqin's own lifetime, although it is said that one of his students, none other than Dahui Zonggao, was so alarmed at the possibility of the written word becoming an obstacle to direct and unmediated realization that he tried to destroy as many copies of it as he could. It is worth noting that Miyun Yuanwu goes so far as to retell the story of the book burning with admiration, implying that the *Blue Cliff Record* marked the beginning of the end of the direct, wordless transmission that began the moment that Sakyamuni raised up a white flower and Mahakasyapa smiled.[10] Baochi Jizong and Zukui Jifu, however, belonged to the sublineage of Hanyue Fazang, who, as we have seen, disagreed vehemently with his teacher about the place of language and texts (as opposed to just blows and shouts) in the cultivation of Chan enlightenment. Confident in their ability to use words to liberate rather than obstruct, Baochi Jizong and Zukui Jifu were particularly fond of this collection. Zukui Jifu in particular appears to have indeed "immersed" herself in the *Blue Cliff Record;* in fact, she even wrote a series of a hundred of her own *songgu* to each of its cases or "precedents," all of which are included in the fifth fascicle of her first discourse record collection

Despite this abundance of writings by Zukui Jifu, however, the dearth of biographical information about her, combined with her total immersion and mastery of the Chan textual tradition, in the end makes her less accessible as a historical person. Although all of the other nuns in this study also make ample use of classical texts in their Dharma talks, most of these talks are at least anchored in the contemporary setting by the name of those requesting the talks or the particular occasions on which they were delivered. There are far fewer markers of this kind in Zukui Jifu's collections, although such markers are not completely absent. As a result, many of these texts largely come across as both ahistorical and impersonal, and, unless the reader is totally conversant in the classical Chan tradition, often impenetrable as well. Of course, this is still interesting, as it shows a woman who has so completely mastered and internalized the textual tradition that her identity has nearly (and I emphasize the "nearly") been lost within it. What keeps her from virtually disappearing in the largely male language of Chan discourse is her friendship, both literary and spiritual, with Baochi Jizong. Perhaps the most striking illustration of this particular combination of friendship, religious aspiration, and literary talent is the *Collection of Harmoniously Resonant Eulogies on Ancient Cases,* which Zukui Jifu wrote in collaboration with Baochi Jizong.

Songgu constitute a literary genre associated primarily with Chan masters and are basically verses written as an expression of a master's response to a famous Chan case or story. This response could be in the form of an interpretation, a confirmation, a negation—or all or none of these. The point is that they were seen as "echoes" of the experience of the great masters of the past, as well as immediate, and as such unique, expressions of the master's own experience. As Yan Dacan put it, after being shown the draft of this collection, "In the bell there is no echo of the drum; in the drum there is no sound of the bell. Yet it is because they retain their individual voices that they are able to harmonize with each other."[11]

What is most interesting about the *Collection of Harmoniously Resonant Eulogies on Ancient Cases,* however, is not only that it represents collaboration between two women Chan masters, but that the precedents for which they wrote their *songgu* were originally chosen by none other than the Song-dynasty woman Chan master Miaozong. The *Collection of Harmoniously Resonant Eulogies on Ancient Cases* is a compilation of poetic eulogies written on, or rather inspired by, forty-three Tang- and Song-dynasty Chan cases, each of which is quoted almost verbatim from its original source. Each of these cases is accompanied first by the *songgu* composed by Miaozong in the Song dynasty and then by those written by her seventeenth-century "successors" Baochi Jizong and Zukui Jifu.

Miaozong's verses may well have been in circulation in her time, either as a self-contained collection or as part of her *yulu* collection. We do not know if they were in circulation in this form during the seventeenth century, but it is most likely that Baochi Jizong and Zukui Jifu excerpted Miaozong's forty-three *songgu* from *Chanzong songgu lianzhu tongji* (A Comprehensive Collection of Eulogies on Ancient [Cases] in Couplet Form from the Chan School), a voluminous compilation of over three thousand *songgu* edited by the Yuan-dynasty monk Puhui. Apart from a single *songgu* attributed to Moshan Liaoran, Miaozong, with forty-three entries, is the only woman Chan master represented in the collection, the same forty-three that we find in Baochi Jizong and Zukui Jifu's *Collection of Harmoniously Resonant Eulogies on Ancient Cases.*[12] Baochi Jizong and Zukui Jifu's decision to write their own commentaries to these forty-three cases apparently received Jiqi Hongchu's enthusiastic support and encouragement—and in fact, he was the one who chose the title of the completed collection. As Zhang Youyu tells us in his preface to this collection,

> [Baochi Jizong] would exchange poems with Abbess Jifu, and although there were two mouths, they were not of a single tongue. The Venerable [Hongchu] happily offered his assistance and his guidance. After they were named Dharma heirs, there was no longer any need for them to take second place to Wuzhuo Miaozong, and so they took [Miaozong's] poetic commentaries and [wrote their own] to harmonize with them.[13]

The compilation of this collection of *songgu* was, Zhang Youyu tells us in his preface, encouraged and supported by Jiqi Hongchu himself: in fact, it is he who came up with the title. Although some of these *songgu* do indeed read beautifully as poems, understanding their content does require a fairly broad familiarity with the allusions and "resonances" of classical Chan literature. The following example, which is based on the well-known story of Zhaozhou's encounter with the old woman of Mount Tai, will help illustrate that Baochi Jizong and Zukui Jifu's verses were designed both as "responses" to the case under consideration (and presumably, with the mind-state of the great Chan master featured in the case) and as "resonances" with each other's verses as well as with that of Miaozong's original poem:

THE CASE:
A monk, who was a disciple of Zhaozhou, was traveling to Mount Wutai and asked an old woman: "Which is the road that leads to Mount Wutai?" The old woman responded: "Just go straight ahead." After the monk had left, the old woman said: "There is another good monk who has gone on his way." Later, when a monk asked Zhaozhou about this, Zhaozhou said: "Wait until I have checked her out." The next day, Zhaozhou went and asked the way to Mount Wutai. The old woman said: "Just go straight ahead." After Zhaozhou had left, the old woman said: "There goes another good monk on the way." When Zhou returned to the monastery, he said to the monk: "I have checked out the old woman of Mount Wutai for you."

WUZHUO MIAOZONG:
Crouching at the foot of the ancient road to [Wu] Tai Mountain,
Traveling monks come and go, meeting with spears and shields.
Zhaozhou holds up the arrows of the great hero
But stops once he has pierced through the skeleton.

BAOCHI JIZONG:
Zhaozhou's eyeballs emit a light;
The old woman's brows are flung to the ground;
Although each appears to have sealed the border,
In the end neither one is able to find a way out.
Leisurely, let us quietly sit on the mountain peak.
Watching as the one falls and the other rises.

ZUKUI JIFU:
Go straight ahead! Go straight ahead!
Distracted, he misunderstands the fingertip.
The road goes south, north, east, and west;
Walking through the grasses and then returning,
How many times can you go around in circles?
What Zhaozhou checked out and saw through, few understand;
Returning to face the spring breezes, he sings and dances alone.
Oh, that wild fox!

Pointing it out, all becomes clear, nothing to be done.
In great peace, grasses and trees exhaust the weapons of war;
The general with a single arrow penetrates the three barriers;
The sun and the moon, both round, beat out a joyful melody![14]

Yet another illustration of the close literary and religious relationship between Baochi Jizong and Zukui Jifu can be found in colophons each wrote for the portrait of the other. Although we have seen numerous such inscriptions written by male monks for portraits of nuns, it is interesting to see how one woman Chan master describes another woman Chan master. The first thing to note is that when describing eminent religious women, both male and female writers use the same comparisons to female exemplars of the past, such as Moshan Liaoran. The difference, as was noted earlier, is that with for male writers it is a matter of comparison, whereas for women it is both comparison and identification. The colophon that Baochi Jizong wrote for the portrait of Zukui Jifu reads as follows:

> Using the method of Moshan,
> She shuts up Guanxi's mouth;
> The old man of Vulture Peak
> Has promised her the lion's roar.
> When she is furious and angry,
> Her nature is like lightning,
> Instantly shattering the void.
> When she is happy and joyful,
> Her words are like spring breezes:
> They agreeably imbue with light
> All that is withered and rotten.
> Availing herself of the "East Mountains walking on the river,"
> She wanders among the clouds that cover the western peaks. [15]
> With the Way of Chan, she does away with models and rules;
> With the Buddha Dharma, she stops the samsaric wheel. [16]
> When I, the abbess of Miaozhan, practiced together with her,
> Never did I see her give her approval when it was not earned.
> Unlike some of those other Chan masters of dubious repute,
> This venerable nun was not one to lightly raise her hand! [17]

We can see from the reference to Channists "of dubious repute" that Baochi Jizong very much desired to emphasize that Zukui Jifu was in fact a "real" Chan master who did not engage in the indiscriminate verification of religious understanding that many considered to be endemic among seventeenth-century Chan masters. Baochi Jizong's reference to the shedding of "models and rules" is a common antinomian Chan conceit but one that, I would suggest, may well have had a different meaning for women used to being encouraged to serve solely as models of wifely duty and motherly virtue.

Zukui Jifu's obsession with the supposedly golden past of classical

Chan is evident throughout her collections. In a series of quatrains entitled "Thinking of the Past on a Spring Day (Chunri huaigu), for instance,
she provides pithy poetic "profiles" of some of the great masters of the
Tang and Song, masters she has clearly come to regard almost as intimates.[18] Thus, on a spring day, when, poetically speaking, a woman might
be thinking of lovers or husbands or of the lost pleasures of days gone by,
we find Zukui Jifu attempting to encapsulate what she considered to be
the essential qualities of some of the great Chan masters of the past, with
a few Bodhisattvas thrown in for good measure.

Following are a just a couple of selections from these quatrains, each
of which begins with the line "Outside the gate, the spring is nearly half
over." The inspiration for the first quatrain in the series is Lingyun Shiqin,
a disciple of the Tang-dynasty master Guishan Lingyou (771–853), who was
said to have achieved enlightenment upon seeing a peach tree in bloom.

> Outside the gate, the spring is nearly half over;
> The peach blossoms coated with rain are red.
> Numinous clouds have still not covered them up,
> Laughing boisterously at the winds atop the cliffs.

The next poem in the series refers to Niutou Farong (594–657), who,
before his enlightenment, sat in meditation inside a secluded cave on
Mount Niutou (near present-day Nanjing). At the time, a hundred birds
would come with flowers in their beaks in homage to his deep spirituality. After his enlightenment under the fourth Chinese patriarch Daoyi
Daoxin, it is said that the birds disappeared. In other words, his enlightenment was a complete one, leaving no traces behind.

> Outside the gate, the spring is nearly half over;
> The fully realized mind is like burnt ashes;
> The loveliest flower leaves no shadow behind,
> And the hundred birds leave not a single track.

The main point to consider is that a series such as this represents a very
different approach from that of women Chan masters such as Qiyuan
Xinggang and Jizong Xingche, who, as we can see from their transmission certificate eulogies *(yuanliu song),* were more interested in the question of how these past masters (and by extension, themselves) fit into the
lineage succession. Like her Dharma grandfather Hanyue Fazang, Zukui
Jifu appears to have been more interested in the various insights that
could be provided by these masters than she was in the matter of how
they (and she) fit into their particular lines of succession.

Zukui Jifu also makes extensive use of the Chan rhetorical device of *daiyun* (speaking in place of). That is to say, in the context of a Dharma talk or informal exchange, the Chan master raises a precedent or case, usually from the classical past, and then poses a question, either to the student or to the congregation as a whole. The latter find themselves unable to reply, and the Chan master, instead of administering a blow or shout, supplies an answer—and sometimes two answers—of her own. Several fascicles of Zukui Jifu's *yulu* are composed of such exchanges, most based on textual sources. Sometimes, however, Zukui Jifu appears to be creating her own case and then commenting on it as well. An example of this is a series of *daiyun* questions found in her *Cliffside Flower Collection*.[19] The first text in this series of "twenty questions" both establishes the context and provides an illustration of such exchanges:

> One day the master was traversing [Lake Dongting], and as they were sitting there in the boat, she raised twenty questions. When those who were traveling with her found themselves unable to respond, she herself provided an answer on their behalf: "The waters of Lake Dongting are wide, and its waves a thousand. If you are unable to find a boat, how will you be able to cross over [*jidu*]?" Answering [again] on their behalf[, she said]: "To pose a question like this in midjourney!" And, again, [she] said: "Cross on over, cross on over [*dulai dulai*]!"

The general gist of this text is fairly clear—especially when one takes into account the term *jidu* is commonly used in Buddhist texts to refer to the metaphorical traversal, through faith and practice, of the sea of samsaric sorrow. What is interesting is Zukui Jifu's deft utilization of a (presumably) actual situation—crossing Lake Dongting with her disciples—to convey a deeper religious teaching.

Another instance of the use of analogies from everyday life, and in particular the everyday life of a gentry woman, is the following poem—or, rather, gatha—in which Zukui Jifu makes use of embroidered silk flowers to deliver a religious message. What is also interesting in this poem—which is addressed to a certain Lady Wang, the woman who actually did the embroidery—is the implicit validation of traditional woman's work.

> Golden needle [and] jade threads have stolen away heaven's work;
> Each and every leaf and each and every petal—not one the same.
> Once the root source is realized, the return is naturally accomplished.
> And one can cause the spring wind to rise from the palm of the hand.

> Spring follows the scissor blades and steals away heaven's work;
> Among the masses of deepest green, there is a drop of red.

Do not say that nothing sweet-smelling and fragrant is lovely;
At the very extreme of fragrance and color is the true emptiness.[20]

Fortunately for us, Zukui Jifu's collections are not completely lacking in more contextualized and even personal sorts of texts, such as Dharma talks delivered on the occasions of tonsure ceremonies or monastic birthdays, and poems and other texts addressed or referring to specific people, places, and events.[21] The names that appear in these texts—the large majority of which, it is worth noting, are names of monastics rather than laymen or women—provide hints of a much larger network of religious and social connections.

It is also clear that both she and Baochi Jizong kept in close and continuous contact with their teacher, Jiqi Hongchu. Not only did they visit him after becoming abbesses of their own convents, but in their Dharma talks and encounters they often relate stories of exchanges attributed to Jiqi Hongchu that they had either personally witnessed or participated in. Zukui Jifu's discourse records include, for example, a personal annotation of two talks in which Jiqi Hongchu elaborates on a teaching regarding the six types of achievement (*liu zhong chengjiu*) and the eight gates (*bamen*) that was particularly associated with him. Other indications that she subscribed not to Miyun Yuanwu's line of blows and shouts but rather to the more varied repertoire of ideas and methods advocated by Hanyue Fazang include her poems extolling the virtues of the principles of each of the five schools, and a brief commentary, with introduction, to a text attributed to Hanyue Fazang entitled *The Twelve Kinds of Sun-Revolving Samadhi of Cloud-Treasury Lodge (Zangyun shi shier zhong rixuan sanmei)*.

The sun-revolving samadhi (Skt. *sūryāvarta-samādhi*) is one of the sixteen states of higher consciousness referred to in the *Lotus Sutra*. Hanyue Fazang further elaborated sun-revolving samadhi into twelve kinds, each of which he associated with a different esoteric symbol. Nine of these symbols are in fact Chinese characters, although they have been endowed with an esoteric meaning by being placed within a circle. The remaining three are composed of an interlocking circle; a circle with a smaller circle at the center, from which a line ending in another small circle extends out to the left; and finally, a circle containing within it two smaller concentric circles, from the four directions of which extend four short lines that touch the circumference of the larger circle but do not extend beyond it.[22] Zukui Jifu's preface reads as follows:

Cast out the golden circles,
[And realize] the supreme truth of the triple storehouse.
Send back the jade proclamations,
[And] see clearly through to the ten directions.

Do not travel along the road of concepts,
[And] your words will be like a flash of lightning.
Before heaven, smash through the gates of passions;
The light of the moon shines from the sea.
I pray that all those gentlemen of attainment
Will match their tallies with this lineage.
Respectfully composed by [Ji] fu.

Although both this preface and Zukui Jifu's commentarial annotations are brief, consisting primarily of exclamations such as "He has stopped up the nostrils" or "By this, one can know the principle," they are evidence of an active—or, rather, interactive—engagement with the teachings and writings of both Jiqi Hongchu and his teacher, Hanyue Fazang.

Although Zukui Jifu does not appear to have composed any transmission certificate eulogies, she did write a series of quatrains, without the usual biographical notices, on the major figures of her lineage, ending with Hanyue Fazang and Jiqi Hongchu. Even more significantly, she includes a much longer series of encomiums on what would appear to be her favorite religious figures, both past and present. This series begins with a piece on Bodhidharma and then moves on to Linji, Yunmen, and Dahui Zonggao. From there she skips forward to Hanyue Fazang and Jiqi Hongchu, her pieces on the latter being the most extensive:

> He does not use the shouts of Linji, he does not practice the blows of Deshan; yet he is able to sweep away all of the brambles and thorns from the past and completely cleanse all of the clevernesses of the four directions. When he is joyful and happy, he plants bamboo on South Mountain in order to make writing brushes; this is his compassionate heart. When he is disturbed and angry, he grinds away at the waves of the Eastern Sea to create an ink that is difficult to describe.

She does not stop here. She follows this piece on her own teacher with a series of poems of praise for no less than six fellow female Chan masters, including Qiyuan Xinggang, Baochi Jizong, and Qiyuan Xinggang's Dharma heir, Yigong Chaoke. As a younger contemporary of Qiyuan Xinggang, Zukui Jifu held the abbess in very high regard. In the following encomium, for example, she alludes to Qiyuan Xinggang's charismatic reputation as a great lineage master:

> Exceptional and extraordinary: in the ten directions there are no walls [that can impede her]; strict and magnificently imposing: in the four directions are no gates [through which she cannot pass]. The staff that she wields—how can one defend oneself against it! Everywhere she is praised

and respected [for her ability] to cut away fetters and shatter nails, as is the duty of a master of the lineage.[23]

Zukui Jifu had probably met Qiyuan Xinggang at some point (although there is no explicit evidence of this). In the following brief quatrain, Zukui Jifu expresses a more personal sense of connection with her:

> The riverbank grasses follow the river's green;
> The village flowers gleam in the sun's crimson.
> There is no need for us to meet face-to-face;
> Over a thousand *li* we share the same breeze.[24]

Zukui Jifu did personally know Qiyuan Xinggang's Dharma heir, Yigong Chaoke, who, as we have seen, had studied for a time with Jiqi Hongchu in Suzhou before going to the Lion-Subduing Chan Cloister in Meixi.[25] Zukui Jifu wrote both a laudatory verse for Yigong Chaoke and the following moving elegy, composed after Yigong Chaoke's death in 1661, to which she appended a brief editorial note saying that "in the past I practiced [*can*] together with this Master":

> Taking leave of our mountain home, we set out on our southern search:
> With our rain capes and our carrying poles, just the two of us.
> Then you entered the Lion Grove and became the one in charge;
> And I plunged into the water like a duck to enjoy a quiet life.
> Clouds and mud have different forms; who is there to blame?
> The eternal snow that fills the breast; each must care for herself.
> On this day, white banners unfurled and sacrificial cups of tea—
> For a white-haired person to weep makes the pain even worse.[26]

In this poem, Zukui Jifu clearly alludes to the difference in religious careers, and perhaps in temperaments, between Yigong Chaoke and herself: she the Mary, as it were, to Yigong Chaoke's Martha. This does not mean that Zukui Jifu lived purely a contemplative life. She was an abbess after all and, judging from the number of her Dharma talks presented on the occasion of a tonsure or ordination, appears to have had quite a few disciples. Nevertheless, in one of her few first-person texts, entitled "A Description of My Aspirations," we sense what appears to be a rather profound alienation from the Chan Buddhist milieu of the day (although it is also true that expressing dismay over the religious decadence of the times appears to have been de rigueur for many monastic writers). In any case, it is worth noting that she singles out for critique the obsession with lineage and Dharma transmission that characterized Miyun Yuanwu and his immediate circles:

The way of the Buddha is both profound and subtle. One's realization
of it can be either shallow or deep, depending on the different methods
one follows. People of later [times] are mediocre and blind to the significance of this. Grabbing their swords, they follow in pursuit of it and vie for
the transmission of the robes. Alas, who is there who is able to touch the
bottom of the river of the Dharma? With their narrow and naïve perspectives, they mislead the rest of us. Unrestrained, they cling to the robes
of antiquity, and their mind-transmissions, carved and engraved, look like
nothing at all. . . . The earth in the east, the heaven in the west, in both
places they've been telling lies. Knocking on the bone in order to extract
the marrow is difficult to sustain, and so they make a habit of distorting the
meaning of things, completely twisting and complicating them. . . . [As for
myself,] I have relied [simply] on not cherishing deluded thoughts, and
have endeavored to model myself on the exemplars of past and present.
The lad Sudhana traveled south to visit with a succession [of teachers],
going to every single gate and hall without turning his back on any. . . .
Worldly discussions, monastic discussions, heated discussions—what point
is there in talking too much, like Feng'gan?[27] Bundling grasses, I can establish a good livelihood for myself; with a single kick, I will shatter both fetters and rice pot.[28]

Elsewhere, Zukui Jifu explicitly refers again to the polemics and sectarian disputes of her day, this time in a poem. The relevant lines read as
follows:

The Buddha has been gone for two thousand years,
And the root vessel each day becomes more tattered.
Five hundred together with three hundred,
Dragons and vipers often become confused.
Self and other take the form of greed and anger;
None of these matters have to do with each other.
Using their scholarly erudition just to attack others,
Forming factions, they fight over robe and bowl.
And in this way the fine children of Sakyamuni
Are nothing more than wolves in sheep's clothing.[29]

Interestingly, Zukui Jifu closes with a recommendation that the disciple to
whom this poem is addressed devote herself to the (presumably less risky)
practice of Pure Land recitation and faith in the Amitabha Buddha.

Zukui Jifu, as noted earlier, used a wide variety of genres and styles,
some more literary than others. Many of them can be found in male
Chan masters' discourse records, but rarely if at all do they appear in

the collections of her female counterparts. One example is her sermons delivered in thanksgiving for rain.[30] It is not clear whether she actually presided over rainmaking rituals—during the seventeenth and particularly the eighteenth centuries, rain rituals were primarily the preserve of the emperor and imperially mandated monks and monasteries.[31] And so it is quite possible that Zukui Jifu's Dharma talk was simply given in conjunction with rain ritual being conducted at a nearby monastery. In any case, the Dharma talk is both lively and engaging, and it is a good example of the merging of Chan and esoteric Buddhism espoused by Hanyue Fazang, as well as of Zukui Jifu's own literary gifts.

> From the blue sky that extends over ten thousand *li* not even a patch of cloud hangs; it needs a cudgeling! This mountain monk has a staff, but today instead of making use of it, she will command Great Teacher Yunmen especially to go and administer a painful blow to the great fish of the Eastern Sea. Then you will see the waves stir up and the billows rise, the clouds turn out and the mist ascend to the utmost, and the Dragon King's palace rock and sway, and the Dragon King will come out onto the road [and demand,] "What does the sky's not raining have to do with me? Your old lame-footed master is really making something out of nothing. My school [of Chan Buddhism] is nothing if not interfering." The Great Master said: "Stop jabbering away; stop jabbering away, and listen to my explanation. Your daughter, King of the Dragons, has already become a buddha, but you still have the face of a beast and are completely lacking in any sense of right and honor. Now this morning throughout the nation the red earth is as if burning, is dying and suffering losses. You are the King of the Dragons, and so naturally you yourself take good care of the bright pearl that is in your safekeeping, dozing away there, quietly submerged in those dead waters." When the Dragon King heard this, he became extremely angry, which created an explosive crash of thunder, immediately followed by [so much] rain it was as if a bowl had been overturned. Great Teacher Yunmen was stuck and there was no place he could retreat, and so he raised his walking staff and said: "Now I will shrink you and put you in this mountain monk's staff and leave. If you all do not believe me, then I will fling it down to the ground." Then [Jifu] said: "And so he got out of the cave astride a dragon, and the drought became a long-lasting downpour."[32]

In this Dharma talk, Zukui creatively combines several images and metaphors about dragons—traditionally considered in China to be the source of life-giving rain; their anger is said to give rise to thunder, lightning, and rain.[33] The Dragon King's Daughter, as we have seen, is featured in the *Lotus Sutra* and is one of the most important of the few stories of female enlightenment to be found in the Mahayana Buddhist scriptural tradition. Her father, the Dragon King, is said to guard a self-illuminating precious pearl in his palace below the sea, and in the Chan tradition, snatching away the pearl and returning home with it is a metaphor for attaining the essence of the Buddhist truth and then applying it to one's everyday life. Many of the dragon stories Zukui Jifu uses are attributed to the great Tang-dynasty master Yunmen Wenyan (864–949). One example is the koan found, among other places, in the *Blue Cliff Record* (case 60): "Yunmen showed his staff to the assembly and said, 'The staff has turned into a dragon and swallowed the universe. Mountains, rivers, the great earth—where are they to be found?'"[34] In case 48 of the *Wumen Guan,* or *Gateless Gate,* we find yet another reference to Yunmen and the connection with rain: "Yunmen held up has fan and said: 'The fan leaps up to the thirty-third heaven, where it grabs Indra on the nostrils; then it strikes the golden carp of the Eastern Sea with a single blow, at which it become a dragon and brings a downpour of rain.'"[35]

Another instance of a type of poem often found in the collections of male Chan masters that I have not found in any of the extant discourse records of other women Chan masters, is Zukui Jifu's poem entitled "Song of the Twelve Hours of the Day." Poems with this title (a traditional Chinese hour was equivalent to two Western hours) can be found in the collections of many male Chan masters. The most famous, perhaps, is the one by Linji's contemporary, Master Zhaozhou, which begins: "The cock crows. The first hour of the day. / Aware of sadness, feeling down and out yet getting up."[36] While Zukui Jifu's version is not quite as iconoclastic as that of her famous predecessor, it does provide a hint of what she considered to be the ideal monastic life.

> Middle of the night—the first hour of the day.
> In my dreams, I go here and there and don't know how to stop myself.
> Treading into pieces the green of the eastern hills and the western peaks;
> Then turning over to find one has been nestled in the bedcovers all
>   along.
>
> The cock crows—the second hour of the day.
> All the routines of everyday life, each one naturally in accord with the
>   other:
> Over there, by the banks of the river, they scrub their faces until they
>   shine;
> Over here, gargling and rinsing the mouth with tea, then swallowing
>   it down.

Dawn breaks—the third hour of the day.
I am alone here among ten thousand forms, and I can bare my body.
If the Buddha and ancestors came, they'd find it hard to overpower me;
Only if a person is herself willing can anyone become intimate with her.

The sun rises—the fourth hour of the day.
In the coral tree groves,[37] the colors are bright and radiant.
There is no need to look elsewhere for the Buddha Gautama;
His golden body, six-feet tall, is in a single blade of grass.

Mealtime—the fifth hour of the day.
In the new pot, fragrant, mouthwatering grains of fresh rice;
When I've finished eating my porridge, I go wash my bowl;
Then tell the prioress to go correct and instruct the others.

Midmorning—the sixth hour of the day.
Do not split up the great emptiness into "this" and "that,"
Bells and clappers in the wind are very good at preaching,
Explaining everything in detail without using a single word!

The sun shifts south—the seventh hour of the day.
Those who love leisure do not pound on Hoshan's drum.[38]
When there's free time, I climb the mountain and stroll about
And, when I'm weary, climb up onto the sitting mat once more.

The sun begins to sink—the eighth hour of the day.
The twelve-sectioned canon can inspire reverence;
Bowing my head, I pay homage to the peerless Great One
And venture to ask why one should stick to basics.

Late afternoon—the ninth hour of the day.
My understanding is still on this side of the river crossing.
I chide myself that my cultivation practice is not stronger;
When all goes well, I am happy; when it doesn't, I get angry!

The sun sets—the tenth hour of the day.
A curve of moon hangs over the willow by the window.
I blow on the kindling, and the furnace fills with smoke;
And four or five flecks of dark ashes fly up over my head.

The golden dusk—the eleventh hour of the day.
Time for the mice to venture out to steal the white honey.

At the foot of my bed they make a racket late into the night,
Which disturbs this mountain monk, so she cannot sleep.

Everyone settled—the twelfth hour of the day.
The mustard seed drinks dry the Fragrant-Water Sea;[39]
Beneath my robes, the *mani* jewel suddenly radiates light,[40]
Singing in unison with the lanterns on the outside pillars.[41]

Although these verses demonstrate well the "vivid immediacy of Chan
literature," the feeling of "being there," this immediacy is, as John McRae
reminds us, "a literary effort contrived through literally centuries of combined effort."[42] There is also little indication that what is being described
is a convent for nuns rather than a monastery for monks—apart from
the third verse, where—if one takes the speaker to be, like the author,
a woman—the reference to undressing for the early morning bath does
hint at some interesting gendered and even sexualized overtones.

But perhaps more revealing is the picture this series of verses paints
of what Zukui Jifu considered to be the ideal monastic life—where her
senior nuns do most of the teaching and she, the abbess, spends time
wandering in the hills, both in her dreams and in whatever leisure time
she can find during the day. In fact, in trying to locate the more personal
side of Zukui Jifu beneath the veil created by her deft literary use of the
Chan textual tradition, one can perhaps point to the handful of poems
written on the occasion of an excursion to a scenic site or a trip through
natural surroundings. Most of these are found in the *Cliffside Flower Collection* and would appear to have been composed when she lived at the
Udambara Flower Convent and enjoyed periods of relative leisure (and
solitude).

IMPROMPTU INSTRUCTION
The wind in the pine accompanies itself: no need for strings and
    songs;
The moon over the water hovers high: no need for a night lamp.
In my eyes and in my ears, nothing but a sublime soughing;
In heaven above and the world below—just a solitary nun.[43]

GATHERING UP FALLEN PINE BRANCHES
The mountains are steep, and there is no thoroughfare;
So what human being could have been to this place?
All through the night the wind gusted with urgency
And caused several pine trees to bend and to break.[44]

RETURNING TO THE MOUNTAINS I LAUGH AT MYSELF
There is no road to the solitary tip of this marvelous peak;
Those who reach it must have reduced their mind to ashes.
Funny how the white clouds have no precise destination
But are blown this way and then that way by the wind.[45]

At this point, it would probably be best to give up trying to "fix" Zukui
Jifu's historical personality, given her determination to create the per-
sona of a prolific but elusive woman Chan master. This determination is
perhaps best exemplified by a six-part colophon that she appears to have
composed for an actual portrait of herself.[46] These verbal self-portraits
show the extent to which Zukui Jifu succeeded in reinventing herself as
a woman Chan master, master of the largely male literary tradition but
still aware of the ambiguity of her gendered position and, in the end,
identifying herself as much with Moshan Liaoran as with any other of her
Dharma ancestors.

ONE
A single scroll of white paper, a few cross strokes of ink-black brush; neither is it a man nor is it a woman. Where did this appearance come from?
Being neither a spirit nor a ghost, what is there that could be transformed?
When there are no words, the spittle accumulates next to the mouth; when
there is no vision, the eyes just become more blurred. She can't help but
laugh at Guanxi with his many flowerbeds—by mistake he's called Linji his
grandfather![47]

TWO
Her mouth as fast as the wind, her disposition as quick as fire. She makes
no distinction between degrees of intimacy, so how would she know anything about "self" and "other"? From the tip of the needle, she uses endless [sorts of] expedients; in the flash of the lightning bolt, the million is
divided into five.[48] Stop boasting about the staff that turned into a dragon;
don't talk about the three mysteries having trapped the tiger. Haven't you
heard the words of Xuansha: "A great adept is the ancestor of the mind.
[Students of today] take this mind as the ancestral source [and] can study
until Maitreya Buddha comes down to be born here [and still never under-
stand]."[49]

THREE
The staff made of the horn of a hare carries the bright moon on its shoulder; the hairy tortoise binds up with cord the clear breezes.[50] This is not a

matter of a marvelous use of miraculous powers or mysterious methods—but who is there who dares to ask them about it?

FOUR
White boulders piled up high, the dark burrow clearly distinguishable. Having seen through shape and form, she can conceal her horns and laugh at the flowing waters [of time]. Laugh at that: the flowing waters are fruitlessly busy. Listen to this: the drifting clouds are naturally lightweight. She knows how to cultivate the [Buddha]-fields even when the crops fail: the one who trusts in [Yan] Hui, will be joyful no matter the circumstances.[51]

FIVE
The mountains of Lake Dongting are lofty and do not reveal their summits;[52] the waters of Lake Tai are deep but do not dampen the feet. Next year, to whom will the clear breezes pass on the transmission? All of the mind-seals of the ancestral teachers have been completely tossed away.

SIX
Face-to-face, neither saying a word. At a time of crisis, the single pole comes first. The gold needle pierces the white moon; the flint sparks shoot into the blue heavens. Bowled over with laughter—there is only the mind-Buddha. Tumbling upside down, she's attained the flesh-Chan. Nowadays, her poverty is even greater than before; should anybody ask, her hands are empty![53]

CHAPTER NINE

From Beijing to Jiangnan

Ziyong Chengru

B y the last quarter of the seventeenth century, the social and political transition was pretty much over, and the Manchu dynasty was firmly established. As we have seen, even Baochi Jizong's son Xu Jiayan had, perhaps reluctantly, traveled to Beijing in 1679 to take up an important office in the Qing court. Linji Chan monks in Miyun Yuanwu's lineage had made the journey even earlier. Muchen Daomin, Miyun Yuanwu's staunch defender and erstwhile ghostwriter, was invited to the capital in 1659 and soon became the favorite of the first Qing emperor (Shunzhi, r. 1644–1661), who bestowed on him the honorary title of Chan Master Hongjue.[1] Yet another of Miyun Yuanwu's twelve Dharma successors, Yulin Tongxiu, was also invited to Beijing in 1659, where he was given the title of Chan Master Dajue Puji. A year later, in the summer of 1660, Yulin Tongxiu helped officiate at the funeral of one of the emperor's favorite consorts, a fervent Buddhist devotee and an enthusiastic patron of Buddhism—and less than five months later, at the funeral of the emperor himself, who died at the age of twenty-three, officially of smallpox. Nor were Muchen Daomin and Yulin Tongxiu alone. In her study of the Beijing of this period, Susan Naquin notes that, in the capital, "monks of (at least) twenty-one different temples associated themselves with the Linji, thus claiming a connection through successive teachers back to [the Tang dynasty].... By the start of the Qing, a monk could claim to belong to the twenty-eighth generation, and by the late eighteenth century, the thirty-fiftieth."[2] Chan master Ziyong Chengru, the last woman Chan master for whom a discourse record collection is preserved in the Jiaxing canon, belonged to this northern branch of the Linji lineage.

As has been the case with all of the seventeenth-century nuns in this study, the general outlines of Ziyong Chengru's life as a Chan master must be teased from the snippets of information contained in, suggested by, or appended to her discourse records. Fortunately, among these materials is a brief biographical account *(xingshi)* in which she herself tells us about her background.³ From this text, we learn that her ancestors were originally from "east of the passes" (the Liaodong area). In the years immediately before and after 1644, many thousands of Chinese who had been living in the Liao River Valley of northeast China joined the Manchus and came "through the pass" to settle in the Beijing area.⁴ Ziyong Chengru's family appears to have been one of these Chinese families. She herself was born around 1645 in Jingmen, in what is today central Hubei Province.⁵ Her father, whose name was Zhou Zhixiang, "followed in the service of the [Shunzhi?] emperor" in the early years of his reign, but "although he performed meritorious service, he was unwilling to accept an official position and [instead] went into retirement, devoting himself to farming and study." Ziyong Chengru does not tell us the nature of the meritorious activities that her father performed for the emperor, but his refusal of an official position and his decision to retire to the countryside to pursue the life of a gentleman farmer would suggest, at least in part, an expedient move. Or then again, it might simply mean that he was a man whose personality was more suited to a life of contemplative seclusion than political service. Her father "was upright and honest, a pure and good man of integrity and cultivation," Ziyong Chengru remarks, and "he had always been a believer in Buddhism."

Like Qiyuan Xinggang, Ziyong Chengru appears to have been an only child. In a text that reflects a combination of autobiographical possibility and hagiographical fiction, she recounts how her father, finding himself still without children at the age of fifty, prayed devoutly to the Bodhisattva, requesting an heir. "This stirred the Bodhisattva's compassion, and I was born," Ziyong Chengru tells us. She also tells us of her early religious inclinations: "As I child, I never engaged in silly talk or laughter, and as soon as I grew a little older, I became determined to leave the world." Again, as in the case of Qiyuan Xinggang, her parents were reluctant to accede to this request from their only child. "When I reached the age of marriage, my parents pushed me to marry," Ziyong Chengru writes, "but being pure-hearted and chaste, I had no desire for things of the flesh, and no love for wealth and status. I wanted nothing more than to [spend my life] following a vegetarian diet and embroidering Buddhist images [*changzhai xiu Fo*]. I was completely determined to attain liberation."⁶

Unlike Qiyuan Xinggang, Ziyong Chengru appears to have been successful in persuading her parents to allow her to enter the religious life rather than marry. In any case, there is no indication that she had to resort to extreme measures such as self-starvation in order to do so. Her account swiftly moves from a statement of her early religious inclinations to a description of her religious training, for despite her professed desire to devote herself simply to "keeping a vegetarian diet and embroidering Buddhist images," she clearly had something very different in mind. She tells us that her tonsure master and first teacher was a monk (or nun?) by the name of Buren and that for twenty years "[I] visited famous masters in order to deepen my understanding and insight." One of the places she visited was Mount Wutai, about 150 miles southwest of Beijing. A cluster of mountains rather than just one (*wutai* means "five terraces"), Wutai had long been an important pilgrimage site, as well as a unique one. As Robert Gimello explains:

> Situated not far south of a stretch of the Great Wall, it marked the boundary between the civilized world of China proper and . . . the vacant expanse now known as Mongolia. [Wutai], therefore, must be seen as a kind of spiritual rampart of the empire. To travel to [Wutai]—particularly in earlier times—was to go to the very edge of China's cultural world, there to risk awesome encounters with things genuinely, if not totally, "other." The severe, wind-swept terrain of the place, together with its dramatic weather, no doubt often served to heighten the sense of adventure and holy dread so commonly felt by the pious visitors from the more secure and domesticated regions of the Middle Kingdom.[7]

Although a northerner, Ziyong Chengru found travel in the Wutai Mountains to be quite a challenge (she does not mention having a companion, but it is unlikely that she was traveling completely by herself). Nevertheless, she appears to have handled the challenge with intrepid determination, according to her own account:

> When I was in the region of Wutai, west of the Liao [River], I experienced much toil and difficulty, but with a resolute spirit, I faced the dangers and encountered tigers and wolves, thieves and bandits. But I was not frightened of fire or swords, natural disasters, or people out to harm me. I regarded everything with complete calm and tranquility.

As early as the fifth century, Mount Wutai came to be regarded as the home of the great bodhisattva Manjusri, known for his eloquence and wisdom, and from the Tang dynasty onward, it grew into a major monastic and pilgrimage center. It was also known as a place where one might be rewarded with sacred visions of Manjusri himself, usually in the form of auspicious and wonderful lights. It seems that Ziyong Chengru was one of the many who claimed to have been granted such a vision. She records the experience in a short poem with a long title—"On Pilgrimage to Mount Wutai, I Lost My Way, but the Bodhisattva Took Compassion on

Me and Manifested Himself so as to Show Me the Way: I Wrote This as a Record of This Miracle":

Peaks and cliffs in folds of green known for their freshness;
Mist and rain so obscure and deep, I lost my way upward.
Treading upon the dark blue hills, a red sun appeared,
And the Dharma King burst forth from out of the void.[8]

It was on Mount Wutai as well that she met Chan master Gulu Fan, the monk under whom she would, as she put it, "die and then come back to life again" (si er fu sheng) and from whom she would finally receive Dharma transmission. He was a Dharma successor of Linji Chan master Yuan'an Benli (1622–1682), one of Muchen Daomin's most well-known Dharma heirs, and was associated primarily with the Long Life Monastery (Changshou an) near Wuchang in Hubei Province—an imperially sponsored monastery, judging from its name. However, Ziyong Chengru appears to have met Gulu Fan at the Wondrous Virtue Monastery (Miaode an) on Mount Wutai—the same monastery where, in 1589, work on the compilation of the Jiaxing canon had first begun before being transferred to the Jiangnan area.[9]

Ziyong Chengru's biographical account includes none of the detailed descriptions of strenuous spiritual practices such as we have for nuns like Qiyuan Xinggang and Jizong Xingche. In her brief description of her meeting with Gulu Fan on Mount Wutai, she does mention being tested on Linji's "three painful blows and his three mysteries and three essentials" and being asked to produce a gatha to demonstrate her understanding of these. However, it does appear, from a comment she makes later during a seven-day intensive meditation retreat, that her primary practice was also huatou cultivation. In this Dharma talk, she refers to the great "ball of doubt" that Dahui Zonggao so strongly emphasized. When this ball of doubt is finally shattered, then and only then, one shares the self-same enlightened ontological status as the saints and sages of the past. She then refers to her own experience: "Thirteen years ago, this mountain monastic embraced [bao] her huatou, neglecting to sleep and forgetting to eat, she was like an idiot, like a cripple, like a person that was dead. Thirteen years later, [she] is [like the] bright sun on a beautiful day, shining on everything without exception."[10]

Whether thirteen years is the time she spent under Gulu Fan's tutelage, or whether that includes all the time she spent on her travels, we do not know. In any case, in due time she became one of Gulu Fan's official Dharma successors, and in 1691, thanks no doubt to a combination of family and religious connections with the imperial family, was named abbess of the Eternal Glory Chan Cloister (Yongqing chanyuan) in Beijing. She also served at several other convents in the imperial city, including the Vast Benevolence Convent (Hong'en si) and the Eternal Life Chan Cloister (Yongshou chanyuan). This latter convent would appear to be the one she describes in the following "impromptu poem":

> The site of this Buddhist convent in the northern city is old,
> And its magnificently placed statues are grand and imposing.
> What is "before" and "after" in the transmission of Dharma?
> Just follow your karmic destiny, whether it is bitter or sweet.
> How wonderful not to engage in conceptions and deliberations,
> Grasping that which seems to exist and yet seems not to be!
> I ask my nuns, wondering if there is anyone who understands:
> If you are going to be firm, then you'll have to match swords.[11]

There is more than one Buddhist establishment by this name in the local gazetteers, but the reference in Ziyong Chengru's poem to the "northern city" (Beicheng) may provide us a clue as to the location of her convent. In the Ming dynasty, Beijing was composed of several cities nested one within the other, with the imperial family residing in the Forbidden City at the center. The Forbidden City was surrounded by the Imperial City, which held the private lakes, gardens, storehouses, and so on associated with the royal family. These in turn were surrounded by the "square older Northern City, representing some 65 percent of the whole, and the attached, newer, rectangular Southern City."[12] With the founding of the Qing dynasty, all of the older Chinese residents of the northern city were forced to move to the southern city, or what would later be called the Outer City, leaving the northern area to immigrants from the northeast (Manchuria and Liaodong), such as Ziyong Chengru's own family perhaps. It is also possible that Ziyong Chengru's convent was located within the Forbidden City itself, given that it clearly enjoyed imperial patronage; in her inaugural Dharma talk, Ziyong Chengru is careful to acknowledge the compassionate Dharma nourishment (*faru*) of her teacher, Gulu Fan, but also the generous beneficence of the emperor as well.

Judging from what she tells us elsewhere, it would seem that although the Eternal Life Chan Convent may have been around for a while, it was very much in need of repair by the time she arrived there, and that she herself built it up by dint of her own determination and the help of wealthy patrons, including many from the imperial family. In the accounts of Dharma encounters and talks in her *yulu* collection ascribed to this period of her life, there are numerous references to visiting groups of laywomen who sponsor vegetarian meals and request Dharma talks.

It is quite possible, then, that she received the support of religious lay associations, which, as Susan Naquin notes, "had existed in Peking since at least the Ming, and were now being created with regularity and enthusiasm by both Chinese and Manchu residents of the capital."[13] There are a number of references as well to visits from members of the imperial family. In one case, we find a contingent of laywomen, no doubt of aristocratic background, led by one of the royal princesses, who is unidentified, although she is referred to as the Great Dharma-Protector Princess (Da hufa gongzhu). Such imperial patronage no doubt went a long way toward establishing the reputation of Ziyong Chengru's convent, not to mention that of the nun herself. As Naquin points out:

> Most of the women of the ruling family came from the Peking area and were more in touch than the emperors with the world outside the palace. Being beyond direct official censure, imperial wives and daughters had greater liberty than their husbands and sons to patronize Buddhist establishments. It was not the custom for them to enter nunneries, so they expressed their piety in visits and gifts. Surely knowledgeable about local beliefs, familiar with a range of clerics (with whom conversation might have been possible), in touch with their relatives, intimate with their female attendants, and in many cases seriously interested in religion, imperial women were able to appreciate what a land endowment, new hall, bestowed name, or mere visit might mean to a temple, its clerics, and its neighborhood.[14]

As an abbess in Beijing, Ziyong Chengru received numerous visitors, both male and female, monastic and lay, Han and Manchu—all with various sorts of concerns and requests. Many of these requests had to do, not surprisingly, with the performance of funeral or death anniversary ceremonies for the departed. Others had to do with religious birthday celebrations for parents or spouses. There were also many tonsure and ordination ceremonies. Ziyong Chengru had at least two official Dharma heirs, and many nuns lived at her convent as well. She also officiated over a form of ritual ordination that appears to have been popular among the aristocratic elite since the late Ming if not earlier. Shen Defu (1578–1642), for example, notes, "When the emperor, the heir apparent, and the various princes of the present reign are born, they all have young boys ordained as monks and have them serve as substitutes [in their place]."[15] Given that Ziyong Chengru herself conducted several such ritual ordinations, it would appear that young women as well as young men could serve as substitutes. We find her, for example, tonsuring a nun at the request of a certain Lady Shu, whose husband held the prestigious position of vice-minister of works. This particular young girl, "donated" by Lady Shu on behalf of her husband, was given the Dharma name "Fochen," and her duty was to "topple down the mountain of [attached] love, and clear away the path of Mara [demons],"[16] or, in other words, to assure that the vice-minister would enjoy a smooth official career. It is not clear how ritualistic such ceremonies were, or whether the young girl was allowed to regrow her hair and return to her family after the ceremony was finished. On another such occasion, arranged by a certain Lady Wu, Ziyong delivers the following Dharma talk:

> With a flick of the hand, the metal blade cuts away a myriad ailments; with her head shaved, this woman [literally, petticoats and hairpins] changes her name to Zusheng [Patriarchs Victorious]. Raising the wick of the lamp of wisdom, wiping clear the mirror of realization, the Buddha nature Vairochana shines forth in ten directions.[17] . . . Yesterday you were still a sojourner in the world of dust; today you have gone out of the world [*fang-wai*, i.e., have become a monastic].[18]

In Ziyong Chengru's *yulu*, amid all the many descriptions of these activities, we find a short reflective poem she wrote when she was forty-nine *sui*, entitled "*Bingzi* [1691] Writing to My Feelings":

> How many glorious seasons have passed!
> Forty and nine years of springtimes.
> Although in this world I have no companion,
> If I ask my mind, I find it is my own intimate!
> The smell of incense disperses the early dawn;
> The closed shutters keep away the dusty world.
> From today, having woken from a foolish dream,
> I am the "Just-as-It-Is Idler" Person of the Way.[19]

Even with the patronage of members of the royal family as well as high officials and their wives, being the abbess of a religious establishment was not particularly easy, between fund-raising and conducting meditation retreats. In this regard, Ziyong Chengru shares many of the institutional concerns of her southern counterparts like Qiyuan Xinggang:

> Laboring hard, I exerted myself and never once was I willing to steal even a half a day of leisure. Abandoning all attachments of body and soul, I resolutely dedicated my life to the attainment of sagehood and the transcendence of the world. Thanks to the power of the Buddha, I was able to move and persuade some Dharma patrons from among the wealthy gentry and district magistrates to help me to build a monastery. Once I had set up

the basic framework, I was able to attract [disciples and donors] who, with their thoughts bent on posterity, [helped] me in the restoration and construction. Even before everything was in order, we held the [three-month summer] silent meditation retreat. Although I had not completed my work, in my heart I wanted to benefit and liberate the people of the world. It is because of this that I occasionally have had to make use of roundabout and cunning means. And it is for this reason that [I was bestowed with the honorary name of] Ship of Compassion and Universal Salvation.[20]

Ziyong Chengru's efforts (which she herself characterizes as sometimes having to be expedient) caught the attention not only of Buddhist laymen and monastics but of the Kangxi emperor himself, who at some point (it is unclear exactly when) bestowed upon her the honorary title of Ship of Compassion and Universal Salvation. This title immediately summons up images of the compassionate "savioress," the bodhisattva Guanyin, and indeed we find an elderly laywoman asking Ziyong Chengru: "The Great Bodhisattva Guanyin has thirty-two manifestations. Which of these forms are you taking on today?" Ziyong Chengru's reply is one befitting a Chan master: "You can look, but here you will not find even a single form!" But, the old woman persists, "if there is no form, then what is it that is ascending to the dais to preach the Dharma?" Ziyong Chengru answers, "For a lion cub to take a bite out of person is like a highbred dog chasing a wily rabbit."[21]

Nevertheless, Ziyong Chengru's imperially bestowed title attracted even more visitors, as much curious as devout, from all parts of China. In fact, one is struck with how many of the recorded accounts begin with Ziyong Chengru asking her visitors, whether male or female, monastic or lay, where they have come from. This is a standard Chan Buddhist opening move, of course, the question being not where they come from geographically but rather the location of their "original home," that is, their Buddha mind. Most of the visitors take her literally, however, and so we can see that although many of them were local (nuns from the Western Hills outside Beijing, for example, or from the Inner Palace itself), others came from nearby provinces such as Henan, and still others came from the Jiangnan area. Ziyong Chengru's discourse records contain the following amusing account of an exchange she had with a skeptical scholar who had traveled a considerable distance to see her:

A first-degree graduate came from the south and entered the hall. He and the Master looked at each other, and then the scholar said: "After having traveled all day to come and visit the 'Ship of Compassion,' who would have guessed that this 'Ship of Compassion' would turn out to be nothing but an old crone!" The Master, emitting an earthshaking roar, then asked: "What is this place? Tell me is it male? Or is it female?" When the scholar could not reply, she said to him: "Come closer and I will tell you." When the scholar was in front of her, she grabbed him and said: "From the day you left Spirit Mountain, there is no place to be sought; from this day on, mother and son have met again." The scholar said, "I trust you completely," and, prostrating himself, took refuge and requested the tonsure.[22]

Another account of an exchange between Ziyong Chengru and a male visitor is highly reminiscent, not accidentally to be sure, of the well-known exchange between the Tang nun Moshan Liaoran and her visitor, the monk Guanxi Zhixian:

A monk asked: "What is the environment [*jing*] of the Eternal Life [convent]?" The Master replied: "In front of the hall there are flowers like jade." "What is the person within this environment like?" asked the monk. The Master replied, "You may scrutinize my face [all you want], but the peak does not reveal itself [*bulou ding*]." "What is your purpose [*yizhi*]?" asked the monk. "One blow [of the stick] leaves one scar," replied the Master.[23]

In 1699, Ziyong Chengru was invited to become abbess of the Rain-Flowers Convent (Yuhua an) in Zhuozhou, just outside Beijing. The invitation came from a group of lay (male) benefactors, and her *yulu* contains a brief account of the installation ceremony, which involved, as it always did for occasions such as this, a ritual tour of the major buildings of the establishment, accompanied by a brief statement. Beginning with the front gate (or mountain gate, as it was called), the tour proceeded to the Weituo Hall, where the Four Wrathful Guardian Gods kept watch, and then to the Great Hall *(dadian)*, ending at the abbot's quarters. Ziyong Chengru's comments about this latter are revealing of her full-hearted acceptance of Miyun Yuanwu's re-creative blows and shouts: "This lion's cave: commoner or sage, both must enter through here. [Even] when the most heroic and spirited monks show up, the great staff will come down on their heads without mercy!"[24]

Her reference to the abbot's quarters as a lion's cave is echoed in an account of an encounter with an uppity monk, this one taking place at the Eternal Peace Convent (Yong'an an) in the Western Hills, which Ziyong Chengru was visiting. We are told that one day a wandering monk came into the abbot's quarters, where Ziyong Chengru was staying, and sat down on the platform. "The wolf has entered into the lion's den," she said. "It is Manjusri who is here," the monk replied. "Just in time for you to wash the feet of this mountain monk!" retorted Ziyong Chengru. "The lion cub has experienced a great conversion [*shizi fa fanshen*]!" was the monk's response. Ziyong Chengru delivered a blow that left the monk speechless, and then drove him out of the room.[25] In this account we see that Ziyong Chengru is being faithful to Miyun Yuanwu's performative re-creation of the blows and shouts of the Tang masters Linji and Deshan. Indeed, blows and shouts appear ubiquitously throughout Ziyong Chengru's Dharma talks, and there is far less mention of the *huatou* investigation that was central to the teaching and practice of Qiyuan Xinggang and her woman Dharma successors. Nevertheless, like them, Ziyong Chengru clearly carried her authority with confidence and aplomb. I would suggest as well that what we see in this metaphysical refusal to be defined, whether as a manifestation of Guanyin or as an old crone, is a more personal and cultural refusal to be limited by traditional notions of women's roles, be they lay or monastic.

It was not always visitors who came to her, however. As we have seen, Ziyong Chengru had done a considerable amount of traveling before becoming an abbess, and she continued to do a lot of traveling afterward as well. The poems she writes on travel are not always possible to date, but we sense in them that despite having spent most of her time consorting with the "rich and famous" in the closed and cloistered world of the Imperial City, she, like Chan master Jizong Xingche, derives an immense pleasure from being on the road. Two short poems, "Traveling in the Mountains" and "A Traveler's Gatha"—the first written in anticipation of memory and the second in remembrance—illustrate this beautifully:

> Staff in hand, I go through the woods, stirring up the fallen reds;
> Suddenly I hear a clear chime carried by the autumn wind.
> I'm afraid that, next time, I won't be able to find this place again.
> I'll try to remember that solitary pine hanging from the cliffside.[26]

> I still think about carrying my travel bundle, in those days gone by,
> Traveling the hills, frolicking in the waters, coming out in cloud country.
> Eyes open and eyebrows raised in astonishment, everything is samadhi,
> And in this great earth, there is nowhere that is not a Wisdom Hall![27]

Ziyong Chengru's travels were, ostensibly at least, not for pleasure but for the purpose of visiting either eminent masters or sacred sites, and preferably both. The immediate scriptural template for such travel was, of course, the popular story in the *Flower Garland Sutra* of the pilgrimage made by the young Sudhana to visit fifty-three "good friends," who offer him the opportunity to deepen his spiritual understanding. Religious travel continued to be important in the seventeenth century and later, and monks would travel to mountains, such as Mount Wutai in Shaanxi (associated with the bodhisattva Manjusri), Mount Jiuhua in Anhui, and Mount Putuo in Zhejiang (the home of Guanyin), as well as to monasteries and stupas associated with famous Chan masters. However, even such travel by male monastics was by no means wholeheartedly endorsed. As Susan Naquin and Chün-Fang Yü point out, "Buddhist monks in general (and Chan monks in particular) asserted that an internal journey might be as conducive to salvation as a physical one, and the latter might even be disruptive and unnecessary."[28] In fact, there is a long tradition in Chan Buddhist texts of undercutting the need for pilgrimages, beginning with Linji himself:

> Followers of the Way, you who are carrying your activities before my eyes are no different from the Buddha and the patriarchs. But you don't believe that and [thus you] go searching for something outside. Make no mistake. There's no Dharma outside, and even what is on the inside can't be grasped. You get taken up with the words from the mouth, but it would be better if you stopped all that and did nothing.... That's better for you than ten years traveling around on pilgrimages.[29]

There was perhaps an important distinction to be made between pilgrimage to holy sites and travel in search of teachers *(canfang)*. Yunqi Zhuhong, perhaps the most important Buddhist figure of this period, felt that the latter was an essential component of Chan religious training, and that the reluctance of many monks to undertake these travels was yet another indication of the sorry state to which Buddhism had been reduced. He writes:

> When the ancients had the slightest doubt in their minds, they would not cheat themselves, but had to find out the answer from a teacher. Thus they did not regard going a long distance as a tiresome task. But nowadays people are otherwise. If it is for seeking out a teacher and asking about the truth, they knit their brows even if they have to cover only the distance of a frog's leap. But if it is for fame and profit, they can easily start a journey of ten thousand *li*.[30]

Nevertheless, concerned as he was with avoiding even the slightest appearance of impropriety (one of his regulations stipulated that no male disciple would take on a female lay disciple under the age of sixty), Yunqi Zhuhong also argued that nuns "should not travel at all!"[31] In this

he concurred with the Confucian assumption that a proper woman ideally should not step over the threshold of the inner chamber, much less
"climb high places or stand on the edge of deep chasms."[32]

Female pilgrimage was also looked upon with little favor by the government authorities, who were worried that unsavory types might be
wandering footloose and fancy-free and, in their eyes, out of control.
Nevertheless, it is obvious that many Buddhist female devotees found in
pilgrimage with like-minded women a rare and enjoyable occasion to get
out of the house and see the sites. There were, in fact, a number of laywomen from elite circles who were well known for having embarked on
extensive pilgrimage travel, not just to one site but to many.[33]

Linji Chan nuns, as we have seen in the case of Jizong Xingche,
appear to have been not at all reluctant to travel, sometimes very long
distances, to meet with eminent masters and visit sites associated with
the Linji lineage. Several decades earlier, for example, the nun Mingxiu
Dongwu, who was a native of Jiangsu and a disciple of Miyun Yuanwu's
Dharma heir, Feiyin Tongrong, traveled to the four great Buddhist mountains *(sida mingshan)*—Emei, Putuo, Wutai, and Jiushan—as well as to Beijing.[34] Famous for both her poetry and her painting, like Ziyong Chengru
many decades later, Mingxiu Dongwu also recorded her impressions in
poems, such as the following:

> The mountain landscape along the He River is fine,
> But one must bear with a rain that goes on forever.
> If you want to see the road that leads to Mount Emei,
> You must rely on the boat of intuitive wisdom.
> Cloud-covered peaks give way to dawn's scene;
> Numinous trees are covered with autumn mist.
> And less than a foot away is a place to gaze upward,
> Where one can then ascend to the first of the heavens.[35]

Not all of the hardships that Ziyong Chengru endured on her travels stemmed from the elements or from bandits, as we can see from the
following poem, entitled "One Day on Pilgrimage, I Sought Refuge in a
Mountain Monastery When Evening Fell but Was Not Admitted; I Composed This to Express My Feelings."

> To travel far in search of knowledge is truly a difficult thing:
> At dusk, I went to a monastery, but was not allowed to stay.
> At midnight, I sat under the elements, my mind one with the stillness.
> Over ten thousand *li* I have rambled and roamed, leaves no sour taste.
> I laugh at these foolish monks who do not see things as I do,

And mistakenly regard those of my kind to be stupid and dull.
The clear breeze and bright moon in the distant wilds;
The hidden birds carrying blossoms pass the bamboo gates.[36]

Ziyong Chengru's greatest aspiration, however, had been to take an extended pilgrimage to the great Chan monasteries and mountains of Jiangnan. Finally, one spring she bid farewell to her disciples in Beijing and boarded a boat headed south, where, she told her disciples, she would "consult the fifty-three" knowledgeable masters, as Sudhana had. To commemorate her departure from Beijing, she composed the following series of ten verses. In them, she refers to the capital by its ancient name of Yanjing, or "capital of Yan." She also uses the term "Jintai," which refers to the Imperial Golden Terrace, one of the famous "Eight Prospects of Yanshan" celebrated by painters and poets in the Ming dynasty. Although the site itself had disappeared by the fifteenth century, it remained very much alive in the poetic and aesthetic imagination of the residents of Beijing. These poems by Ziyong Chengru are filled with anticipation, but also, perhaps, a reluctance to leave both her disciples and the northern landscape that had always been her home. Although it is almost impossible to date any of Ziyong Chengru's writings, it would appear from this poem that she fully intended to return to Beijing the following autumn.

Yesterday my disciples spoke to me of the grief of separation
As they poured out the endless sorrow that was in their hearts.
I've ordered the flowers in the courtyard not to be too anxious,
Lest they startle the pearly dewdrops on the autumn blooms.

I bought myself a light boat in anticipation of going south.
A bright moon fills my breast; my empty heart feels foolish!
In front of the cliffs, hidden birds sing out time and again,
Saying, "When you reach the south, consult the fifty-three!"

Last night the numinous blossom in my dream split in two;
But when I awoke, it was as before—vast and without a trace.
A heavenful of luminous moon, as clear as if just bathed;
The jade waters of the Yan hills all lift the traveler's spirits.

Do not slight the lazy and foolish: both come from no mind.
Clouds emerge without thinking, birds just sing their songs.
The wind pierces the flowers' shimmer, their fragrance so fine.
What need to seek for anything more than surprises like these!

It is just that I love the Yan Mountains and their jade waters,
Where clear breezes and bright moon complement each other.
The birds in the trees know how things will turn out in the end;
Flying close to my carriage, from afar they seal a vow with me.

A skiff of a boat floats in the vastness under the bright moon;
In northern lands or southern skies the landscape is the same.
Stop nattering on, my disciples, about how fond of me you are;
When fall comes, you can expect the geese to return as before.

Two sleevefuls of springtime light as I leave the Forbidden City;
One breastful of anxious thoughts poured out toward the south.
The mountains of Yan on my mind as grieving clouds thicken,
But if you wait until high autumn, then its colors will become clear.

The lightweight sail hangs high among the five-colored clouds;
Ten thousand miles of road to travel, as far as the eye can see.
Its two banks of reed flowers reach beyond the edge of the sky;
The sun's glow rises above me at the gateway to the eastern sea.

A willow-colored overcoat reminds me it is a cold time of year;
And peach reds still recall the sorrowful feelings of separation.
Filling all the world's jade waters, one bright moon in the sky;
If you stay and wait on Golden Terrace, you can see it very well.

The Chan mind is not solitary, as clouds in the wilds know;
Reed moon and plum blossom, to whom can I send them?
The sorrow of parting is meaningful and so hard to dismiss;
But if the way is in tune with no-mind, it will go as it should.[37]

Ziyong Chengru's voyage south paralleled, although on a completely different scale, the Kangxi emperor's famous southern excursions, taken in 1684, 1689, and then again in 1705. In fact, thinking perhaps that the Kangxi emperor would appreciate her feelings upon experiencing for the first time the warm lushness and changeable weather of the south, sometime in 1701 she composed several short verses for him, one of which reads as follows: [38]

This year, what fortune to have met with the southern sun!
During the day, it changes several times from cloudy to clear.
And beneath the sail, the paper window is dry and then wet,
As the stone paths in front of the boat are wet and then dry.[39]

On her journey south, Ziyong Chengru passed through Anhui, where she visited the Buddhist sacred mountain Mount Jiuhua. One of the more well-known pilgrimage destinations on this mountain later became the Ganlu Monastery, or Sweet Dew Monastery, but when Ziyong Chengru spent the night there, it was not that old, having been established in 1667 at the instigation of Yulin Tongxiu.[40]

> Pushing through brambles, cutting through trees, the road spirals
> around.
> The chimes of the Chan "family air" sound; the evening smoke lies level.
> When I arrived here, I was afraid that I wouldn't have a place to stay,
> Until I was able to make out the solitary lamp of the Sweet Dew.[41]

The night she spent on Mount Jiuhua was not the most comfortable, although she was still reluctant to leave:

> Last night at the top of the mountain, it was bone-piercing cold;
> My entire body felt miserable, and I didn't get any sleep at all.
> Now this time as I take my leave, I grieve that it is not easy to get here;
> Carrying the rain and welcoming the wind, I descend the nine peaks.[42]

Once she arrived in Jiangsu and Jiangnan, Ziyong Chengru was particularly anxious to visit the funerary stupas of her lineage ancestors, in particular that of Muchen Daomin in Zhejiang and that of Yuan'an Benli in Ningbo, where she was welcomed warmly and asked to deliver a Dharma talk. In the exchange that supposedly took place after this talk, we see some of the same familiar gender-related allusions and references, in what almost seems like a testing of this female Linji Chan master come from the north:

> The monk asked: "Thirty blows—are they [actions] of a man or of an enlightened person?" Ziyong Chengru replied: "Just as long as the fellow isn't beaten to death." The monk then said: "The Great Way is not divided into male and female; why is there any need for me to ask you [these questions]?" Ziyong replied: "The nun was originally a woman." The monk said: "Then when you speak, the congregation assembles like clouds. In the end, who is the gentleman hero among women?" Ziyong [Chengru] said: "Each and every person has the sky over [his or her] head; each and every one has the earth under [his or her] feet." The monk then gave a shout. Ziyong [Chengru] said: "What is the point of recklessly shouting like that?" The monk then bowed respectfully, and Ziyong [Chengru] said: "The Dharma does not rise up all alone—it cannot emerge without reli-

ance on the environment, and it is neither distant nor is it far. I've come
from a distance of three thousand *li* to the mountain of my ancestors, and
have humbly accepted the request of the abbot, [who is] the senior monk
and my Dharma uncle, to ascend this platform and speak of the principles
of the lineage. I am ashamed only that my wisdom, insight, and knowledge
are shallow. If I dare to take up this challenge, I must surely turn and bor-
row the light and dark, form and emptiness, of the mountains and hills
and the great earth; the call of the magpies and the cries of the crows. The
water flows and the flowers blossom, brilliantly preaching without ceasing.
In this way there is no restraint, and there may even be some fresh and
refreshing phrases.[43]

At this point, Ziyong Chengru's itinerary becomes a little difficult to
reconstruct. She appears to have received numerous invitations from lay
benefactors to visit and to give Dharma talks. In just such a talk, delivered
at the request of a group of Buddhist laymen headed by a certain Layman
Sun, Ziyong Chengru notes:

On my journey here from the capital, this mountain monastic has [endured]
wind and frost and [passed through] great areas of wilderness; but what
place is not home to a patch-robed monk, a place to settle the body and
mind? My original plan was simply to come on pilgrimage [*chaoshan*]; I did
not expect that today I would receive an invitation from Layman Sun to
ascend this lotus seat and preach these words of Dharma.[44]

Ziyong Chengru's original intention may well have been to return
to Beijing as soon as she had completed her southern pilgrimage (just
as Jizong Xingche expressed her intention to return to Hengshan), but
she was persuaded instead to become the abbess of a recently restored
convent called the Jade Empyrean Chan Cloister (Bixia chanyuan) in the
scenic Wu Mountains, bordering the southern edge of the famous West
Lake outside of Hangzhou. The invitation, the text of which is included
in her *yulu*, was extended by a group of twenty-eight lay donors, At the
head of the list was the author of the invitation, Zhao Jishi (1628–1706),
who was from the newly emergent merchant class rather than the traditional elite. He also appears to have amassed a good amount of money,
and in his old age he retired to the city of Beijing, where he spent his last
years enjoying the company of like-minded friends, such as the famous
dramatist Kong Shangren (1648–1718), and cultivating his garden,
which was called Yi Garden.[45] On the invitation list, Zhao Jishi's name is
followed by that of Ling Shaomin, a Hanlin official whose primary claim
to fame was his being one of the twenty-seven compilers and editors of

the great *Kangxi Dictionary*, published between 1710 and 1716. In other words, the men who lent their names, and apparently also their money, to the refurbishment of the Jade Empyrean Chan Cloister represent a group of literati officials who, whatever their feelings about serving the Manchu regime, sought and succeeded in making use of their considerable talents at court. Moreover, men like Zhao Jishi also traveled a great deal, both on official business and for pleasure, and had their feet firmly planted in two worlds, Beijing in the north and Jiangnan in the south. In this regard, it is not hard to see why, if they were at all sympathetic toward Buddhism, they would welcome a woman such as Ziyong Chengru, given her extensive traveling between north and south and her close connections at court and elsewhere.

Zhao Jishi's text reflects these cross-regional connections. He notes her place in the Linji Chan lineage of Miyun Yuanwu; her long years of cultivation, leading to her enlightenment experience and her confirmation as a Dharma heir; and her various travels to Buddhist holy mountains and sacred sites, culminating in her journey south. But he also goes into considerable detail about all of the high officials and palace ladies of wealth and status who flocked around Ziyong Chengru in Beijing as if she were the bodhisattva Guanyin herself. Finally, he recounts how he and his cohorts expended much time, energy, and money to convert what appears to have been a somewhat dilapidated hermitage into a real working convent, "cutting away the thistles and brambles in order to build an abbot's quarters" for this esteemed female lineage-holder from the north.[46]

It is unclear whether or not Ziyong Chengru ever made it back to Beijing, as she had promised her followers there that she would, or whether she spent her last days at the Jade Empyrean Chan Cloister. It is also unclear when exactly she passed away, although we are told that it occurred on the twentieth day of the twelfth month. The only account we have is that of an exchange between Ziyong Chengru and her disciple Jingxuan. It is a perfect Chan performance, but oddly poignant nevertheless, especially when we consider that Jingxuan was one of her senior students, serving both as her personal attendant and as one of the nuns responsible for keeping a record of their teacher's Dharma talks and other activities (her name appears as the compiler of the second fascicle of Ziyong Chengru's discourse record collection.).

Jing was very anxious about the Master's departure into nirvana. The Master said: "From the beginning there has been neither birth nor death—so what nirvana will there be?" But Jing's grief did not abate. The Master then gave a shout, and Jing silently went into a trance. The Master then called her out of it and asked, "At this moment is there still any nirvana, or is there still not any nirvana?" Jing said: "Your disciple from the beginning has experienced neither birth nor death, so what nirvana can there be?" The Master then said, "Since there is no birth or death, how can there be a nirvana?" Jing did not know what to say. The Master asked: "This is what it is like before the dream." Jing replied: "What is it like after the dream?" The Master said: "When you are in a dream, you still speak the language of dreams."

Finally, as she was obliged to do as a Chan master, Ziyong Chengru composed one last gatha:

Summoning the ordinary: who does not know it?
All of a sudden, I have grasped the sword
And split open the dying words of the immortals;
Fathers are never able to transmit it to their sons.[47]

The extant version of Ziyong Chengru's discourse record collection, which appears to have been added to the Jiaxing canon during one of its last printings, is made up of a single fascicle, although it may have originally been longer. The collection itself was assembled by various disciples (including two named Dharma heirs, Foliang and Fodeng) with the help of other nuns as well as lay patrons. It was, however, Ziyong Chengru herself who had first taken the initiative to have it printed. In 1699, before leaving Beijing, she had taken a copy of what had been compiled so far to show to Linji Chan master Chaoyong and to ask him to write a preface for it.

Chaoyong, who was originally from Jiangnan, had taken the tonsure in 1650 from Chan master Daotian Anjing and had served as abbot in various monasteries in the Jiangnan area before being invited by the Qing emperor to serve as abbot of the prestigious Supreme Response Monastery (Shenggan si), located in the Western Hills. He was also a good friend of Ziyong Chengru's teacher, Gulu Fan. Although Chaoyong compiled a number of works, including a thirty-fascicle anthology of poetry by monastics, he is best known for his compendium of brief biographies of (primarily) Linji teachers, entitled *Complete Books of the Five Lamps (Wudeng quanshu)*. In this important collection, which was printed in 1697, two years before Ziyong Chengru's visit, he included the names (and a few selections from their writings) of more than thirty-five women Linji Chan masters, including Ziyong Chengru.[48]

Although Chaoyong had probably read a few of her pieces (as evidenced by his inclusion of them in the *Complete Books*), when Ziyong Chengru went to visit him, it was probably the first time he had actually met her face-to-face. Impressed by what he saw, and by the texts that she gave him to read, he agreed to write a preface and to assist in the publication of the discourse records. "Since the coming of the Great Dharma from the west," he began,

> there have been nuns [*biqiunis*] who have been capable of carrying on the true way, and practicing and teaching the true enlightenment, shouting and striking without emptiness, and effecting the Dharma transformation of others. After the First Patriarch's Dharma heir Zongchi, and Gao'an [Dayu]'s Dharma heir Moshan Liaoran, there was no one, but in our own times there have been the esteemed Chan masters Jinsu [Shiche Tong]sheng's Dharma heir Qiyuan [Xing]gang; Longchi [Wanru Tong]wei's Dharma heir Jizong [Xing]che; Xuedou [Shiqi Tong]yun's Dharma heir Weiji [Xing]zhi; and Tiantong [Linye Tong]qi's Dharma heir Yinyue Lin.[49] Forging and hammering, they established their gates and halls; those who study them later are amazed at their diligence and admire their labor, penetrating the essence and exhausting principle. Even among those who are students of the inkslab and famous for their virtue, there are none who can find fault. Each of them passed [this on] to their students, who helped each other. Their style of teaching spread and circulated through Jiang[su], Zhe[jiang], Qi [Shandong area], and Chu [Hubei area]. In establishing their reputation [and] taking care of their convents, their discipline was firm and severe [and] they were elegant and refined, their greatness there for all to see. It will be over twenty years since I first came to the capital. Here too, famous women from great families [have been known to] retreat into the mountains to ask after the Way and to seek instructions for illumination. However, those who have genuinely practiced and have actually become enlightened—casting away their shells, fully penetrating the thusness of things, and completely dedicating their lives—have in the end been very few. And among the nuns, those who, like the Chan masters of the south, have been able to fully experience the truth and achieve transcendence, breaking through the deluded thoughts of life and death and thus able to serve as spiritual exemplars, are not many.[50]

All of the women Chan masters referred to in this passage—Qiyuan Xinggang, Jizong Xingche, Weiji Xingzhi, and Yinyue Lin—belonged to the first generation of women Dharma heirs in the Linji Chan revival of the early and mid-seventeenth century. Although clearly beginning to recede into seemingly distant memory, they had solidly taken their place in the thread-thin but enduring lineage of Moshan Liaoran and, before her, the nun Zongchi. And, in large part due to the efforts of Chaoyong himself, they had taken their place in the Linji lineage as well.

Wang Zhi, a literatus-official from Hebei Province, writes in his postface to Ziyong Chengru's *yulu:* "When I read the hymns and verses she wrote about her pilgrimage to the south, I [found them] simple and clear, lofty and limpid *(jianjie gaolang)*."[51] The monk Shilin Yu, author of yet another postface and a Dharma heir of Muyun Tongmen, was impressed primarily for her spontaneous eloquence; when she spoke of the Dharma, he says, it "poured forth from her breast without the slightest premeditation" *(Cong xiongjin zhong wuyi wei chu liuchu)*. She was, he says, generally regarded as "Miaozong come again."[52]

A Brief Epilogue

By the early eighteenth century, the Manchu Qing dynasty was firmly in place, and many of the cultural and social boundaries and borders that had been loosened or blurred by the traumatic contingencies of the transition began to snap back into place. Starting as early as the famous special examination of 1679, literati men began to be lured back into government service, and energies that had once been poured into patronage of Buddhist monasteries began to be rechanneled into the more traditional pursuits of the Confucian literati. It also meant a restoration of Confucian orthodoxy and learning, which, unlike the metaphysical subjectivity of Wang Yangming and his followers, was marked by a new concern with so-called evidential scholarship *(kaozheng)*. And while Buddhist activities by no means ceased, the Linji Chan revival initiated by Miyun Yuanwu nearly a century before gradually slipped into obscurity and even oblivion.

In his study of seventeenth-century Linji Chan, Jiang Wu offers a number of possible reasons for this disappearance. Above all, he argues, the main figures in this movement, such as Miyun Yuanwu, Feiyin Tongrong, Hanyue Fazang, and others were "involved in too many controversies that were nasty, notorious, and detrimental to the harmony of the Buddhist world."[1] The fault lines created by their incessant infighting would eventually lose them support among both monastic and lay followers and would undermine their entire project. The final blow came when the Yongzheng emperor (1678–1735) personally took it upon himself to standardize Chan Buddhist teachings and practice—an intervention that resulted in the denunciation of Hanyue Fazang and his school (who, not incidentally, was closely allied with many loyalist literati) as heterodox.[2]

But, as Jiang Wu persuasively argues, ultimately, the reason was that the seventeenth-century Chan Buddhist effort to "reinvent" a past was based almost entirely on a largely romantic and imaginary reading of the classical Chan textual tradition and was largely ungrounded in actual monastic training and routine. The rhetoric of classical Chan, emphasizing at it did the unmediated apprehension of ultimate truth found considerable support among seventeenth-century literati, both men and women, many of whom felt alienated from the "real world" anyway. When, however, the turmoil and turbulence of the seventeenth century subsided, and the literary and intellectual world became dominated by a revived neo-Confucianism and the evidential scholarship of the eighteenth century, literati interest and engagement in this form of Buddhism also faded. Even to this day, only minimal reference can be found to the seventeenth-century Linji Chan revival—and the men and women Chan masters associated with it—in scholarly and Buddhist writings, although it did in fact leave its mark, as Wu demonstrates, on the development of modern Chan Buddhism.

Assuming that Jiang Wu is correct in his assessment, to what extent did our seventeenth-century women Chan masters participate in, benefit from, and contribute to the revival of seventeenth-century Linji Chan in general, and the creation of these three legacies in particular? The first thing to note is that this was a time when more and more educated women were becoming active participants in the literary world through reading, writing, editing, and having works published, and they, like their male literati counterparts, were attracted and intrigued by this "textual" Chan revival. In particular, I would suggest, it was the imaginative textual re-creation of the Linji Chan ideal (or rhetoric if you will) of gender equality, combined with the obsession of Miyun Yuanwu and his circle for increasing the number of Dharma transmissions, that some of these women found most attractive. For, although to some it may have represented nothing more than an ideal, to our seventeenth-century women Chan masters it was not merely a matter of rhetoric. Rather, it was the imaginative acceptance of this ideal that enabled them to take their place as legitimated women Chan masters and to exercise their skills as religious leaders. In other words, the rhetoric of heroism and equality that was reimagined as part of the seventeenth-century revival of Chan Buddhism provided women with an opportunity to "do what men do"—that is, pursue active and respected public lives as Chan masters.

As Jiang Wu notes, beneath the rhetoric of beating and shouting, seventeenth-century Chan masters may not have been particularly original in terms of their contributions to doctrine, but they were "extremely talented" when it came to "managing monastic affairs and initiating new construction and renovation projects."[3] In this, as Timothy Brook persuasively argues, they had the enthusiastic support of many local gentry elite, who, deprived of traditional sources of power and prestige, devoted much of their energies to the patronage of monasteries, some even going so far as to become monks themselves.

As we have seen, several of our seventeenth-century women Chan masters apparently shared these same entrepreneurial gifts, if on a somewhat small scale. Although nuns like Baochi Jizong and Zuikui Jifu appear to have been more interested in the "textual worlds" of Chan, Qiyuan Xinggang and her disciples clearly were deeply concerned also with institution building, both literal and symbolic. Thus they devoted much energy, albeit sometimes reluctantly, to fund-raising and to convent building and renovation. They were also very concerned that that their names and their efforts on behalf of the lineage be appreciated and acknowledged, and that their disciples would carry on their work. And like their male monastic counterparts, they too enjoyed the enthusiastic support of local gentry.

In his book *Praying for Power*, Brook notes that although women were "a powerful factor inducing men of the gentry to direct their philanthropy toward Buddhist monasteries," in general, "monastic patronage . . . tended to be a male activity." He explains that Buddhism was generally regarded as an acceptable "sphere for female religiosity . . . as long as it remained subordinated to Confucian patriarchy." Although women continued to visit monasteries in groups on pilgrimage or festival days, the undercurrent of male anxiety regarding women's visits to monastic establishments prevented women from being afforded any of the "cultural opportunities to establish the sorts of connections to monasteries that gentry culture permitted to men."[4] While this was no doubt true of the larger, public monasteries *(si)* that are the focus of Brook's study, as we have seen in the story of the founding of the Lion-Subduing Chan Cloister, it would also appear that both men and women played a very active role in the patronage of smaller, local cloisters and convents. Some male literati were involved on behalf of or together with their female relatives, but others clearly had established their own relationships of mutual respect and regard with these abbesses, with whom they engaged in conversation and correspondence. As for the literati's wives and mothers, often they did not just encourage their male relatives to greater philanthropy but themselves took the lead in these efforts. As Dong Hance notes in a temple inscription he wrote for the Myriad Good Works Convent, "my departed mother together with the wife of official Yan, and her sisters-in-law, all had faith in Buddhism and considered themselves comrades. . . . There was no good deed that they did not undertake, and having undertaken it, they made sure it was carried through."[5]

But what about the second legacy, that of networking? Although none of our seventeenth-century convents acquired the prestige of the regular Dharma-transmission temples, it is clear that abbesses like Qiyuan Xinggang clearly had this model in mind when they considered matters such as succession to the abbacy. As we have seen, on a more personal level, being acknowledged as a legitimate lineage-holder was very important to women like Qiyuan Xinggang and Jizong Xingche, both of whom proudly composed their own transmission certificate eulogies. For women traditionally deemed to belong to the "inner quarters," belonging to a lineage meant the ability to overcome barriers of both time and space. Being officially acknowledged as a woman Chan master meant that a woman could legitimately take her place in a long line of Chan masters, most of whom were male, stretching back to the Tang dynasty and, before that, to Bodhidharma and the Buddha himself. And because of the filial connotations of the Chan lineage notions, it also legitimated, if not required, travel to pay respects to the person or the remains of one's lineage ancestors. Thus women Chan masters like Jizong Xingche and Ziyong Chengru had no difficulty justifying leaving their home convents and embarking on long journeys to the Jiangnan region to visit the monasteries and funerary stupas of their Dharma grandfathers, fathers, and uncles. In other words, these women Chan masters were afforded a much larger religious "family," within which they could move with far more ease than they ever could have within their own biological families. Literati women of this period were also developing similar sorts of networks, usually with other women but not always within the immediate family, by means of their writing and publications. In a sense, then, one could say that these seventeenth-century nuns were simply expanding on these kinds of networks, including among them connections not only with female relatives, monastics, and gentry laywomen but also with male monastics and laymen as well.

Finally, there is the question of reintegration. As we have seen, our women Chan masters rarely engaged directly in the polemics that raged around them; if anything, they explicitly deplored them. Like their male counterparts, they often chose "to present themselves as authentic and iconoclastic Chan monks," but unlike many of these monks, women Chan masters such as Qiyuan Xinggang also tended to openly emphasize "their virtuosity in conventional Buddhist training."[6] Perhaps because they were women, they (and their disciples and followers) appear to have considered it to be just as important or even necessary also to emphasize such things as monastic discipline, frugal efficiency, and religious charity. Thus in the *yulu* of most of our nuns, underneath the requisite "performances" of blows and shouts we can see many other aspects of their religious lives, including engaging in the arduous practice of *huatou* cultivation and solitary retreat *(biguan)*, conducting intensive meditation retreats, and performing numerous kinds of rituals and ceremonies, such as funerals, death anniversaries, prayers of thanksgiving for rain, and the consecrations of statues and bells. They also had to deal with the very

real problems of convent upkeep and how to feed and house a growing number of visitors. We also see that although they did seem to favor
huatou cultivation, they did not hesitate to advocate the practice of Pure
Land devotions to their followers when they thought that method would
be more helpful. In this respect, then, it can be said that they contributed
to what Jiang Wu refers to as the seventeenth-century Chan Buddhist process of creating a standard monastic practice composed of "a mixture of
meditation, esotericism, and Pure Land."[7]

It would seem, then, that both the imaginative possibilities afforded
by the Linji Chan revival in the seventeenth century, and the return to
"the standard form of Buddhist monasticism" (together with the restoration of Confucian orthodoxy) in the eighteenth, had different implica-
tions for women and men. Generally speaking, when, in the eighteenth
century, male literati began to return in even greater numbers to the
work of preparing for civil exams and appointments to official positions,
the only proper place for an elite woman, including a pious woman, once
again became the home. Although always somewhat controversial, the
notion that a gentry woman who publicly demonstrated her religious
authority and insight in the Dharma hall might be as praiseworthy as one
who exercised her moral influence privately from within the inner chambers appears to have slowly but surely faded away. Certainly there continued to be eminent nuns who ran their convents with the same pious
dedication and determination demonstrated by these seventeenth-century women. But with the evaporation of the seventeenth-century "reinvention of Chan," it became far less common for women to be officially
recognized as lineage holders, Dharma successors, and legitimated Chan
masters. Also lost was the opportunity, provided by the Chan tradition of
the *yulu,* for religious women to leave behind relatively extensive records
of their lives and their work, records that for all their adherence to conventional religious generic experiences, have the advantage of having
been composed, selected, and compiled by religious women themselves.
In short, for women who may have harbored religious ambitions such as
those demonstrated by the women we have met in this book, the failure
of the Linji Chan reinvention meant a return to the margins and, in the
words of Caroline Walker Bynum quoted at the beginning of this study,
to the "stories that men liked to tell."

Notes

Preface

1. Caroline Walker Bynum, "Religious Women in the Later Middle Ages," in *Christian Spirituality: High Middle Ages and Reformation,* ed. Jill Raitt, Bernard McGinn, and John Meyendorff (New York: Crossroad, 1987), p. 50.

2. Ibid., p. 136.

3. Although there are a number of important articles on Buddhist nuns in English, the most noteworthy being the studies on Song-dynasty female monastics by Miriam Levering and E. Ding-hwa Hsieh, there are only a very few monograph-length studies on premodern Chinese nuns. These include (in English) Valentina Georgieva's "Buddhist Nuns in China: From the Six Dynasties to the Tang" (Ph.D. diss., Leiden University, 2000); and Kathryn M. Tsai's *Lives of the Nuns: Biographies of Chinese Buddhist Nuns from the Fourth to Sixth Centuries* (reprint ed., Honolulu: University of Hawai'i Press, 1994); and (in Chinese) Cai Hongsheng's *Nigu tan* (Guangzhou: Zhongshan daxue chubanshe, 1996) and Li Yuzhen's *Tangdai de biqiuni* (Taiwan: Xuesheng shuju, 1989). Most of these studies are about nuns from the Song dynasty and earlier, very few of whose own works remain extant.

4. Anne Winston-Allen, *Convent Chronicles: Women Writing about Reform in the Late Middle Ages* (University Park: Pennsylvania State University Press, 2004), p. 16.

5. Xavière Gauthier, "Existe-t-il une écriture de femme?" [Is there such a thing as women's writing?], trans. Marilyn A. August, in *New French Feminisms,* ed. Marks and de Courtivron, pp. 162–163; cited in Sidonie Smith, *A Poetics of Women's Autobiography: Marginality and the Fictions of Self-Representation* (Bloomington: Indiana University Press, 1987), p. 18.

6. Winston-Allen, *Convent Chronicles,* p. 20.

7. S. Smith, *Poetics of Women's Autobiography,* p. 18.

8. A recent example of just such a re-creation is Sallie Tisdale's book entitled *Women of the Way: Discovering 2,500 Years of Buddhist Wisdom* (San Francisco: HarperSanFrancisco, 2005). "Stories" of Buddhist nuns, often accompanied by detailed "illustrations," have appeared in Chinese as well. See, for example, Hong Beimou's *Zhongguo mingni* [Famous nuns of China] (Shanghai: Shanghai chubanshe, 1995).

Chapter One: Setting the Stage

1. The fictional examples of this are countless, but one of the more well-known is the Ming-dynasty novel, *Monks and Nuns in a Sea of Sins (Senghai niehai)*. For an English translation of this novel, see Richard F. S. Yang and Howard S. Levy: *Monks and Nuns in a Sea of Sins* (Washington: Warm-Soft Village Press, 1971). Cai Hongsheng's *Nigu tan* is, to a large extent, primarily a study of the (often negative) images of nuns to be found in literary and other sources.

2. Jo Ann Kay McNamara, *Sisters in Arms: Catholic Nuns through Two Millennia* (Cambridge, Mass.: Harvard University Press, 1996), p. 4.

3. *Women and Monasticism* (1896; reprint, New York: Russel and Russel, 1963), p. viii; cited in Winston-Allen, *Convent Chronicles*, p. 240, n. 19.

4. Lei Ruoxin, "Zhongguo gudai nigu susu xintai fenxi," *Nandu xuetan* 26, no. 1 (January 2006): 35.

5. Ibid.

6. Ibid., p. 36.

7. "Jiu xia jiu Zhao ni'ao mi hua, jizhong ji Jia xiucai baoyuan," in *Pai'an jinqi* (1628; Jinan: Qilu shushe, 1995), p. 95.

8. Included in Zhang Yingchang (1790–1869), comp., *Qingshi ze* (Zhonghua shuju, 1983), p. 995.

9. Andrea S. Goldman, "The Nun Who Wouldn't Be: Representations of Female Desire in Two Performance Genres of 'Si Fan,'" *Late Imperial China* 22, no. 1 (2001): 72.

10. Ibid., p. 74.

11. McNamara, *Sisters in Arms*, pp. 4–5.

12. Timothy Brook, *Praying for Power: Buddhism and the Formation of Gentry Society in Late-Ming China*, Harvard-Yenching Institute Monograph Series (Cambridge, Mass.: Harvard University Press, 1993), p. 73.

13. Wai-yee Li, "Heroic Transformations: Women and National Trauma in Early Qing Literature," *Harvard Journal of Asiatic Studies* 9, no. 2 (December 1999): 363–364. For an excellent overview of the cultural context of this transitional period, including the issue of religion and gender, see Wai-yee Li's introduction to *Trauma and Transcendence in Early Qing Literature*, ed. Wilt L. Idema, Wai-yee Li, and Ellen Widmer, Harvard East Asian Monographs (Cambridge, Mass.: Harvard University Asia Center, 2006), pp. 1–70.

14. Here, and in the remainder of this study, the romanized *zi* (style name) will be used to indicate a person's literary cognomen.

15. A selection of Xia Shuji's poems can be found in Wang Duanshu's *Mingyuan shiwei* (1667), 26:8b–9b. Wang Duan also devotes a chapter to Xia Shuji in her *Ming sanshi jia shixuan* (1820), 2:8, 1–6.

16. Brief biographies of these two women, as well as a few examples of their poems, can be found in Wanyan Yunzhu's *Guochao guixiu zhengshi ji* (1831), *fulu*,

9b–10a. See also Zhenhua, *Xu biqiuni zhuan,* in *Biqiuni zhuan quanji* (Taipei: Fojiao shuju, 1988), p. 86; and Hu Wenkai, *Lidai funü zhuzuo kao,* rev. ed. (Shanghai: Shanghai guji chubanshe, 1985), p. 821.

17. Cai Hongsheng, "Lingnan sanni yu Qingchu zhengju," *Zhongshan daxue xuebao* 1 (1994): 61–68. Cai Hongsheng is one of the few scholars from the PRC who has devoted a full-length scholarly monograph to the study of nuns in China *(Nigu tan).* Although this monograph contains, to my mind, an inordinate amount of discussion regarding the fictional (and often negative) images of nuns, in his 1994 article on these "loyalist nuns" he explicitly notes that the all-too-familiar traditional images of sex-starved or licentious nuns are "objectively speaking, for the most part artistic fabrications *(yishude xugou)* and have little to do with historical facts" (p. 67). For more on Buddhism in Guangdong during the transition period, see his *Qingchu Lingnan Fomen shilüe* (Guangzhou: Guangdong gaodeng jiaoyu chubanshe, 1997).

18. Li, introduction to Idema et al., *Trauma and Transcendence,* p. 27.

19. Here and in the rest of this book, *jinshi* (advanced scholar) is followed by a date for the year someone earned, usually through examination, the highest possible metropolitan degree.

20. "Fushi Yigong chanshi yulu xu," *Fushi Yigong chanshi yulu, J.* 39:1a.

21. See Wilt L. Idema and Beata Grant, *The Red Brush: Women Writers of Imperial China,* Harvard East Asian Monographs (Cambridge, Mass.: Harvard University, 2004; 2nd ed., 2007), pp. 347ff.

22. There are now a significant number of important studies on women's writing of the late imperial period, including a number of scholarly monographs. The seminal work is Dorothy Ko's *Teachers of the Inner Chambers: Women and Culture in China, 1573–1722* (Palo Alto, Calif.: Stanford University Press, 1994). See also Ellen Widmer and Kang-i Sun Chan, eds., *Writing Women in Late Imperial China* (Palo Alto, Calif.: Stanford University Press, 1997); Susan Mann, *Precious Records: Women in China's Long Eighteenth Century* (Palo Alto, Calif.: Stanford University Press, 1997); Ellen Widmer, *The Beauty and the Book: Women and Fiction in Nineteenth-Century China,* Harvard East Asian Monographs (Cambridge, Mass.: Harvard University, 2003); and Grace Fong, *Herself an Author: Gender, Agency, and Writing in Late Imperial China* (Honolulu: Hawai'i University Press, 2008).

23. Jiang Wu, *Enlightenment in Dispute: The Reinvention of Chan Buddhism in Seventeenth-Century China* (New York: Oxford University Press, 2008).

24. He Xiaorong, *Mingdai Nanjing shiyuan yanjiu* (Beijing: Zhongguo shehui kexue chubanshe, 2000), p. 125. As Victoria Cass notes, in the Ming dynasty (and later) nuns were often lumped together with those characters that, according to a popular household adage, one should never allow to cross the threshold into one's home: "Don't invite in, for any reason, a nun, a monk, an adept, a wet-nurse or a granny money-lender." Cited in *Dangerous Women: Warriors, Grannies and Geishas of the Ming* (Lanham, Md.: Rowman and Littlefield, 1999), p. 47.

25. For studies of two of these figures, see Chün-Fang Yü, *The Renewal of Buddhism in China: Chu-hung and the Late Ming Synthesis* (New York: Columbia University Press, 1981); and Sung-peng Hsü, *A Buddhist Leader in Ming China* (University Park: Pennsylvania University Press, 1979).

26. "Miyun chanshi yulu xu," *J.* 10:1a.

27. Qian Qianyi, "Wulin chongxiu baoguaoyuan ji," in *Qianmuzhai quanji* (Suihai zhai, 1910), 42:5–6; Quoted in Wu, *Enlightenment in Dispute,* pp. 159–160. As Wai-yee Li points out, the decision of a significant number of late-Ming literati to take the tonsure as an expression of their loyalist sympathies was often mixed with "unresolved contradictions," and there was a largely performative side to their donning of monastic robes. She quotes a poem by Qian Biandeng (1612–1695) on Fang Yizhi (1611–1671)—both literati-turned-monks—the last two lines of which read, in Li's translation, "He takes pride in being able to make likely Sanskrit chants/An old monk who has the actor's authentic flair." In an editorial note, Qian Biandeng adds," I laughed at him for having the intonation of old monks on the stage of the theater" (Li, introduction to Idema et al., *Trauma and Transcendence,* pp. 11–12). Although Qian Qianyi's critique of the revivalists' blows and shouts can be read as a partisan critique of religious hypocrisy, and Qian Biandeng's parody of Fang Yizhi's as a sympathetic recognition of the need for assuming different guises for survival, the common focus on performance is worth noting. Certainly, it may explain why so many seventeenth-century literati (including men like Fang Yizhi) were attracted to Miyun Yuanwu's re-creative efforts to revive a largely text-based and performative version of what he imagined to be traditional Linji Chan practice.

28. Lan Jifu, "Jiaxing dazang de tese jiqi shiliao jiazhi," in *Fojiao de sixiang yu wenhua: Yinshun daoshi bazhi jinliu shouqing wenji* (Taipei: Foguang chubanshe, 1991), p. 263.

29. The majority of sixty-five Buddhist nuns in the monk Baochang's *Biographies of Buddhist Nuns (Biqiuni zhuan),* compiled in 516, were women from relatively high-ranking families. In most of their biographies some reference is made to their literacy as well as to their eloquence and preaching skills, although only in a single case does Baochang actually quote from one of their poems. See Idema and Grant, *Red Brush,* pp. 153–156.

30. Miriam L. Levering, "Dōgen's *Raihaitokuzui* and Women Teaching in Sung Ch'an," *Journal of the International Association of Buddhist Studies* 21, no. 1 (1998): 103.

31. Miriam Levering has done extensive research on both of these women. See ibid., pp. 77–110; and her "Miao-tao and Her Teacher Ta-hui," in *Buddhism in the Sung Dynasty,* ed. Peter N. Gregory and Daniel Getz (Honolulu: University of Hawai'i Press, 1999), pp. 188–219; and "Women Ch'an Masters: The Teacher Miao-tsung as Saint," in *Women Saints in World Religions,* ed. Arvind Sharma (Albany: State University of New York Press, 2000), pp. 180–204.

32. For discussions of these women, both historical and legendary, see Miriam Levering, "The Dragon Girl and the Abbess of Mo-shan: Gender and Status in the Ch'an Buddhist Tradition," *Journal of the International Association of Buddhist Studies* 5, no. 1 (1982): 19–35; and Ding-hwa E. Hsieh, "Images of Women in Ch'an Buddhist Literature of the Sung period," in *Buddhism in the Sung*, ed. Peter N. Gregory and Daniel A. Getz Jr. (Honolulu: University of Hawai'i Press, 1999), pp. 148–187.

33. Zhenhua, *Xu biqiuni zhuan*, p. 86. This is a collection, published in 1921, of brief biographical notices of nuns such as those found in late seventeenth-century collections of Buddhist biographies such as the *Wudeng quanshu*, as well as various local and temple gazetteers. Page numbers refer to the reprint edition of this text in *Biqiuni zhuan quanji* (Taipei: Fojiao shuju, 1988).

34. Zhenhua, *Xu biqiuni zhuan*, 3:44.

35. "Shi ni Zhixue," *Baichi chanshi yulu, J.* 28:106a.

Chapter Two: Images of Nuns in the Writings of Seventeenth-Century Monks

1. "Yu Xuxian daoren," *Muren shenggao, J.* 35:489b–c.

2. "Zhang mu Huang ruren muzhi ming," *Muzhai chuxueji* 85:3 (*Jindai Zhongguo shiliao congkan* ed., pp. 1441–1444).

3. Qian Qianyi, "Zuotuo biqiuni Chaoyin taming," *Muzhai youxueji bu,* p. 508.

4. Cited in Alison Weber, *Teresa of Avila and the Rhetoric of Femininity* (Princeton, N.J.: Princeton University Press, 1990), p. 36.

5. Ibid.

6. Interestingly, Wengu Guangyin visited Huanyou, the Dharma master of Miyun Yuanwu. Huanyou felt they had a good Dharma connection, but Wengu Guangyin was unwilling to study with him. Zhenhua, *Zhongguo fojiao renming dacidian,* p. 937.

7. "Shi ni Jingguang," *Gushan Yongjue heshang guanglu, J.* 27:631a–b.

8. Ibid.

9. Muchen Daomin was one of the most active participants in the fierce polemical debate between Miyun Yuanwu and Hanyue Fazang. On the other hand, although Muchen Daomin started out as a Ming loyalist and was highly respected and lauded for this patriotic stance, in the end he became known as a political turncoat. In 1659 he was invited to preach at the Qing court, where he was given the honorary title "Chan Master Hongjue." This lost him much of the respect he had once enjoyed among his literati followers in the Jiangnan area.

10. "Yuanqing Hu daoren," *J.* 26:393b–c.

11. "Huzhou Chanding an biqiuni Daxian mu xieming," *J.* 26:366b–367a.

12. Miriam Levering, "Lin-chi (Rinzai) Ch'an and Gender: The Rhetoric of

Equality and the Rhetoric of Heroism," in *Buddhism, Sexuality and Gender,* ed. Jose Ignacio Cabezon (Albany: State University of New York Press, 1992), p. 137.

13. *Dahui Pujue chanshi yulu, T.* 47, no. 1998A, p. 909b.

14. Quoted in Levering, "Lin-chi (Rinzai) Ch'an and Gender," p. 139. For a more extended study of the use of this term in seventeenth-century Chan texts, see Beata Grant, "*Da Zhangfu:* The Rhetoric of Heroism in Seventeenth-Century Chan Buddhist Writings," in *Nan Nü: Men, Women and Gender in China* 10:2 (forthcoming).

15. Levering, "Lin-chi (Rinzai) Ch'an and Gender," p. 142.

16. Ibid., p. 144

17. *T.* 30, no. 1577, p. 265b.

18. *Huayan jing tanxuan ji, T.* 35, no. 1733, p. 261b.

19. Ibid., p. 261b.

20. *Dafang guangfo Huayanjing shu, T.* 35, no. 1735, p. 716b.

21. Ibid., p. 716b.

22. *Song gaoseng zhuan, T.* 50, no. 2061, p. 737c.

23. "Meixi an xu," *Tiantong Hongjue Min chanshi yulu, J.* 26:476a.

24. "Ti biqiuni Liaofan," *Xiangyan Xixin Shui Chanshi yulu, J.* 39:720b.

25. "Ti Daoyu biqiuni xiang," *Faxi Yin chanshi yulu, J.* 28:811a.

26. *Classic of Poetry (Shijing)* 1:14 (152). James Legge translation.

27. *Lienü zhuan,* 1:13.

28. *Xiuye Lin Chanshi yulu, J.* 36:598b.

29. "Wei ni tifa," *Xingkong Tai Chanshi yulu, J.* 39:577a.

30. *Baichi chanshi yulu, J.* 28:53a.

31. Hsieh, "Images of Women," p. 170.

32. "Shi Huang daopo," *Baichi chanshi yulu, J.* 28:94b.

33. Translation by Burton Watson, *The Zen Teachings of Master Lin-chi: A Translation of the* Lin-chi Lu (New York: Columbia University Press, 1993), p. 106.

34. Hsieh, "Images of Women," p. 172.

35. There are several of these accounts in *Gaoshan Maozhu chanshi yulu, J.* 29:123a.

36. Hsieh, "Images of Women," p. 176.

37. "Shi niseng Sixiu," *Lianfeng Chanshi yulu, J.* 38:369a.

38. "Shi Fanjing Zong yanzhu Yanguan," *Yuan'an Li chanshi yulu, J.* 37:393c.

39. "Pumen Fan Jingzong yanzhu fenggang," *Yuan'an Li chanshi yulu, J.* 37:401b.

40. The term *foshi* is normally used to refer to Buddhist death-related rituals. Here, however, it clearly refers to a far wider range of Buddhist activities.

41. Mount Taibai, also known as Qingling Peak, is in Shaanxi Province and, at twelve thousand feet, is the highest point in eastern China. Rufeng, or Nipple Peaks, may refer to the two unusual nipple-shaped formations in Guizhou Province that even today are considered a scenic tourist spot. The Wulei Mountains

are in Zhejiang Province; the Wulei Monastery dates back to the ninth century and earlier. In 1645 it was headed by Muchen Daomin, who transformed it into a Linji Dharma-transmission temple. For the next several decades, it was one of the largest and most prosperous temples in all of China. The Mount Ruiyan referred to here may be the one in Fujian Province.

42. "Puming Jing anzhu fenggang," *Yuan'an Li chanshi yulu, J.* 37:401c.

Chapter Three: The Making of a Woman Chan Master

1. Some of the material in this and subsequent chapters has been published previously in my article "Female Holder of the Lineage: Linji Chan Master Zhiyuan Qiyuan Xinggang (1597–1654)," *Late Imperial China* 17, no. 2 (December 1996): 51–76.

2. Susan Mann, trans., "Two Biographies by Zhang Xuecheng (1738–1801)," in *Under Confucian Eyes: Writings on Gender in Chinese History,* ed. Susan Mann and Yu-yin Cheng (Berkeley: University of California Press, 2001), p. 218.

3. "Fushi Qiyuan Gang chanshi xingzhuang," *Fushi Qiyuan chanshi yulu, J.* 28:437b–439b. Unless otherwise noted, all subsequent quotations are from this source.

4. During the last years of the Ming, Wu Zhu had held a series of important official positions. Later, together with the famous loyalist poet Chen Zilong (1608–1647), who at the time was serving as prefectural judge of Shaoxing, Wu became very active in the effort to quell the rebellions that threatened the Zhejiang and Jiangsu area. After the fall of Beijing, he retreated to Meixi "and had nothing more to do with things of the world" (*Meili zhi* 9:5b).

5. *Jiaxing fuzhi* (1840) 79a.

6. According to the traditional Chinese system, every newborn child is automatically a year old, and, regardless of when they were born, another year is added to their age on each subsequent lunar New Year. In this study, the term *sui* refers to this traditional form of indicating age.

7. "Taming," *Fushi Zhiyuan chanshi yulu, J.* 28:439b–440a.

8. This dramatic response to parents' recalcitrance has a long history in China. Threats of suicide were the primary weapon used by women who found themselves powerless to achieve their aspirations in any other way. In fact, as early as the fourth century, we find the future nun Sengji fasting in order to coerce her mother into allowing her to become a nun. See Tsai, *Lives of the Nuns,* pp. 27–38. As recently as the 1980s, Wen-jie Qin tells us, a woman fell into a semiconscious state in order to persuade a male Buddhist teacher to give her permission to enter the convent. Wen-jie Qin, "The Buddhist Revival in Post-Mao China: Women Reconstruct Buddhism on Mt. Emei" (Ph.D. diss., Harvard University, 2000), p. 228.

9. "Fu Chang weng jushi," *Fushi Qiyuan chanshi yulu, J.* 28:430a.

10. Wuming, *Liandeng huiyuan* 10, in X. 136:298.

11. Hong Beimou, *Zhongguo mingni.*

12. Of course, a man wishing to leave his family to become a monk could claim—as at least one seventeenth-century Chan master is described as having done—that he was following the example of the Sakyamuni Buddha, who left parents, wife, and child in order to seek liberation. Mahaprajapati, who is said to have sought permission from the Buddha to inaugurate a nun's sangha, presumably did not leave the palace until after the death of her husband.

13. The original term *anshen liming* means "to establish oneself according to heaven's will"—in other words, to have so fully established one's life in accord with the will of heaven as to be imperturbable and unmoved by external circumstances. Originally, this was a Confucian phrase (Confucius: "At the age of twenty I had established myself, at the age of forty I had no [disturbing] emotions, and at the age of fifty I know the will of heaven"). As used by the Buddhists, it meant that, thanks to spiritual practice, one's (nonexistent) mind was at peace.

14. "Fu Yuan daopo," *Miyun chanshi yulu, J.* 10:46c. A *li* is the equivalent of approximately one-third of a mile.

15. As Jiang Wu notes, "at the end of the sixteenth century, Chan practice was widely understood as meditation, especially the meditation on critical phrases *(huatou)* advocated by Dahui Zonggao." Wu, *Enlightenment in Dispute*, p. 40.

16. Cited in Yü, *Renewal of Buddhism in China*, p. 173.

17. This particular *huatou* appears to have been first popularized by Chan master Yungu Fahui (1500–1579)—who was also from Jiaxing—and it was used often by Hanshan Deqing, who studied with Fahui, as well as by Yunqi Zhuhong and many others. See Chün-fang Yü, "Ming Buddhism," in Denis Twitchett and Frederick W. Mote, eds., *The Cambridge History of China*, vol. 8, part 2, 1368–1644 (Cambridge: Cambridge University Press, 1988), pp. 926–927. Again, this points to continuity in terms of Chan practice—despite the rhetoric of blows and shouts—even among Miyun Yuanwu's immediate Dharma heirs.

18. "Ni Shangji Ben qing shangtang," *Tianwang Shuijian Hai heshang liu hui lu, J.* 29:257c.

19. Although primarily associated with Daoist alchemical practice, this notion of nourishing the spiritual embryo can be found in Buddhist texts as well. Victor Sōgen Hori notes that in the Japanese Zen tradition, after a monk completes formal koan training, he must then engage in a second stage of training called *shōtai chōyō* (Ch. *shengtai changyang*), or "the long nurturing of the sacred fetus." This stage, also known as post-satori training, involves a period of seclusion sometimes lasting many years. As Hori points out, there is a connection here not only with notions of nourishing the "sacred fetus" found in Daoist alchemical practice (both inner and outer) but also with Confucian ideals of living in seclusion "in order to reemerge and assume public responsibility at a later time." Whether or

not this is what Qiyuan Xinggang had in mind, in retrospect this is precisely how it worked out for her. See Hori, *Zen Sand: The Book of Capping Phrases for Kōan Practice* (Honolulu: University of Hawai'i Press, 2003), pp. 27–29.

20. See John Kieschnick's discussion of the many-layered meanings of the wish-fulfilling scepter in his *Impact of Buddhism on Chinese Material Culture* (Princeton, N.J.: Princeton University Press, 2003), pp. 145–146.

21. Wen-jie Qin found the same initial hostility and resistance from present-day male monastics on Mount Emei. She recounts the travails that a woman named Yan Ci went through first to become a student of Master Pu Chao, the head of the Mount Emei Buddhist Association, and then to establish what would be the first convent on Mount Emei. Yan Ci recounts that when she went to see Master Pu Chao and asked to be allowed to become a nun, the first thing he did was to cast a divination, which revealed that she was indeed meant to become a nun. She continues: "But he told me that he did not plan to accept women into the monasteries because women are petty by nature and like to cry. He said that a few years previously he had published an article in a newspaper announcing that Mt. Emei had never had nuns in its history. I argued back saying that since the Buddhist scriptures teach that even small creatures like snakes and ants have Buddha-nature, women can also become enlightened. Astonished at hearing this, Master Pu Chao said to me: 'You are a young girl with great ambition!' But he insisted that because there wasn't any official policy on accepting women into the monasteries, he would not take me in." Qin, "Buddhist Revival," p. 228.

22. For a discussion of this genre, see Hasebe Yūkei, *Min Shin Bukkyō kyōdanshi kenkyū* (Tokyo: Dōhōha shuppan, 1993), pp. 353–354. Hasebe mentions Qiyuan Xinggang's texts but does not seem to have realized that her female Dharma heir Yigong Chaoke also composed a *yuanliu song*, which is contained in her *yulu*. The third woman Chan master who wrote a *yuanliu song* was Jizong Xingche, who is discussed in chapter 6. See also Jiang Wu, "Building a Dharma Transmission Monastery in Seventeenth-Century China: The Case of Mount Huangbo," *East Asian History*, no. 31 (June 2006).

23. The practice of *biguan* was associated with the Linji Chan monk Gaofeng Yuanmiao. Beginning in 1266, he spent nine years meditating in virtual solitude on Mount Longxu in Ling'an. During this period he wore "a single robe both winter and summer" and forsook the comforts of "fan or stove." In 1279 he went into retreat a second time—partly to avoid the chaos that accompanied the collapse of the Southern Song dynasty—this time to the Tianmu Mountains of Hangzhou. He built a small hut for himself, where he lived in seclusion until his death in 1295. His practice of solitary confinement was called "enclosure as if dead" *(siguan)*. In fact, this practice continued into the mid-twentieth century in China. Holmes Welch describes how a monk embarking on such a retreat would take up residence in a room or small building: "the doors would be locked, and two

boards would be nailed over the doorway like an 'X,' inscribed with the date and the particulars." Welch, *The Practice of Chinese Buddhism, 1900–1950* (Cambridge, Mass.: Harvard University Press, 1967), p. 321.

24. Li Li'an, "Mingmo Qingchu Chanzong de jiben zouxiang," *Zhongguo zhexue shi* 3 (1999): 83.

25. Quoted in Yü, *Renewal of Buddhism in China*, p. 176.

26. "Chuguan shizhong," *Fushi Qiyuan chanshi yulu, J.* 28:426b.

27. Patricia B. Ebrey, *The Inner Quarters: Marriage and the Lives of Chinese Women in the Sung Period* (Berkeley: University of California Press, 1993), p. 125.

28. Anne Carolyn Klein, *Meeting the Great Bliss Queen: Buddhists, Feminists and the Art of the Self* (Boston: Beacon Press, 1995), p. 83.

29. Ibid., p. 85.

30. Meixi is also referred to as Meili in some gazetteers and other texts. In order to avoid confusion, I will use "Meixi" only.

31. Although a *chanyuan* was still considered a minor religious establishment in comparison with most (male) public monasteries, or *si*, it was larger and more prestigious than a simple *an*, which could refer to anything from a purely familial chapel or a small hermitage to a fair-sized convent. Like the term *chanshi*, which can be translated either as "meditation master" or "Chan master"), the term *chanyuan* can be translated as either "Chan cloister" or "meditation cloister." It also seems to refer more unambiguously to a religious institution with primarily, though not necessarily exclusively, Chan affiliations. To preserve a sense of these distinctions, loose as they are, in this book the term *an* (which in the original is sometimes but not always prefaced by the character *ni*, for "nun") will be translated simply as "convent," and the term *chanyuan* as "Chan cloister."

32. Even today along the riverbank one hundred connected buildings remain, said to have been built around 1560 by Dong Bin for the exclusive use of the servants of the Dong clan women.

33. "Mu xiu Jishan an yin," *Nanxun zhenzhi* 9:18. This convent would be repaired again in the eighteenth century and was still in existence in the nineteenth. In *Meili zhi* 11:19, there is mention of a chaste nun from this convent by the name of Sibao, who, along with a nun from a nearby convent, drowned herself in the river in 1860 rather than endure the humiliation of the invading Taiping troops.

34. According to information provided in a local gazeeteer, on the last day of the tenth month, lay Buddhists, the majority of whom were women, would keep a nightlong vigil at this temple, during which time they would recite the name of the Buddha with their rosaries. *Nanxun zhenzhi* 12:1b–10a.

35. A Meixi native, Wang Ting had served in various official posts around the country and earned a reputation for his philanthropy. Around 1668 his father died, and he retired to Jiaxing. There he devoted himself to his scholarly and literary pursuits, in particular his poetry, for which he became quite well known.

He was also a major patron of monasteries and convents in the area and was a pro-lific writer of prefaces, inscriptions, and pleas for funds. His wife was a woman of considerable piety. The Wang Convent (Wang an), a small hermitage, had been built for her just south of the Lion-Subduing Chan Cloister. Although originally designed primarily for Madame Jiang's personal devotions, it appears to have gained a considerable reputation for its Chan practice. According to one source, "both monastics and lay would come there to take refuge, and it was nearly as flourishing as the Lion-Subduing Chan Cloister itself." After his wife's death, it appears to have reverted to a scenic spot and was commonly referred to as the Wang garden. *Meili zhi* 4:25b. Wang Ting's inscription "Chongxiu Fushi Chanyuan ji" is found in *Meili zhi* 4:21b–22a.

36. Dong Sizhao's father was Dong Daochun (*jinshi* 1583); his mother was a daughter of the celebrated essayist Mao Kun (1512–1601). A highly educated woman, Dong Sizhao's mother was also the sister of the even more celebrated his-torian, poet, and dramatist Mao Wei (1575–1640). Dong Sizhao counted among his five brothers the more famous scholar and poet Dong Sizhang (1568–1628) and the Ministry of Rites official Dong Sicheng (1560–1595).

37. Dong Hance passed the second-degree examinations with distinction but never held office. In 1645 he played a valiant role in staving off bandits and rebel troops and preventing them from completely overrunning his hometown. Despite his loyalist sentiments, in 1673 he went to the capital in the hopes of acquiring an official position for himself. However, he appears to have run afoul of some political enemies and wound up in prison instead. When he was released, he returned to Nanxun and devoted the remainder of his life to his literary and religious pursuits, both Buddhist and Daoist. *Nanxun zhenzhi* 19:5b.

38. A fund-raising appeal written by Dong Hance for yet another convent in Nanxun provides a glimpse of the religious "heroism" some of these nuns exemplified for loyalists like himself. In this inscription, he laments the overall decline and decay of Buddhism (mirroring the unsettled political situation) and bemoans in particular the insidious corruption that erodes the purity of Bud-dhism, like "worms eating away at the flesh of the lion." In conditions such as this, he says, "those who are able to extricate themselves from the depths of the mud of the five obstructions [*wuzhang*] are few. If [liberating oneself was difficult] for men [*zhangfu*], how could it not be even more so for women?" Dong continues with high praise for the nuns who live in the Grass Convent (Cao an), where they preserve the true teaching, and he emphatically reassures his readers (and poten-tial donors) of the worthiness of supporting the convent and its work. "Xundong Cao an mu yin," *Nanxun zhenzhi* 9:24b–25a.

39. *Nanxun zhi* 24:9b.

40. Dong Hance, "Wanshan an ji," *Nanxun zhenzhi* 28:8–10.

41. Under Muyun Tongmen's charismatic leadership, the Southern Antiquity Monastery became a flourishing community of Buddhist practice. Wang Ting, who

wrote a preface to this monk's discourse record collection, remarks on the bur-
geoning revival of Linji Chan Buddhism that he himself had witnessed: "I remember how thirty years ago, the world did not know very much about things having
to do with the Chan school. It [all] began with the elder Miyun [Yuanwu] . . . ,
preaching and teaching at Jinsu [Monastery]. . . . When I look around me, there
are only a few who have been able to continue what he began, and the monk
Muyun [Tongmen] is the best." *Meili zhi* 16:4b.

    42. *Wudeng quanshu* 76:292b.
    43. "Fayu," *Fushi Qiyuan chanshi yulu, J.* 28:427a.
    44. See *Xu chuandenglu, T.* 51, no. 2077, p. 469b.

Chapter Four: Qiyuan Xinggang as Abbess, Dharma Teacher, and Religious Exemplar

    1. For an excellent discussion of this portrait in the context of Chan portrai-
ture in general, see Su Meiwen, "Nüxing chanshi de daoying: You 'Xiezhen yu
mingyan' tanxi Qiyuan chanshi zhi xingxiang," *Foxue yanjiu zhongxin xuebao* 10
(2005): 253–286.
    2. "Ti zi xiang," *Fushi Qiyuan chanshi yulu, J.* 28:432a.
    3. "Qiyuan Gang zhi Chanshi," *Bushuitai ji, J.* 26:393b. *"Sulu"* is an allusion
to one of the recorded encounter dialogues between Miaozong and Dahui Zonggao.
    4. "Taming," *Fushi Qiyuan chanshi yulu, J.* 28:439b.
    5. Their son, Wu Yuanqi (*jinshi* 1678), would later become a well-known fig-
ure in cultural and political circles. As a Buddhist layman, he also kept up his
connections with many monks and nuns, including several of Qiyuan Xinggang's
own Dharma heirs.
    6. This was not the only time that Madame Qian made use of dreams to com-
municate her piety. We are told that when she was about to die, she bade her family recite the name of the Buddha, while she herself sat in the lotus position and
appeared to pass away. However, after a short while, she revived and proceeded to
tell her startled family that she had had been taken to the underworld. There, she
said, "[I] called out that I was the disciple of [Qiyuan Xinggang], and nowhere
did I encounter any obstacle. All I saw was the Buddha, who welcomed me and
then told me to return to the living [and tell everyone what she had witnessed]."
Madame Qian remained among the living for three additional days and then
finally passed away for good. However, her support of Qiyuan Xinggang did not
end with her death. When her son, Yuanqi, had a dream of his deceased mother,
dressed in white robes and bowing in the direction of the Lion-Subduing Chan
Cloister, he requested that Qiyuan Xinggang conduct a special funeral service for
her. On the evening after the service, he again had a dream of his mother. This
time she was sitting in a sedan chair, "her face like jewels elegant and lovely, and

the smoke of incense swirling around her." Nor was the connection to remain a purely religious one. Wu Zhu's daughter married Hu Shengzhou, Qiyuan Xinggang's nephew.

7. "Ti Zheke Xu jushi ougeng tu can," *Fushi Qiyuan chanshi yulu, J.* 28:431c.

8. Li, introduction to Idema et al., *Trauma and Transcendence,* p. 26.

9. In the gazetteer notice, she is lauded for having remained constantly at her husband's side to bring him calm and consolation during his difficult time in office. It is also said that after his death her grief was such that she longed to die, although she did not go so far as to commit suicide. *Jiaxing fuzhi* (1682) 64:316.

10. Qiyuan Xinggang also maintained a correspondence with Wu Zhongmu's cousin, Wu Qianmu (style name "Pouzhong"), who, like Wu Zhongmu, devoted himself to the care of his bereaved mother after the death of his father.

11. "Fu Zhu laoshuren," *Fushi Qiyuan chanshi yulu, J.* 28:429c.

12. "Zhu Chaochen cheng song," *Fushi Qiyuan chanshi yulu, J.* 28:427.

13. "Wu laofuren bingzhong ling lang Zhongmu jushu qi fayu kaishi," *Fushi Qiyuan chanshi yulu, J.* 28:427a.

14. In 1677, Zhu Yizun set up residence in Meixi, where he built a garden and a studio that he named the Pushu ting, or Airing Books Pavilion (later the name of one of his collected works). Portions of the garden and the pavilion still exist today.

15. *Jingzhiju shihua,* in *Xuxiu siku quanshu: Jibu* (1698; reprint, Shanghai guji chubanshe, 1995–1999), 23:760–761.

16. Ibid., 23:761.

17. "Mengxia guanzhong xianyong," *Fushi Qiyuan chanshi yulu, J.* 28:429b.

18. "Fu biaosao," *Fushi Qiyuan chanshi yulu, J.* 28:430a.

19. "Jintai fashi zai Tianing si jiangjing Shi wang," *Fushi Qiyuan chanshi yulu, J.* 28:427b.

20. "Zhanxu xiong guofang," *Fushi Qiyuan chanshi yulu, J.* 28:427b.

21. *Meili zhi* 4:27a.

22. "He Zheng Yundu Qiuting yin," *Fushi Qiyuan chanshi yulu, J.* 28:429b.

23. "Fu Zheng Yundu jushi," *Fushi Qiyuan chanshi yulu, J.* 28:429b.

24. "Fu Zheng jushi," *Fushi Qiyuan chanshi yulu, J.* 28:430c.

25. This ritual had often been associated with the state—for five years, from 1368 to 1372, the founding Ming emperor had sponsored elaborate *shuilu* ceremonies for the souls of those who had died in the chaotic years of the fall of the previous dynasty. In the late sixteenth century, Yunqi Zhuhong's *Shuilu yigui* [Ritual Instructions for the Deliverance of Creatures of Water and Land] was, as Daniel B. Stevenson explains, "not his creation but a recodification *(chengding)* of a manual of the same title written about 1260 by Zhipan, author of the monumental *Comprehensive Record of the Buddhas and Patriarchs (Fozu tongji)*" (Stevenson, "Text, Image and Transformation in the History of the *Shuilu Fahui,* the Buddhist Rite for Deliverance of Creatures of Water and Land," in *Cultural Intersections in*

Later Chinese Buddhism, ed. Marsha Weidner [Honolulu: University of Hawai'i Press, 2001], p. 34). Zhipan's version was "a minor work virtually unknown outside the immediate region of southern Zhejiang," and in choosing to promulgate this ritual text, rather than the Jinshan rituals currently in vogue, Yunqi Zhuhong "in effect rejected the charisma of established tradition in preference for a highly marginalized version of the rite," which nevertheless, he felt, looked far more "as a Buddhist rite should" (ibid.). Zhipan's version is no longer extant, but Zhuhong's emended *Shuilu yigui* remains the one still in use today.

26. Ibid., p. 34.

27. "Fushi qiyuan Gang chanshi yulu," *J.* 28:438c.

28. Brook, *Praying for Power*, p. 87.

29. "Fushi qiyuan Gang chanshi yulu," *J.* 28:438b.

30. For excellent studies on philanthropy and charity, both Buddhist and otherwise, during this period, see Joanna F. Handlin Smith's work, including "Social Hierarchy and Merchant Philanthropy as Perceived in Several Late-Ming and Early-Qing Texts," *Journal of the Economic and Social History of the Orient* 41, no. 3 (1998): 417–451; and "Benevolent Societies: The Reshaping of Charity during the Late Ming and Early Ch'ing," *Journal of Asian Studies* 46, no. 2 (1987): 309–337.

31. "Fushi qiyuan Gang chanshi yulu," *J.* 28:438b.

32. Ibid.

33. "Wei Xigan faxiong heshang mu Jueshi juhuo," *Fushi Qiyuan chanshi yulu, J.* 28:432c.

34. "Shanseng ji yu Dong an anpinle dao," *Fushi Qiyuan chanshi yulu, J.* 28:427a.

35. "Mengxia guanzhong xianyong."

36. Bernard Faure, *The Rhetoric of Immediacy: A Cultural Critique of Chan/Zen Buddhism* (Princeton, N.J.: Princeton University Press, 1991), 184.

37. Alan Cole, "Upside-Down/Right Side Up: A Revisionist History of Buddhist Funerals in China," *History of Religions* 35, no. 4 (1996): 332.

38. Faure, *Rhetoric of Immediacy*, p. 185.

39. Ibid., pp. 189–190.

40. Ibid., p. 187.

41. Welch, *Practice of Chinese Buddhism*, p. 342. Interestingly, Welch also quotes an informant who does not appear to be shaken by the apparent contradiction between the theoretical notion of emptiness and the practical concern for what happens to the "no-self" after death: "The great monk can be peaceful because he knows that life is illusory, that his pain is illusory, and so he can keep control of himself, just as an ordinary person may realize in a dream that it is a dream."

42. Holmes Welch tells a story he heard about the death of the Venerable Dingxu, who died in Hong Kong of cancer in 1962. Apparently, eighteen hours after his death "his body was still soft, as if he were simply asleep." Ibid.

43. Buddhist saints were believed to leave crystalline fragments or relics in the ashes of their cremated bodies as proof of their great sanctity, but in the case of a buddha, his entire body was a relic. For an extended discussion of the significance of relics and the cult of relics in Chan Buddhism, see Faure, *Rhetoric of Immediacy*, pp. 133–178.

44. "Ku benshi Qi laoheshang," *Cantong Yikui Chaochen chanshi yulu, J.* 39:9b.

45. Here the Jetavana Forest (Qilin) is an allusion to Qiyuan (Jetavana Park) Xinggang.

46. "Diao ni Qiyuan chanshi," *Baichi chanshi yulu, J.* 28:111b.

Chapter Five: Passing on the Lamp

1. "Yichuan faxiong fushi you sheng seng ji," *Fushi Yigong chanshi yulu, J.* 39:3a.

2. "Yichuan Faxiong heshang fengkan," *Fushi Yigong chanshi yulu, J.* 39:6a.

3. *Cantong Yikui Chaochen chanshi yulu, J.* 39:1b.

4. *Fazhi* is one of the few religious kinship terms that can be read in the feminine as well as the masculine, since in Chinese, *zhi* (written with the woman radical), is used to refer to the child of a brother, regardless of whether that child is male or female.

5. "Mian Shanhu ni Yiyin fazhi," *Baichi chanshi yulu, J.* 28:110c.

6. "Zun Shanhu Yiyin faxiong chanshi," *Cantong Yikui Chaochen chanshi yulu, J.* 32b–33a.

7. This and subsequent quotations, unless otherwise noted, are from Mingyuan Weiyi's "Cantong Yikui Chaochen chanshi xingzhuang," in *Cantong Yikui Chaochen chanshi yulu, J.* 39:1a–4a.

8. As Vincent Goossaert notes, in the late imperial period such seven-day retreats where men and women stayed within the temple were the target of particular censure by local authorities as well as journalists writing for the *Shenbao*. See his forthcoming article "How the Late Imperial Chinese State Attempted to Prevent Women from Visiting Temples," in *Nan Nü: Men, Women and Gender in China* 10, no. 2 (2008).

9. "Ji Yigong faxiong," *Cantong Yikui Chaochen chanshi yulu, J.* 39:8b–9a.

10. "Fushi Yigong chanshi yulu xu," *Fushi Yigong chanshi yulu, J.* 39:7a.

11. "Ba," *Fushi Yigong chanshi yulu, J.* 39:6a.

12. "Wan Yigong faxiong," *Cantong Yikui Chaochen chanshi yulu, J.* 39:10b.

13. "Cantong an jiming," *Cantong Yikui Chaochen chanshi yulu, J.* 39:15b.

14. *Jiaxing fuzhi* (1682) 17:27a. It is interesting to note that in Yuan's section on Daoists and Buddhists, in which we find Qiyuan Xinggang's biographical notice, the nuns are combined seemingly arbitrarily with the monks, instead of being relegated to the end of the section, as was often the case in later gazetteers.

15. "Cantong Yikui Chaochen chanshi xingshi," *Cantong Yikui Chaochen chanshi yulu.* Unless otherwise noted, all of the subsequent longer biographical quotes in this chapter are from this source.

16. One of Yikui Chaochen's elder sisters, who had married a certain Jin Huan, appears to have been widowed at the age of twenty *sui. Pinghu xianzhi* 21:2b. I am not positive that this Madame Sun was Yikui Chaochen's sister, but she is mentioned as being the great-granddaughter of Sun Zhi. Another Madame Sun, explicitly noted as being the daughter of Sun Hongzu, Yikui Chaochen's uncle, died at the hands of battling troops in Hubei, together with thirty other family members, including her children. See *Pinghu xianzhi* 19:18b.

17. One of the first discourses in Poshan Haiming's discourse records was delivered in commemoration of Yikui Chaochen's deceased great-grandfather Sun Zhi, at the request of two of her uncles, Sun Hongzha and Sun Hongfu. See *Poshan chanshi yulu, J.* 26:2b.

18. *Jiaxing fuzhi* (1682) 17:27b. I have found no mention of this monk in later Jiaxing gazetteers.

19. There is a brief biography of Sun Zilin in the *Jiaxing fuzhi* (1682) 17:21b– 22a.

20. The second wife of Yunqi Zhuhong, Venerable Lady Tang took the tonsure after Zhuhong left her to become a monk, and she became known for her religious accomplishments. See Chün-Fang Yü's discussion of their relationship in *Renewal of Buddhism in China,* pp. 12–16.

21. This is a reference to the story of Liu An (d. 122 BCE), the prince of Huainan and the patron of a group of scholars who composed the *Huainanzi,* a philosophical work with a strong Daoist coloring. Later legend turned Liu An into a magician who succeeded in preparing the elixir of immortality and ascended to heaven with his entire household, including those chickens and dogs who happened to have swallowed some of the elixir.

22. It is curious to note that the Jiaxing gazetteer contains a brief biographical notice for Yikui under the heading "Sun Zhennü" (Chaste Maiden Sun), with no mention of either her marriage or her widowhood but simply stating that she was determined to preserve her chastity. *Jiaxing fuzhi* (1682) 14:87b.

23. This practice was quite popular (although not always condoned) during the late imperial period. It reflects a combination of Confucian filial piety, Buddhist notions of bodhisattvahood, and Chinese medical notions that a child's flesh could bring healing to a parent's illness. See Qiu Zhonglin, "Buxiao zhi xiao—Tang yilai gegu liaoqin xianxiang de shehuishi chutan," *Xin shixue* 6, no. 1 (1995): 49–94; and Reiko Ohnuma, "The Gift of the Body and the Gift of the Dharma," *History of Religions* 37, no. 4 (1998): 321–359.

24. See Brook, *Praying for Power,* pp. 54–88, for a succinct discussion of the breakdown of the "high embankment" between Buddhism and Confucianism.

25. "Cantong qi" is also the title of a well-known poem by the Zaodong monk

Shitou Xiqian (700–790), in which case "the Three" may refer simply to the diversity of Buddhist teachings, which in the end are one.

26. "Cantong an jiming," 15b–c.

27. Jingnuo Chaoyue, whose secular surname was Liu, was the daughter of a county magistrate from Renhe (Zhejiang Province). She entered the monastic life as a young girl and studied for many years with Xiongsheng Weiji before finally becoming her senior Dharma heir. Like her teacher, Jingnuo Chaoyue earned a reputation for compassionate but strict discipline and impeccable behavior and attracted hundreds of lay followers. She was also known for being a talented poet and having left a *yulu,* apparently no longer extant.

28. "Ku Xiongsheng fashu da heshang," *Cantong Yikui Chaochen chanshi yulu, J.* 39:12a.

29. "Zeng Dongyun Chanyou," *Cantong Yikui Chaochen chanshi yulu, J.* 39:10c.

30. "Shou Dongyun Chanshi wushi," *Cantong Yikui Chaochen chanshi yulu, J.* 39:11c.

31. "Da Gui Suoying Gao furen wen zuo shufa," in Wang Qi, comp., *Chidu xinyu,* 2 vols. (1668; reprint, Taipei: Guangwen, 1996), 3a–4b.

32. Yikui Chaochen was actually related by marriage to one of the members of this well-known trio of women poets—Gui Shufen, Shen Hui, and Huang Dezhen (*zi* Yuehui). Huang Dezhen was married (although widowed early) to Sun Zengnan (*zi* Rangshang), who, like Yikui Chaochen, was a third-generation descendant of Sun Zhi's and thus most likely her cousin.

33. Xu Naichang, ed., *Guixiu cichao* (Nanking, 1909), 4.5a–b.

34. "Zishu xinglue shun tu," *Cantong Yikui chanshi yulu, J.* 39:18a.

35. "Yimao Dong tanyue qing shi fuzhu Fushi shengzuo," *Cantong Yikui Chaochen chanshi yulu, J.* 39:11a.

36. "Zishu xinglue shun tu," *Cantong Yikui Chaochen chanshi yulu, J.* 39:18a.

37. Ibid.

38. "Cantong an jiming," *Cantong Yikui Chaochen chanshi yulu, J.* 39:15b.

39. Ibid.

40. "Shijiawen Fo kaiguang Zaichu xitang qing xiaocan," *Cantong Yikui Chaochen chanshi yulu, J.* 39:11a.

41. As Chün-Fang Yü describes in her study of Yunqi Zhuhong, *The Renewal of Buddhism in China,* much of this eminent monk's formidable energies were expended in setting up comprehensive rules and regulations for the monastic life. He felt that the lack of such discipline in his time was responsible for the bad reputation that Buddhism had begun to acquire. For a detailed description of these regulations, see Yü, *Renewal of Buddhism,* pp. 192–222.

42. An interesting twist to this delegation of authority is that there seems to have been a conscious realization that in fact the Joining-the-Three Convent represented two different but naturally complementary lineages, one of them the

Linji Chan lineage represented by Qiyuan Xinggang and her teachers and the other, the Three-Teachings lineage, represented by Sun Zilin himself. Thus we find him advising his sister as follows: "The way I see it, senior nun Fayuan [Mingling] should in matters of doctrine and theory continue the orthodox lineage of [Linji], and [Mingyuan] Weiyi should, in matters of practice, uphold the way of Joining-the-Three [*cantong*]. The Master said: 'That is right, that is right!'"

43. Faure, *Rhetoric of Immediacy,* 188.

44. The nine bonds that keep people tied to the world: love, hate, pride, ignorance, wrong views, possessions (or attachments), doubt, envy, and selfishness.

45. "Yiwei qiu qian yiri qinti cishi jie," *Cantong Yikui Chaochen chanshi yulu, J.* 39:34a.

46. *Jiaxing fuzhi* (1682) 17:21b. Sun and Zhi clearly represented the continuation of the so-called Taizhou school of neo-Confucian thought, which flourished in eastern Zhejiang during the years of the late Ming. This school was known for not only its affinity toward the liberal philosophy of Wang Yangming but its affinity for, and indeed adoption of, Chan Buddhist ideas as well. The famous Confucian scholar, political statesman, and Ming loyalist Huang Zongxi (1610–1695) was by no means lacking in respect for Buddhist teaching or teachers (recall that he did write the epitaph for Linji master Hanyue Fazang, Jiqi Hongchu's Dharma father). Nevertheless, he was critical of the blurring of boundaries between Confucian and Buddhist thought, especially as exemplified in members of the Taizhou school such as Zhou Rudeng (1547–1629) and Huang Daozhou (1585–1646)— the very sort of men Shi Bo and Sun Zilin regarded as their teachers. "During the Wanli era," Huang Zongxi writes, "Confucians were giving public lectures all over China, and so Buddhists like Zibo Zhenke and Hanshan Deqing came to prominence in the same way. Monks like Miyun and Zhanran followed in the wake of Zhou Rudeng and Tao Wangling. Confucianism and Buddhism became like meats on a skewer, each taking on the flavor of the next." See "Zhang Ren'an xiansheng muzhiming" [Epitaph for Master Zhang Ren'an], cited and translated in Brook, *Praying for Power,* p. 826.

47. *Meili zhi* 11:17b.

48. One of her poems is included in the voluminous anthology of Qing poetry by Xu Shichang (1858–1939), *Wanqing yishui hui* (Taipei: Shijie shuju, 1963) p. 3360b. Interestingly, she is also celebrated today as a famous Jiading poet.

49. *Meili zhi* 4:21a.

50. "Dong Wei you Bore an," *Nanxun zhi* 9:27.

Chapter Six: From Hengzhou to Hangzhou

1. "Xingshi," *Jizong Che chanshi yulu, J.* 28:453b.

2. Tan edited Master Hanshan's *Dongyou ji* [Records of Travel to the East] in 1617 and also wrote a commentary to Hanshan's autobiography *(Hanshan Laoren*

nianpu zixu shulu shu) in 1650. Elsewhere, in a poem addressed to him, Jizong speaks of meeting with Tan and of her great admiration for his unflagging travels on behalf of Hanshan Deqing, as well as his great literary talents. See "Ciyun da Tan Sao'an jushi," *Jizong Che chanshi yulu, J.* 28:465a.

3. "Jizong chanshi yulu xu," *Jizong Che chanshi yulu, J.* 28:441a.

4. Yan Dacan was also the person primarily responsible for getting these *yulu* printed, at Jizong Xingche's request. He appears to have been a rather flamboyant figure who was first introduced to Chan Buddhism by Wengu Guangyin (1566–1636) but claimed to have had his first experience of enlightenment on his own after reading a famous koan by the Tang master Fayan Wenyi (885–958). He was able to have this experience confirmed by a number of the more eminent Buddhist masters of the time, including Hanshan Deqing, Tianyin Yuanxiu (1575–1635), and Miyun Yuanwu. Ultimately he became a formal student of Miyun Yuanwu's senior student, Feiyin Tongrong (1593–1661). His biographical account in the *Wudeng quanshu* paints a picture of a "wild Channist" who had no compunction about striding into temples and beating on the temple drums rather than lighting incense. After the fall of the Ming dynasty, Yan Dacan lived in retirement for several decades and attracted visitors both lay and monastic. In the fall of 1671, with no sign of illness, he invited all of his friends to his home for a vegetarian feast, over which he presided, sitting cross-legged and talking and laughing as usual. As soon as the feast was over, he gave out an earthshaking shout and pushed over several tables. The guests all rose in consternation to see what had happened, and found he had died. He was eighty-one *sui*. See Peng Shaosheng's *Jushi zhuan* 54:562; and *Wudeng quanshu* 71:245d.

5. Yan Dacan, "Jizong Che chanshi yulu shuu," *Jizong Che chanshi yulu, J.* 28:442a.

6. Wang Duanshu, *Mingyuan shiwei* (1667) 10:26.5a.

7. Kang-i Sun Chang, "Ming-Qing Women Poets and Cultural Androgyny," *Tamkang Review* 30, no. 2 (1999): 12–25; reprinted in *Critical Studies* (special issue on feminism/femininity in Chinese literature), ed. Peng-hsiang Chen and Whitney Crothers Dilley (2002): 21–31.

8. Grace Fong, "A Feminine Condition: Women's Poetry on Illness in Ming-Qing China," in *From Skin to Heart: Perceptions of Emotions and Bodily Sensations in Traditional Chinese Culture*, ed. Paolo Santangelo and Ulrike Middendorf (Wiesbaden: Harrassowitz Verlag, 2006), pp. 131–150. See also Binbin Yang, "Women and the Aesthetics of Illness: Poetry on Illness by Chinese Women Poets of the Qing" (Ph.D. diss., Washington University in St. Louis, 2007).

9. *Nanyue chuandeng lu* is a collection of biographies and recorded sayings of 133 great Tang-dynasty masters of the Nanyue Huairang lineage of Chan Buddhism, followed by a collection of teachings by masters of the Song, Yuan, and Ming periods.

10. Published in 1600, this was a selective anthology of what Yunqi Zhuhong

felt to be the most useful of the great masters' teachings on Chan practice. Although Yunqi Zhuhong often lamented the dearth of such masters in his own time—and, as we have seen, he had little patience with what he regarded as the antics of teachers such as Miyun Yuanwu—he included in his collection a number of Ming-dynasty masters as well.

11. This line appears in Yunqi Zhuhong's account of the Yuan-dynasty Linji master Gaofeng Yuanmiao, who is said to have had an enlightenment experience one day when he happened to lift his head and read these two lines in a colophon inscribed on a painting of the Song-dynasty master Wuzu Fayan (1024–1104). See *Changuan cejin, T.* 48, no. 2024, p. 110a.

12. "Fu ni Jizong," *Shishuang Erdan Zun chanshi yulu, J.* 27:580b.

13. "Shi ni Jizong," in *Nanyue Shanci Ji chanshi yulu, Zhonghua dazangjin di'er ji,* 106:14b–15a.

14. Ibid., p. 15a.

15. "Jizong Che chanshi yulu xu," *Jizong Che chanshi yulu, J.* 28:442b.

16. This is an allusion to a famous line (often quoted in classical Chan texts) attributed to the early Buddhist monk Sengzhao (384–414): "I share the same roots with heaven and earth; I share the same body as the myriad phenomena."

17. "Ji Hengyang Liushi xiongdi," *Jizong Che chanshi yulu, J.* 28:469a.

18. Huineng, the so-called Sixth Patriarch of Chan Buddhism, is associated with the Nanhua Monastery in Caoqi (Guangdong Province). Thus "Caoqi" is sometimes used as another name for the so-called sudden enlightenment school of Southern Chan. The phrase "not much to it" *(buduo zi)* is from the oft-repeated story of Linji Yixuan, who is said to have made this comment about the teachings of Huangbo—and, by extension, of Buddhism—immediately after his own enlightenment.

19. "Shi Jizong shangzuo," *Wanru chanshi yulu, J.* 25:496b.

20. See "Song Yuan shouzuo xigui," *Yuanwu Foguo chanshi yulu, T.* 47, no. 1997, pp. 781a–b.

21. The characters *xuyang* mean, literally, "to rear" or "to raise." I have translated the word here as an exhortation to Jizong Xingche to rear or cultivate herself, but it is possible that Wanru Tongwei is instead giving her the authorization to cultivate others—that is, students of her own.

22. Among the signatories to Jizong Xingche's invitation were Zhou Maolan and Zhou Maozao, sons of Zhou Shunchang (1584–1626), who was executed because of his opposition to the powerful eunuch Wei Zhongxian and was known as one of the "Seven Heroes of Donglin"; and Xu Yuanpu, son of the loyalist martyr and poet Xu Xichang, an ardent bibliophile who joined the Fushe in 1629 and converted his father's old studio into a monastery in 1646. Also on the list of Fushe members are two sons of the literatus-poet and loyalist Yao Ximeng; poet and literatus Xu Shupi (1596–1683), who joined the Fushe in 1629 and lived in retirement on the slopes of Mount Longchi after the fall of the Ming; and Huang

Kongshao (b. 1589), who held official posts in Yunnan, among other places, but after 1644 renounced public office and took up Chan Buddhism.

23. This is one of the primary arguments Brook makes in his excellent study, *Praying for Power: Buddhism and the Formation of Gentry Society in Late-Ming China.*

24. *Jizong Che chanshi yulu, J.* 28:442b.

25. "Shi zhi Danghu Shanhu an Yiyin chanshi tongzhong tanhu qing shang-tang," *Jizong Che chanshi yulu, J.* 28:447a–b; and "Shanhu chanyuan Yigong yuan-zhu tong zhu hufa shenjin qing jiyyuan kai lu shangtang," *Jizong Che chanshi yulu, J.* 28:447b–c.

26. The second of these two talks was delivered on the occasion of the "open-ing of the furnace" *(kailu),* which usually occurred around the tenth month of the lunar year and marked the start of the winter season. Traditionally, the head of the monastery or convent delivered a special Dharma talk on this day. Thus the fact that Jizong Xingche delivered this talk at the request of, and in place of, the abbess Yigong suggests that she was a very honored visitor indeed.

27. "Shi Zixiu Gao jushi," *Jizong Che chanshi yulu, J.* 28:466c.

28. "Yu Huang Chaoyun jushi," *Jizong Che chanshi yulu, J.* 28:469a–b.

29. "Seng Yixiu Shi jushi," *Jizong Che chanshi yulu, J.* 28:465a.

30. "Yu Chen Fangsan jushi," *Jizong Che chanshi yulu, J.* 28:465c.

31. Among her many "words of instruction" addressed to women is even one addressed to "Qian Muzhai furen." This may have been Qian Qianyi's first wife, although it could also have been his more famous second wife, Liu Rushi, a Bud-dhist devotee well known in her own right as a poet and loyalist.

32. "Shi Xiang Hanlin furen," *Jizong Che chanshi yulu, J.* 28:452b.

33. "Jizong Che chanshi yulu xu," 28:1a.

34. "Duanwu shizhong," *Jizong Che chanshi yulu, J.* 28:449c–450a.

35. "Zeng Yizhen daoren," *Jizong Che chanshi yulu, J.* 28:464b–c.

36. "Tu zhongyin," *Jizong Che chanshi yulu, J.* 28:465c.

37. "Xie huai," *Jizong Che chanshi yulu, J.* 4:10a.

38. "Guo Gaochao Pudu ni an jie su," *Jizong Che chanshi yulu, J.* 4:24a.

39. My translation of this line—*chiti cheng ru tougang ao*—is tentative.

40. "Mengxia jianggui Chu song hua xianxiong you Yue," *Jizong Che chanshi yulu, J.* 28:466a.

41. "Nanyue shanju zayong," *Jizong Che chanshi yulu, J.* 28:462a–b.

42. *Wudeng quanshu* 93:420c.

43. *Jizong Che chanshi yulu, J.* 28:442a. Ai Zhong of the Han dynasty was famous for the large, sweet, and juicy pears that he grew in his orchard. "Eating an Ai fam-ily pear" subsequently became a commonly used simile for describing the experi-ence of reading an exceptionally fresh and lively piece of writing.

44. Ibid., 28:443a.

45. *Mingyuan shiwei* 10:26.5a. Wang Duanshu also places Jizong Xingche's poetry on a par with that of the Tang poets Meng Jiao (751–814) and Jia Dao

(779–843). The comparison that most readily comes to mind, however, is with the poetry of Han Shan (Cold Mountain), the Buddhist recluse poet who lived at least a century earlier than Meng and Jia. Jizong Xingche refers to Han Shan in her poems, and she clearly shared his love of mountain life.

Chapter Seven: From Wise Mother to Chan Master

1. Jiqi Hongchu came from a loyalist family. His father changed their surname because, although written differently, it had the same pronunciation as that of the notorious rebel leader Li Zicheng (1606–1645), whose traitorous actions led to the suicide of the last Ming emperor, on Coal Hill in Beijing on April 25, 1644. It is said that even after becoming a monk, every year on this date Jiqi Hongchu would don robes of mourning, light incense, and silently and tearfully bow in the direction of Beijing. As Wai-yee Li points out, the nineteenth day of the third month became a code word in many early Qing writings, lamenting the fall of the Ming. See Li, introduction to Idema et al., *Trauma and Transcendence,* p. 2, n. 1.

2. Xu Fang supported himself by selling his calligraphy and paintings, but, determined to maintain his seclusion, he is said to have placed these items on the back of his donkey, which he would send on alone into the city. Other well-known loyalists who were followers of Jiqi Hongchu include Xiong Kaiyuan (*jinshi* ca. 1621–1627) and Dong Yue (1620–1686), attributed author of the 1640 novel *Xiyouji bu* [*Supplement to the* Journey to the West]. Both of these men eventually took the tonsure with Jiqi Hongchu. Even the aged statesman Qian Qianyi struggled up Mount Lingyan in 1664, the last year of his life, to pay his respects to the monk on the occasion of his birthday.

3. "Huai ren shi jiushou," in Qian Zhonglian, *Qingshi jishi,* 1:723.

4. "Songgu hexiang ji xu," *Songgu hexiang ji, J.* 28:565a.

5. Wang Shilu's now only partially extant anthology of women's writings, *Ranzhi ji* (1672), appears to have included excerpts from her discourse records.

6. *Mingyuan shiwei* 10:26.5a.

7. Ibid., 10:26.4b.

8. "Lingshi heshang wushi shou song," *Lingrui chanshi Yanhua ji, J.* 35:758c.

9. Jin Shanrong's wife, Lady Zhong (d. 1671) became a recluse of sorts after her husband's death. She is said to have moved into a small building with nothing more than four walls and a window and never set foot out of it. In the difficult years of famine she is said to have used her own money to help out those of her extended family who were poor. She also earned a notice as a *lienü,* or exemplary woman, in the local gazetteers.

10. *Jiaxing fuzhi* (1682) 7:44b–45c; *Jiaxing fuzhi* (1878) 50a–51b.

11. *Guochao huazheng xulu* (Jiangdu: Zhushi cangban, 1739).

12. Yu Jianhua, *Zhongguo meishujia renming cidian* (Shanghai: renmin meishu chubanshe, 1981), p. 557a.

13. Ibid., p. 555a. Since this line is not found in either of the other two primary sources cited by the author of this biographical dictionary—the *Guochao guixiu zhengshi ji* and Zheng Geng's *Guochao huazheng xulu*—it may come from the third primary source (which I have not seen), Xu Yuanwen's *Jin Taifuren zhuanlue*.

14. *Guochao guixiu zhengshi ji*, 2.7b.

15. See Wai-yee Li's excellent introduction and "Confronting History and Its Alternatives in Early Qing Poetry: An Introduction," both in Idema et al., *Trauma and Transcendence*.

16. James Legge, *The Chinese Classics* (1898), vol. 4 , part 2, 5:5 (p. 343).

17. *Jiaxing fuzhi* (1682) 64:16b. It is unclear when exactly Xu Zhaosen died, although it was probably sometimes during the tumultuous years of the 1650s. Nearly half a century later, in 1699, Xu Jiayan published a collection of his own poetry, to which he appended a selection of twenty poems composed by his father that Jiayan had "saved from burning," in this case by storing them away in the prodigious memory for which he had been famous even as a child. *Baojing zhai shiji* (Jinan: Qi Lu Shushe chubanshe, 1997), pp. 309–554.

18. Mann, *Precious Records,* pp. 182–183. As Grace Fong also observes: "It is through the analogy of repeated practice, discipline, and concentration that embroidery takes on religious meanings. Its practice is in some ways akin to religious recitation, the accumulation of merit through endlessly repeating the name of the Buddha, and chanting or copying a sutra." Fong, "Female Hands: Embroidery as a Knowledge Field in Women's Everyday Life in Late Imperial and Early Republican China," *Late Imperial China* 25, no. 1 (2004): 19–20.

19. In 1678 the Kangxi emperor announced that the court was soliciting names for membership in this commission, and he called on local officials to nominate "scholars of broad learning and outstanding eminence" *(boxue hongru)* to sit for a special examination conducted at the capital in 1678. One hundred eighty-eight men were summoned for the examination; fifty were awarded the special degree, among them Xu Jiayan. Most of these men had already gained a reputation as scholars even before sitting for the exam. Along with a new title for himself, his mother, who by this time had passed away, was honored posthumously with the title of "Jin Taifuren" (Commandery Grand Mistress)—the head of this commission, the scholar Xu Yuanwen (1634–1691), even wrote a brief biography of her entitled *Jin Taifuren zhuanlue*. I have not yet been able to locate this text, which is mentioned in a biographical notice for Jin Shuxiu in *Jiaxing fuzhi* (1682) 2.7b–2.8a.

20. In the 1879 Jiaxing prefectural gazetteer, Jin Shuxiu appears in the "wise mother" *(xianmu)* category of exemplary women. Ibid.

21. "Songgu hexiang ji xu," 28:565a.

22. "Zeng Zhang furen," *Baochi Zong chanshi yulu J.* 35:712c.

23. The English translation of this text by Ruth Fuller Sasaki, Yoshitaka Iriya,

and Dana R. Fraser is entitled *A Man of Zen: The Recorded Sayings of Layman P'ang* (New York and Tokyo: Weatherhill, 1971 and 1976). In a footnote to their translation of this particular passage (p. 73), they state, "It was customary for a temple priest to write on a slip of paper the donor's name, the gift and its purpose, and the date. This would then be displayed in public so that the donor's merit would become known to others, i.e., 'transferred.'"

24. *Z.* 69:1336.

25. "Ji Luoyang Hou furen," *Baochi Zong chanshi yulu, J.* 35:712c.

26. "Dong an heshang seng," *Baochi Zong chanshi yulu, J.* 35:712c.

27. *Baochi Zong chanshi yulu, J.* 35:709c.

28. "Dong an xitang guo fang," *Baochi Zong chanshi yulu, J.* 35:709c.

29. See Miriam Levering, "A Monk's Literary Education: Dahui's Friendship with Juefan Huihong," *Chung-Hwa Buddhist Journal* 13, no. 2 (2000): 369–384.

30. During the last decade of his life, Huihong compiled a collection of eighty-four biographies of Chan masters, entitled *Chanlin sengbao zhuan* [Chronicles of the Sangha Jewel within the Groves of Chan]. For more on Huihong in English, see Robert M. Gimello, "Mārga and Culture: Learning, Letters, and Liberation in Northern Sung Ch'an," in *Paths to Liberation: The Mārga and Its Transformations in Buddhist Thought*, ed. Robert E. Buswell Jr. and Robert M. Gimello (Honolulu: University of Hawai'i Press, 1992); and George Keyworth, "Transmitting the Lamp of Learning in Classical Chan Buddhism: Juefan Huihong (1071–1128) and Literary Chan" (Ph.D. diss., University of California, Los Angeles, 2001).

31. "Nianfo jie shi tu," *Lingrui chanshi Yanhua ji, J.* 35:759a.

32. For a comprehensive study of Hanyue Fazang's life and his disagreements with Miyun Yuanwe, see Lian Duanji, "Hanyue Fazang (1573–1635) xing wan Ming Sanfang zongpai de jianli," *Zhonghua Foxue xuebao* 7 (1996): 167–208.

33. "Lingyan Tuiweng lao heshang zan," *Lingrui chanshi Yanhua ji, J.* 35:573b.

34. So intense was Miyun Yuanwu's outrage that in 1639, three years after Hanyue Fazang's death, he wrote yet another polemical text in which he accused Hanyue Fazang of being a bastard, a child with not one but three different fathers and thus no proper father at all. In accusing Hanyue Fazang in this way, Miyun Yuanwu was following a largely Confucian model, but of course Tang Chan writers did not speak in these terms; rather, they spoke of going beyond the Buddha and the patriarchs. However, by the late Ming, Confucian ideology had so seeped into Chan circles that Yuanwu himself took this respect for seniority and lineage for granted.

35. The late Ming Buddhist master Zibo Zhenke was actually the person primarily responsible for reviving interest in Juefan Huihong's writings as well as his ideas. These texts also became the centerpiece of one of the many polemical battles between Miyun Yuanwu and Hanyue Fazang. For a detailed discussion of these issues, see Liao Cheng-Heng, "Huihong Juefan zai Mingdai: Songdai

chanxue zai wan Ming de shuxie," *Zhongguo yanjiuyuan lishi Wenyan yanjiu suo ji kan* 75, no. 4 (2004): 797–837.

36. Dale S. Wright, *Philosophical Meditations on Zen Buddhism* (New York: Cambridge University Press, 2000), pp. 84–85.

37. Ibid., p. 85.

38. "Xu," *Baochi Zong chanshi yulu, J.* 35:705a.

39. "Miaozhan ni Baochi Zong chanshi zan," *Lingrui chanshi Yanhua ji, J.* 35:753c. The image of the wooden man and the stone woman are often used in Chan poetry to symbolize that paradoxical freedom of liberation. A well-known example are the lines from "Song of the Precious Mirror Samadhi," by Dongshan Liangjie (807–869), which read: "When the wooden man starts to sing, the stone woman gets up to dance."

40. This is a reference to a popular story (originally from the *Surangama Sutra*) about Yajnavdatta of Sravasti, who one day looked in the mirror and noticed that the person reflected in it had a head. Panicking that he himself had lost his head, he ran through the streets asking if anyone had seen it. Here, of course, the story means that one can see the externals but miss the real person.

41. I am unsure of the translation (much less the meaning) of these two lines.

42. This is an allusion to Bodhidharma's disciple Huike, said to have understood the "bone" (or in some versions, the "marrow") of his master's teaching.

43. "Zi zan," *Baochi Zong chanshi yulu, J.* 35:713a.

44. "Qing Lingrui heshang zhu Miaozhan qian tuiyan shangtang chanyuan yu," *Baochi Zong chanshi yulu, J.* 35:707a.

45. "Zhu Haiyan Nanxun chanyuan yu," *Baochi Zong chanshi yulu, J.* 35:707a.

46. "Baochi chanshi jichen xiaozi Xu Yan Xu Ran deng qing shangtang," *Lingrui ni Zukui Fu chanshi Miaozhan lu, J.* 35:717b.

47. Xu Jiayan's published collection of writings, *Embracing the Scriptures Poetry Collection (Baojing shiji)* contains the titles of a text written to "two scrolls of landscape painting executed by my departed mother and presented to a lady" and an account of the awarding of posthumous titles to his mother and his wife upon his elevation to the Hanlin Academy in 1679. Neither appear to make any reference to her life as a Chan master.

Chapter Eight: Reviving the Worlds of Literary Chan

1. Li Mo had, like many of his literati counterparts, held office during the first decades of the seventeenth century, but after 1644 he went into retirement, spending the last decades of this life in the Suzhou area. His name also appears on the list of lay patrons who extended an invitation to Jizong Xingche to assume leadership of the Wisdom Lamp Convent in Hangzhou.

2. I have not been able to identify this particular monk, also known as

Jiangxin Daozhe, but am assuming that he was, like Zukui Jifu, a disciple of Jiqi Hongchu.

3. "Lingrui chanshi yulu xu," *Lingrui ni Zukui Fu chanshi Miaozhan lu, J.* 35:715a.

4. For a biography of Lady Xian in English, see "Madame Xian," in *Notable Women of China: Shang Dynasty to the Early Twentieth Century,* ed. Barbara Bennett Peterson (Armonk and London: M. E. Sharpe, 2000), pp. 165–170. Lady Xian has become an important cultural icon and even today is worshipped as a goddess on Hainan Island. See *The First Hero among Women: Lady Xian* [Jinguo yingxiong diyiren—Xian furen] (Guangzhou: Guangzhou renmin chubanshe, 2005).

5. "Lingrui chanshi yulu xu."

6. It is not clear where exactly this convent was located, but, judging from the many references to Lake Dongting, it was very likely situated somewhere on the banks, or perhaps even on one of the islands within this large and scenic lake in northeastern Hunan.

7. "Lingrui chanshi *Yanhua ji* shu," *Lingrui chanshi Yanhua ji, J.* 35:741b.

8. *Lingrui chanshi Yanhua ji, J.* 35:741c.

9. Thomas Cleary and J. C. Cleary, trans., *The Blue Cliff Record* (1977; reprint, Boston and London: Shambhala Press, 1992), p. 43.

10. "Yu Hanyue shangzuo," in *Tiantong zhishuo* 1:5 (Harvard University microfilm, original in Tōkyō Daigaku Tōyō Bunka Kenkyūjo).

11. "Songgu hexiang ji xu," *Songgu hexiang ji, J.* 28:215a.

12. Puhui's collection can be found in Z. 65:1295. It is said that it took him over two decades to compile it. He based his work on a core collection of cases entitled *Collection of Couplets of Eulogies on Ancient Cases of the Chan School (Chanzong songgu lianzhu ji),* which was first compiled by the Song-dynasty monk Faying, who himself had spent thirty years on the project before finally publishing it in 1175. Faying's original collection contained 2,100 verses by 122 Chan masters; Puhui added 493 cases and 426 authors, for a total of 3,050 verses. I am most grateful to Miriam Levering for alerting me to this collection and pointing out that the cases and Miaozong's *songgu* can all be found in it; although they are not all grouped together in one place, they do appear in the same order as they do in *Collection of Harmoniously Resonant Eulogies on Ancient Cases.*

13. "Songgu hexiang ji xu."

14. The three barriers here may represent the three organs that make distinctions: the eye, the ear, and the mouth.

15. Someone asked: "What is the place from whence all the buddhas come?" Master Yunmen said: "[Where] the East Mountains walk on the river." The meaning of these two parallel lines, then, appears to be that, given that she has attained enlightenment—that is, she has arrived at "the place from whence all the buddhas come"—she is able to move and act freely in the world.

16. I am reading the characters *jue chuniu* (literally, cutting off the pivot or

central axis) as a reference to putting an end to the three poisons—greed, anger, and ignorance—said to keep the cycle of life and death spinning.

17. "Lingrui heshang zan," *Baochi Zong chanshi yulu, J.* 35:712c–713a.

18. "Chunri huaigu," *Lingrui Yanhua ji, J.* 35:754b.

19. "Shi yiri duhu," *Lingrui Yanhua ji, J.* 35:745c–746b.

20. "Wang furen hicai xian mudan shen jing shi yi er jie," *Lingrui chanshi Yanhua ji, J.* 35:756b.

21. Many of these are from the Xu family, which suggests that Zukui Jifu may have been related to Baochi Jizong in some way. It would also explain why the former Jin Shuxiu, wife and then widow of Xu Zhaosen, would have sought her out at the Miaozhan Convent. I have, however, found no concrete evidence that this was indeed the case.

22. There is a reference to this text, together with a diagram, in a work by the late seventeenth-century monk Jiyin Xiangyu, who had studied intensively with Jiqi Hongchu about the same time as Zukui Jifu. In this text, Jiyin Xiangyu makes an attempt (yet again) to establish a lineage of Chan Buddhism, beginning with the earliest figures all the way down to approximately 1689. Although he belonged to Hanyue Fazang's lineage, he apparently made a real effort to offer a balanced treatment of both Hanyue Fazang's and Miyun Yuanwu's contributions: "Without Tiantong [Yuanwu], we would not be able to see the breadth and expanse of Linji [Chan]; without Sanfeng [Hanyue], we would not be able to see the subtle nuances of Linji [Chan]." Cited in Shi Jianyi, "Hanyue Fazang zhi chanfa yanjiu," *Zhonghua foxue bao* 11 (1998): 217.

23. "Dong an ni Qiyuan chanshi zan," *Lingrui chanshi Yanhua ji, J.* 35:753c.

24. "Ji Dongan zhuren," *Lingrui chanshi Yanhua ji, J.* 35:758b.

25. In fact, it is quite likely, although again I have not been able to find any documented evidence, that Zukui Jifu had, like Yigong Chaoke, entered the religious life as a young girl and had been raised in a convent. This would certainly explain the lack of detailed information about her family background.

26. "Diao Fushi Yigong chanshi," *Lingrui chanshi Yanhua ji, J.* 35:758c.

27. Feng'gan was a Tang-dynasty monk who was known for his poetry and for being one of the three recluses (together with Hanshan and Shide) of Guoqing Monastery of the Tiantai Mountains. There is a story about an official whom Feng'gan had instructed to look up Hanshan and Shide when he went to Tiantai. He found the two men sitting around, talking and laughing, and he bowed to them respectfully, but they just spit and cursed at him. When the other monks in the monastery asked the official why he was even bothering with these crazy fellows, Hanshan and Shide grabbed the official and said, "Feng'gan talks too much" *(Feng'gan raoshe).* They then left the temple and were never seen again. Some of Feng'gan's poems are included with those of Hanshan.

28. "Shu zhi," *Lingrui chanshi Yanhua ji, J.* 35:758a.

29. "Nianfo jie shi tu," *Lingrui chanshi Yanhua ji, J.* 35:759a.

30. In China such rituals were originally associated with Daoist and shaman traditions, but they became associated as well with Tantric teachers such as Amboghavajra, who was called upon several times by the Tang emperor to conduct special rainmaking ceremonies. In this way, rainmaking became part of the Buddhist ritual repertoire as well and, as such, was performed by Buddhist monks down through to the modern period.

31. See Evelyn S. Rawski, *The Last Emperors: A Social History of Qing Imperial Institutions* (Berkeley: University of California Press, 1998), pp. 220–230.

32. "Zheyu shangtang," *Lingrui ni Zukui Fu chanshi Miaozhan yulu, J.* 35:722a.

33. Brian Ruppert, "Buddhist Rainmaking in Early Japan: The Dragon King and the Ritual Careers of Esoteric Monks," *History of Religions* 42, no. 2 (2002): 143–174. There are a great number of stories and legends about dragons in Buddhist lore. It is said, for example, that they were once human beings who, because of their stupidity and bad temper, took on the form of an animal. There are all sorts of dragons, some respectful of the Dharma and bringing beneficial rains, others disrespectful of the Dharma and bringing rains that cause flooding and destroy crops. Dragon kings belong for the most part to the first category, and there are said to be seven of them. In one legend, the Dragon King of the Ocean is said to have once taken on the shape of a human being in order to engage in spiritual cultivation, but because it could not retain his human form when it was sleeping, the Buddha commanded that at certain times, such as when being born, when about to die, when sleeping, and when angry, it had to revert to its original dragon shape.

34. *Biyan lu,* case 60; Cleary and Cleary, *Blue Cliff Record,* p. 341.

35. *Wumen guan, T.* 48, 299:1.

36. James Green, trans., *The Recorded Sayings of Zen Master Joshu* (Walnut Creek, Calif.: AltaMira Press, 1998), p. 171.

37. "Coral tree" is another name for the *pārijāta* tree, said to grow in front of the palace of Indra and regarded as the king of heavenly trees.

38. This is an allusion to case 65 of the *Biyan lu,* or *Blue Cliff Record.* Cleary and Cleary's translation: "Ho Shan imparted some words saying, 'Cultivating study is called "learning." Cutting off study is called "nearness." Going beyond these two is to be considered real going beyond.' A monk came forward and asked, 'What is "real going beyond?"' Shan said, 'Knowing how to beat the drum.' Again he asked, 'What is the real truth?' Shan said, 'Knowing how to beat the drum.' Again he asked, '"Mind is Buddha"—I'm not asking about this. What is not mind and not Buddha?' Shan said, 'Knowing how to beat the drum.' Again he asked, 'When a transcendent man comes, how do you receive him?' Shan said, 'Knowing how to beat the drum'" (*Blue Cliff Record,* p. 365). In the context of this poem, the reference to pounding on Hoshan's drum would seem to indicate the uselessness in asking questions, even very subtle ones, or, from the perspective of an

abbess, not having to reply to persistent students with the phrase "Knowing how to beat the drum" but simply enjoying a quiet couple of hours walking in the hills.

39. According to Buddhist mythology, each of the many worlds contains nine mountains and eight seas. Mount Sumeru is the mountain in the center, surrounded by the eight mountains and eight seas, and all of this—aside from the eighth sea, which is filled with saltwater—is filled with the fragrance of the eight merits.

40. "Shi'er shi ge," *Lingrui chanshi Yanhua ji, J.* 35:759b–759c. The *mani* jewel, like the mirror, reflects all the colors of the world without itself having any color and symbolizes complete and perfect liberation. It is also symbolic of the Buddha within, as in Sengzhao's saying, "Within, there is a jewel. It is hidden inside the human body." Cited in Urs App, *Master Yunmen: From the Record of the Chan Master "Gate of the Clouds"* (Tokyo: Kodansha International, 1994), p. 207.

41. *Luozhu*—the exposed pillars outside of the Dharma hall. Along with other inanimate parts of the monastery, including walls, tiles, lamps, and lanterns, the pillars belong to the category of inanimate objects. In Chan terminology, the term *luozhu* is used to refer to the absence, in a positive sense, of emotional attachment.

42. John R. McRae, *Seeing through Zen: Encounter, Transformation, and Genealogy in Chinese Chan Buddhism* (Berkeley: University of California Press, 2003), p. 100.

43. "Ou shi," *Lingrui chanshi Yanhua ji, J.* 35:759a. The character I have translated here as "nun" is *seng*, which refers to monks or monastics in general, and not *ni*, which more specifically refers to nuns.

44. "Shi duo song," *Lingrui chanshi Yanhua ji, J.* 35:759b.

45. "Gui shan zi chao," *Lingrui chanshi Yanhua ji, J.* 35:759b.

46. "Zi ti," *Lingrui chanshi Yanhua ji, J.* 35:754a.

47. Since there is no subject in the original Chinese, these colophons could be translated in the first person as well. However, I feel that the third person is more appropriate.

48. An allusion to case 60 of the *Blue Cliff Record*, "Yunmen's Staff Changes into a Dragon." See Cleary and Cleary, *Blue Cliff Record*, pp. 341–346.

49. An allusion to a commentary to case 56 of the *Blue Cliff Record*, "Qin Shan's One Arrowpoint Smashes Three Barriers." See Cleary and Cleary, *Blue Cliff Record*, pp. 328–329.

50. When swimming in water covered with water grasses, the tortoise can appear to have fur. This is a Chan metaphor for illusion.

51. An allusion to a passage from the *Analects (Lunyu)* 6:9: "Virtuous indeed is Hui! One basket of food, one gourd of water, and a narrow alley. Others are unable to endure this kind of hardship, but as for Yan Hui, it does not change his happiness. Virtuous indeed is Hui!"

52. An indirect allusion to Moshan, who also did not "reveal her summit."
53. "Zi ti."

Chapter Nine: From Beijing to Jiangnan

1. See Arthur Hummel, *Eminent Chinese of the Ch'ing Period (1644–1912)* (Taipei: Literature House, 1964), p. 257.

2. Susan Naquin, *Peking: Temples and City Life, 1400–1900* (Berkeley: University of California Press, 2000), p. 54. It is also important to remember that the nun Wenjian Guxin (d. 1322), an official Dharma heir of Linji master Gaofeng Yuanmiao (1238–1295), was the abbess of two major convents in Beijing.

3. "Xingshi," *Ziyong Ru chanshi yulu, J.* 39:831a.

4. By the late sixteenth century, the fertile area east of the Liao River had been settled not only by Chinese emigrants but also by non-Chinese Jürchen peoples who practiced both agriculture and trade and for the most part adopted Chinese ways. In fact, Liaodong was considered by the Ming to be Chinese. In 1616, however, the Jürchen leader Nurhachi, through both military and other means, tried to establish himself as ruler of Liaodong, urging those "who lived west of the Liao River to join him in his new kingdom." By 1625 he had gained control of all the territory east of the Liao River. Under Nurhachi's successors, many Chinese were brought into the civil service, and, in the words of Jonathan Spence, "a swelling number of Chinese defectors from the Ming cause, many of them officers who had brought their own troops along with them, sought service with the new khan." In subsequent years, at least eight full Chinese "banners" were created—and the Jürchen of the northeast China adopted the new name "Manchu." See Jonathan D. Spence, *The Search for Modern China* (New York: W. W. Norton, 1999), pp. 26–27, 30. It may be that Ziyong Chengru's family belonged to one of the Chinese banner families.

5. The only clue to her date of birth is a poem (translated later in this chapter) dated 1696 *(bingzi)* in which she refers to having lived in the world for "forty-nine springs." *Ziyong Ru chanshi yulu, J.* 39:821b.

6. Xingshi," 831a.

7. Robert M. Gimello, "Chang Shang-yin on Wu-t'ai Shan," in *Pilgrims and Sacred Sites in China,* ed. Susan Naquin and Chün-fang Yü (Berkeley: University of California Press, 1992), p. 99.

8. "Canfang riwan tou shansi buna gan fu," *Ziyong Ru chanshi yulu, J.* 39:822a. There are many accounts of pilgrims who have had this vision of sacred light, including, as it happens, the contemporary nun Yan Fa, who describes the experience she had on a pilgrimage to Wutai in 1995 with her mother and some friends: "One morning we were on our way to a temple; suddenly something appeared in the sky. I saw Wenshu Pusa [Manjusri] with a few attendants in midair about fifty meters away from us. It looked as if they were going some-

where and had stopped to look at us. They wore colorful clothes like what we see in paintings and were glowing with a golden light." Qin, "Buddhist Revival," p. 396.

9. "Shang Taishan guo Miaode an liqin benshi laoren," *Ziyong Ru chanshi yulu, J.* 39:821b. Although "Taishan" could refer to Mount Tai, I am assuming that, given the name of the monastery, which was very well known in Chan Buddhist circles, Ziyong Chengru meant "Wutai shan," a place she visited several times.

10. "Qiqi Zhao furen qing xiaocan," *Ziyong Ru chanshi yulu, J.* 39:820b.

11. "Yongshou jishi," *Ziyong Ru chanshi yulu, J.* 39:821c.

12. Naquin, *Peking,* p. 6.

13. Susan Naquin, "Sites, Saints, and Sights at the Tanzhe Monastery," *Cahiers d'Extrême-Asie* 10 (1998): 195.

14. Ibid., p. 154.

15. Quoted in Yü, *Renewal of Buddhism in China,* p. 155.

16. "Wu furen song tiseng luofa qing xiaocan," *Ziyong Ru chanshi yulu, J.* 39:820b.

17. Susan Naquin notes that Mongols who visited Peking "seemed to have also given currency to the idea that Peking was the home of Vairochana, transcendent Buddha, incarnation of the Law, and symbol of the Wheel-Turning King." She adds, "This link between Peking and an idealized Chakravartin ruler probably originated with—and certainly served the interests of—the Qing throne." Naquin, *Peking,* p. 473.

18. "Wu furen song tiseng luofa qing xiaocan," *J.* 39:820b.

19. "Bingzi ganhuai," *Ziyong Ru chanshi yulu, J.* 39:821b. Here she is giving herself a new name: "Ruru xian daoren." The characters for "ru" in "Ruru," often translated as "Thusness" or "Suchness," are identical to those for the "ru" in Ziyong Chengru's name.

20. "Xingshi," 831a–b.

21. Here she makes use of an allusion to a famous story from the *Zhanguoce* (Accounts of the Warring States Period), which tells of a legendary dog called Hanlu, who goes in pursuit of a very clever hare by the name of Dong Guoling. They chase each other around the mountain three times, and in the end both run themselves to death. In other words, their chase is a complete waste of energy, from which no one emerges the victor.

22. "Xi sanriyou, you yi nanfang xiushi jintang xiangjian," *Ziyong Ru chanshi yulu, J.* 39:821b.

23. "Seng wen ruhe shi Yongshou jing," *Ziyong Ru chanshi yulu, J.* 39:823b.

24. "Fangzhang yue," *Ziyong Ru chanshi yulu, J.* 39:822b.

25. "Zai Xishan Yong'an si you yige xingjiao seng hejing fangzhang," *Ziyong Ru chanshi yulu, J.* 39:821a.

26. "Shan xing," *Ziyong Ru chanshi yulu, J.* 39:821c.

27. "Xingjiao jie," *Ziyong Ru chanshi yulu, J.* 39:821c.

28. Susan Naquin and Chün-Fang Yü, eds., introduction to *Pilgrims and Sacred Sites in China* (Berkeley: University of California Press, 1992), p. 15.

29. Burton Watson, *Zen Teachings of Master Lin-chi*, p. 53.

30. Quoted in Yü, *Renewal of Buddhism in China*, p. 174.

31. Naquin and Yü, introduction to *Pilgrims and Sacred Sites in China*, p. 20.

32. From the *Book of Filial Piety for Woman*, attributed to a certain Ms. Zheng of the eighth century but, because of the spread of printing, widely circulated in the Ming and Qing. See Patricia Ebrey, trans., "The Book of Filial Piety for Women, Attributed to a Woman Née Zheng (ca. 730)," in *Under Confucian Eyes: Writing on Gender in Chinese History*, ed. Susan Mann and Yu-yin Cheng (Berkeley: University of California Press, 2001), p. 65.

33. Perhaps the best example is the woman poet Wang Wei (d. 1647) from Yangzhou. Orphaned at the age of seven, she became not a nun but a courtesan and traveled around the Jiangnan area on her boat, visiting with male literati and exchanging poetry with them. Later she became the concubine of a Ming loyalist with whom she appears to have spent many happy years until her death. Wang Wei had a special love for mountains and rivers and was also a Buddhist devotee. Her fondness for poetry, nature, and Buddhism came together in her pilgrimages to various famous spots in the Jiangnan area. In their *Collected Poems of the Successive Reigns*, Qian Qianyi and Liu Rushi tell us that at one point, before her marriage and while still at the height of her fame as a courtesan, she "experienced sudden enlightenment and converted to the joys of Chan. With a linen pack and a bamboo staff, she traveled throughout the Yangzi region. She climbed Mount Dabie, visited the famous sights of Yellow Crane Tower and Parrot Isle, went on pilgrimage to Mount Wudang, and climbed the Tianzhu Peak. Traveling up the Yangzi, she ascended Mount Lu and visited the straw-thatched cottage of Bo Juyi [772–846], and at Wuru she sought instruction from the great master Hanshan Deqing [1546–1623]. Upon her return, she had a pond for the release of living fish constructed in Hangzhou, and calling herself the Person of the Way of the Straw Cape, she intended to live out her life in this manner [as a recluse]." *Liechao shiji xiaozhuan* (1698; reprint, Shanghai: Gudian wenxue chubanshe, 1957), p. 760

34. This information is found in a modern, popularized retelling of the lives of famous Buddhist nuns—*Zhongguo mingni*, by Hong Beimou. However, the author, who refers to Mingxiu as "Mingben," provides no footnotes or references whatsoever, and I have as yet been unable to verify this information.

35. Xu Shichang, *Qingshi hui, J.* 199:31a.

36. "Canfang riwan tou Shansi buna gan fu," 822a.

37. "Jingdu biezhong songxing zanshi shishou," *Ziyong Ru chanshi yulu, J.* 39:825a–b.

38. It is not clear when exactly Ziyong Chengru presented these poems to the emperor, since their visits to the south do not appear to have coincided.

39. "Huangshang you cheng," *Ziyong Ru chanshi yulu, J*. 39:826c.

40. The story is that when the Xuanhua emperor died, Chan master Yulin was sent to the Ksitarbha Temple (Jin dizang) on Tiantai, the highest peak of Jiuhua Mountain, he stopped by this place and was impressed by its beauty. A local Chan monk who had been living in seclusion in a nearby cave for over twenty years heard of Yulin's wish and began the work of raising funds to build the temple. The legend was that the day they started to work, big drops of sweet dew hung from all of the pine trees, an auspicious omen indeed.

41. "Chao Jiuhua yexing su Ganlu an," *Ziyong Ru chanshi yulu, J*. 39:828b.

42. "Xiashan yuti," *Ziyong Ru chanshi yulu, J*. 39:828c.

43. *Ziyong Ru chanshi yulu, J*. 39:827b.

44. "Taokou Sun jushi lingzhong hufaqing shangtang fayu," *Ziyong Ru chanshi yulu, J*. 39:826c.

45. Originally from Anhui, he was raised in Hangzhou, where his family moved when he was young. He took the second-level degree in 1651, and although he never passed the highest examinations, in 1668 he was named district magistrate of Jiaocheng in Shanxi Province. Over the next several decades, he served in the Ministry of Revenue and as tax collector in Yangzhou, where he acquired a reputation for his efforts to reform the system.

46. Zhao Jishi does not, however, seem to have been a particularly devout Buddhist. In fact, I would suggest that his interest in Ziyong Chengru, genuine as it may have been, represents an interest in the anomaly of a "holy" woman with both spiritual authority and, thanks to her royal connections, considerable secular prestige. In terms of his own writing, he was above all a collector of stories and information. Among his more well-known works are the Huizhou local gazetteer and a collection of miscellaneous writings in twelve fascicles that is a curious assemblage of anonymous popular stories and tales, bits and pieces of historical and semihistorical trivia, stories about ghosts and demons, jokes and humorous tales, notes on word usage, and many other things. It also includes, for example, brief biographical accounts of men known for their loyalty or their filiality (a reflection of his work as a compiler of local gazetteers) and, interestingly enough, accounts of "anomalous women of the inner chamber."

47. *Ziyong Ru chanshi yulu, J*. 39:830c.

48. Curiously, he fails to mark her name with the character *ni* for "nun," as he almost invariably does for the other women in his collection. This has led some later scholars, including the modern Japanese scholar Yuichi Hasebe, to assume that Chan master Ziyong Chengru was a man. It is also interesting to note that when Chaoyong's collection was published, it stirred up a tremendous polemic, not because he included women masters but because he was thought to have taken liberties with the Zaodong lineage.

49. Yinyue Lin (1607–1683), née Huang, was from an elite Shaoxing (Zhejiang) family. Married at the age of sixteen, she became a disciple at age thirty (we

are not told if her husband died or not) and later became a Dharma heir of Linji Chan master Linye Tongqi (1595–1652). She left a *yulu* collection, although this appears to be no longer extant. A few of her poems are included in an anthology of women's writings compiled by Wang Duanshu (1621–ca. 1706). In an editorial note, Wang Duanshu remarks that Yinyue Lin's example provides evidence for those who need it that "the ability to realize the Great Way has nothing to do with whether one is a man or a woman." Linye Tongqi himself says of his woman disciple: "In former days there was a certain nun Moshan / who said the Way has neither male nor female form / I consider your effective skills [*jiyong*] to be no less than hers / And well suited to be a model for those to come." "Yu Yinyue Lin yanzhu," *Linye Qi chanshi yulu, J.* 26:653b.

50. "Ziyong Ru chanshi yulu xu," *Ziyong Ru chanshi yulu, J.* 39:819a.

51. "Ba," *Ziyong Ru chanshi yulu, J.* 39:832a.

52. Ibid., 827c.

Epilogue

1. Wu, *Enlightenment in Dispute,* p. 245.

2. Ibid. p. 257.

3. Wu identifies three major institutional changes within Chinese Buddhism that can be attributed to these seventeenth-century masters: expansion, networking, and reintegration. Expansion refers to the extraordinary flourishing of Chan during this period, in which monasteries (many of which still exist today) were built and refurbished on a grand scale and the interchange and cooperation between monastics and a disillusioned elite became more intimate than ever before. Networking refers to the emphasis on Dharma transmissions and creation of an institutional network of Dharma transmission monasteries, a network that continued in some areas into the Republican period. Reintegration refers to the way in which seventeenth-century Chan Buddhism "behind its discourse of sudden enlightenment . . . assimilated and reconfigured [diverse] Buddhist heritages through institutionalizing tools such as the compilation of monastic codes and liturgical manuals that are still followed by modern Buddhists." Ibid., p. 270.

4. Brook, *Praying for Power,* p. 190.

5. "Wanshan an beiji," *Nanxun zhi* 38:7b–8a.

6. Wu notes that when writing Hanyue Fazang's biography, his students omitted that Hanyue Fazang was not only a Chan master but also a master of Vinaya and esoteric ritual. In other words, although the iconoclastic Chan style of spontaneous beating and shouting was indeed enacted publicly in monasteries, it was soon ritualized and retained only its symbolic meaning. See Wu, *Enlightenment in Dispute,* p. 247.

7. Ibid.

Selected Bibliography

Anonymous works, gazetteers, discourse records, and major collections of primary sources are listed by titles.

App, Urs. *Master Yunmen: From the Record of the Chan Master "Gate of the Clouds."* Tokyo: Kodansha International, 1994.

Atwell, William S. "From Education to Politics: The Fushe." In *Unfolding of Neo-Confucianism,* edited by W. T. de Bary, pp. 333–367. New York: Columbia University Press, 1975.

Baichi chanshi yulu. 30 fasc. *J.* 28:1–163.

Baochi Zong chanshi yulu. 2 fasc. *J.* 35:705–713.

Berling, Judith. "Bringing the Buddha Down to Earth: Notes on the Emergence of Yülu as a Buddhist Genre." *History of Religions* 27 (1987): 56–88.

———. *The Syncretic Religion of Lin Chao-en.* New York: Columbia University Press, 1981.

Borell, Ari. "*Ko-wu* or *Kong-an?* Practice, Realization, and Teaching in the Thought of Chang Chiu-ch'eng." In *Buddhism in the Sung,* edited by Peter N. Gregory and Daniel A. Getz, Jr. Kuroda Press. Honolulu: University of Hawai'i Press, 1999.

Bossler, Beverly. "Women's Literacy in Song Dynasty China." In *Qingzhu Deng Guangming jiaoshou jiushi huadan lunwenji,* pp. 322–352. Shijiazhuang, 1997.

Brook, Timothy. "At the Margin of Public Authority: The Ming State and Buddhism." In *Culture and State in Chinese History: Conventions, Accommodations, and Critiques,* edited by Theodore Huters, R. Bin Wong, and Pauline Yu, pp. 161–188. Stanford, Calif.: Stanford University Press, 1997.

———. "Funerary Ritual and the Building of Lineages in Late Imperial China." *Harvard Journal of Asiatic Studies* 49, no. 2 (1989): 465–499.

———. *Geographical Sources of Ming-Qing History.* Ann Arbor: Center for Chinese Studies, University of Michigan, 1988.

———. *Praying for Power: Buddhism and the Formation of Gentry Society in Late-Ming*

China. Harvard-Yenching Institute Monograph Series. Cambridge, Mass.: Harvard University Press, 1993.

———. "Rethinking Syncretism: The Unity of the Three Teachings and Their Joint Worship in Late-Imperial China." *Journal of Chinese Religions* 21 (1993): 13–44.

Bushuitai ji. 32 fasc. *J.* 26:309–437.

Buswell, Robert E., Jr. "The 'Short-Cut' Approach of Kan-hua Meditation: The Evolution of a Practical Subitism in Chinese Ch'an Buddhism." In *Sudden and Gradual: Approaches to Enlightenment in Chinese Thought,* edited by Peter Gregory. Honolulu: University of Hawai'i Press, 1987.

Bynum, Caroline Walker. "Religious Women in the Later Middle Ages." In *Christian Spirituality: High Middle Ages and Reformation,* edited by Jill Raitt, Bernard McGinn, and John Meyendorff. New York: Crossroad, 1987.

Cai Hongsheng. "Lingnan sanni yu Qingchu zhengju." *Zhongshan daxue xuebao* 1 (1994): 61–68.

———. *Nigu tan.* Guangzhou: Zhongshan daxue chubanshe, 1996.

———. *Qingchu Lingnan Fomen shilüe.* Guangzhou: Guangdong gaodeng jiaoyu chubanshe, 1997.

Cantong Yikui Chaochen chanshi yulu. 1 fasc. *J.* 39:7–18.

Cass, Victoria. *Dangerous Women: Warriors, Grannies and Geishas of the Ming.* Lanham, Md.: Rowman and Littlefield, 1999.

Chang, Kang-i Sun. "Ming-Qing Women Poets and Cultural Androgyny." *Tamkang Review* 30, no. 2 (1999): 12–25. Reprinted in *Critical Studies,* special issue on feminism/femininity in Chinese literature, edited by Peng-hsiang Chen and Whitney Crothers Dilley (2002): 21–31.

Chen Yuan. *Chen Yuan shixue lunzhu xuan.* Shanghai: Shanghai renmin chubanshe, 1981.

———. *Mingji Dian Qian Fojiao kao.* Beijing: Zhonghua shuju, 1959.

———. *Qingchu sengzheng ji.* Beijing: Zhonghua shuju, 1962.

———. *Zhongguo Fojiao shiji gailun.* Beijing: Zhonghua shuju, 1962.

Ch'ien, Edward. *Chiao Hung and the Restructuring of Confucian Orthodoxy.* New York: Columbia University Press, 1986.

———. "The Conception of Language and the Use of Paradox in Buddhism and Taoism." *Journal of Chinese Philosophy* 9, no. 3 (1982): 307–328.

Chou, Yi-Liang. "Tantrism in China." *Harvard Journal of Asiatic Studies,* 3–4 (1945): 241–332.

Cleary, Thomas, and J. C. Cleary, trans. *The Blue Cliff Record.* Boston and London: Shambhala Press, 1992.

Cole, Alan. "Upside-Down/Right Side Up: A Revisionist History of Buddhist Funerals in China." *History of Religions* 35, no. 4 (1996): 332.

Dudbridge, Glen. "Women Pilgrims to Tai Shan: Some Pages from a Seventeenth-Century Novel." In *Pilgrims and Sacred Sites in China,* edited by Susan Naquin and Chün-fang Yü, pp. 39–64. Berkeley: University of California Press, 1992.

Ebrey, Patricia B. *The Inner Quarters: Marriage and the Lives of Chinese Women in the Sung Period.* Berkeley: University of California Press, 1993.

Faure, Bernard. *The Power of Denial: Buddhism, Purity, and Gender.* Princeton, N.J.: Princeton University Press, 2003.

———. *Chan Insights and Oversights: An Epistemological Critique of the Chan Tradition.* Princeton, N.J.: Princeton University Press, 1993.

———. *The Rhetoric of Immediacy: A Cultural Critique of Chan/Zen Buddhism.* Princeton, N.J.: Princeton University Press, 1991.

Faxi Yin chanshi yulu, 12 fasc. *J.* 28:777–828

Ferguson, Andrew, trans. *Zen's Chinese Heritage: The Masters and Their Teachings.* Boston: Wisdom Publications, 2000.

Fong, Grace. "Female Hands: Embroidery as a Knowledge Field in Women's Everyday Life in Late Imperial and Early Republican China." *Late Imperial China* 25, no. 1 (2004): 1–58.

———. "A Feminine Condition: Women's Poetry on Illness in Ming-Qing China." In *From Skin to Heart: Perceptions of Emotions and Bodily Sensations in Traditional Chinese Culture,* edited by Paol Santangelo and Ulrike Middendorf, pp. 131–150. Wiesbaden: Harrassowitz Verlag, 2006.

———. *Herself an Author: Gender, Agency, and Writing in Late Imperial China.* Honolulu: Hawai'i University Press, 2008.

Foulk, T. Griffith. "The 'Ch'an School' and Its Place in the Buddhist Monastic Tradition." Ph.D. diss., University of Michigan, 1987.

———. "The Form and Function of Koan Literature: A Historical Overview." In *The Koan: Texts and Contexts in Zen Buddhism,* edited by Steven Heine and Dale S. Wright, pp. 15–45. New York: Oxford University Press, 2000.

———. "Myth, Ritual, and Monastic Practice in Sung Ch'an Buddhism." In *Religion and Society in T'ang and Sung China,* edited by Patricia Ebrey and Peter Gregory, pp. 147–208. Honolulu: University of Hawai'i Press, 1993.

Foulk, T. Griffith, and Robert H. Sharf. "On the Ritual Use of Ch'an Portraiture in Medieval China." *Cahiers d'Extrême-Asie* 7 (1993–1994): 149–219.

Fushi Qiyuan chanshi yulu. 2 fasc. *J.* 28:421–440.

Fushi Yigong chanshi yulu. 1 fasc. *J.* 39:1–6.

Gaoshan Maozhu chanshi yulu. 14 fasc. *J.* 29:91–158.

Ge Zhaogang. *Chanzong yu Zhongguo wenhua.* Shanghai: Shanghai renmin chubanshe, 1995.

Georgieva, Valentina. "Buddhist Nuns in China: From the Six Dynasties to the Tang." Ph.D. diss., Leiden University, 2000.

Gimello, Robert M. "Chang Shang-yin on Wu-t'ai Shan." In *Pilgrims and Sacred Sites in China,* edited by Susan Naquin and Chün-fang Yü, pp. 89–149. Berkeley: University of California Press, 1992.

————. "Mārga and Culture: Learning, Letters, and Liberation in Northern Sung Ch'an." In *Paths to Liberation: The Mārga and Its Transformations in Buddhist Thought*, edited by Robert E. Buswell Jr. and Robert M. Gimello, pp. 471–486. Honolulu: University of Hawai'i Press, 1992.

Goldman, Andrea S. "The Nun Who Wouldn't Be: Representations of Female Desire in Two Performance Genres of 'Si Fan.'" *Late Imperial China* 22, no. 1 (2001): 72.

Goossaert, Vincent. "Counting the Monks: The 1736–1739 Census of the Chinese Clergy." *Late Imperial China* 21, no. 2 (2000): 40–85.

Grant, Beata. "*Da Zhangfu:* The Rhetoric of Heroism in Seventeenth-Century Chan Buddhist Writings." In *Nan Nü: Men, Women and Gender in China* 10:2 (2008), forthcoming.

————, trans. *Daughters of Emptiness: Poems of Chinese Buddhist Nuns.* Boston: Wisdom Publications, 2004.

————. "Female Holder of the Lineage: Linji Chan Master Zhiyuan Qiyuan Xinggang (1597–1654)." *Late Imperial China* 17, no. 2 (December 1996): 51–76.

————. "Severing the Red Cord: Buddhist Nuns in Eighteenth-Century China." In *Buddhist Women across Cultures*, edited by Karma Lekshe Tsomo. Honolulu: University of Hawai'i Press, 2001.

————. "Through the Empty Gate: The Poetry of Buddhist Nuns in Late Imperial China." In *Cultural Intersections in Late Chinese Buddhism*, edited by Marsha Wiedner, pp. 87–114. Honolulu: University of Hawai'i Press, 2001.

————. "Who Is This I? Who Is That Other? The Poetry of an Eighteenth-Century Buddhist Laywoman." *Late Imperial China* 15, no. 11 (1994): 1–40.

Green, James. *The Recorded Sayings of Zen Master Joshu.* Walnut Creek, Calif.: AltaMira Press, 1998.

Guo Peng. *Mingqing fojiao.* Fujian: Fujian renmin chubanshe, 1982.

Gushan Yongjue heshang guanglu, 30 fasc. J. 27:585–745

Hasebe Yūkei. *Min Shin Bukkyō kyōdanshi kenkyū.* Tokyo: Dōhōha shuppan, 1993.

He Xiaorong. *Mingdai Nanjing shiyuan yanjiu.* Beijing: Zhongguo shehui kexue chubanshe, 2000.

Hengshan xianzhi. 1875.

Hengzhou fuzhi. 1875.

Hong Beimou. *Zhongguo mingni.* Shanghai: Shanghai chubanshe, 1995.

Hori, Victor Sōgen. *Zen Sand: The Book of Capping Phrases for Kōan Practice.* Honolulu: University of Hawai'i Press, 2003.

Hsieh, Ding-hwa E. "Buddhist Nuns in Sung China (960–1279)." *Journal of Sung-Yuan Studies* 30 (2000).

————. "Images of Women in Ch'an Buddhist Literature of the Sung Period." In *Buddhism in the Sung*, edited by Peter N. Gregory and Daniel A. Getz Jr., pp. 148–187. Honolulu: University of Hawai'i Press, 1999.

———. "Yuanwu K'o-ch'in's (1063–1135) Teaching of Ch'an Kung-an Practice: A Transition from Literary Study of Ch'an Kung-an to the Practical K'an-hua Ch'an." *Journal of the International Association of Buddhist Studies* 17 (1994): 66–95.

Hsü, Sung-peng. *A Buddhist Leader in Ming China.* University Park: Pennsylvania University Press, 1979.

Hu Wenkai. *Lidai funü zhuzuo kao.* Rev. ed. Shanghai: Shanghai guji chubanshe, 1985.

Hummel, Arthur W., ed. *Eminent Chinese of the Ch'ing Period (1644–1912).* Taipei: Literature House, 1964.

Hurvitz, Leon. "Chu-hung's One Mind of Pure Land and Ch'an Buddhism." In *Self and Society in Ming Thought,* edited by Wm. Theodore de Bary, pp. 451–476. New York: Columbia University Press, 1970.

Idema, Wilt L., and Beata Grant. *The Red Brush: Writing Women of Imperial China.* Cambridge, Mass.: Harvard University Asia Center, 2004; 2nd ed., 2007.

Idema, Wilt L., Wai-yee Li, and Ellen Widmer, eds. *Trauma and Transcendence in Early Qing Literature.* Harvard East Asian Monographs. Cambridge, Mass.: Harvard University Asia Center, 2006.

Jen, Yu-wen. "Ch'en Hsien-chang's Philosophy of the Natural." In *Self and Society in Ming Thought,* edited by W. T. deBary. New York: Columbia University Press, 1971.

Jiaxing Dazangjing. 40 vols. Reprint of *Zhonghua dazang jing di er ji.* Taipei: Xinwenfeng chubanshe, 1987.

Jiaxing fuzhi. 1682.

Jiaxing fuzhi. 1840.

Jizong Che chanshi yulu. 4 fasc. J. 28:441–470.

Keyworth, George. "Transmitting the Lamp of Learning in Classical Chan Buddhism: Juefan Huihong (1071–1128) and Literary Chan." Ph.D. diss., University of California, Los Angeles, 2001.

Kieschnick, John. *The Eminent Monk: Buddhist Ideals in Medieval Chinese Hagiography.* Honolulu: University of Hawai'i Press, 1997.

———. *The Impact of Buddhism on Chinese Material Culture.* Princeton, N.J.: Princeton University Press, 2003.

Klein, Anne Carolyn. *Meeting the Great Bliss Queen: Buddhists, Feminists and the Art of the Self.* Boston: Beacon Press, 1995.

Ko, Dorothy. *Teachers of the Inner Chambers: Women and Culture in China, 1573–1722.* Palo Alto, Calif.: Stanford University Press, 1994.

Lan Jifu. "Jiaxing dazang de tese jiqi shiliao jiazhi." In *Fojiao de sixiang yu wenhua: Yinshun daoshi bazhi jinliu shouqing wenji.* Taipei: Foguang chubanshe, 1991.

Lei Ruoxin, "Zhongguo gudai nigu susu xintai fenxi," *Nandu xuetan* 26, no. 1 (January 2006): 31–36.

Levering, Miriam. *Ch'an Enlightenment for Laymen: Ta-hui and the New Religious Culture of the Sung.* Ph.D. diss., Harvard University, 1978.

———. "Dōgen's *Raihaitokuzui* and Women Teaching in Sung Ch'an." *Journal of the International Association of Buddhist Studies* 21, no. 1 (1998): 77–110.

———. "The Dragon Girl and the Abbess of Mo-shan: Gender and Status in the Ch'an Buddhist Tradition." *Journal of the International Association of Buddhist Studies* 5, no. 1 (1982): 19–35.

———. "Lin-chi (Rinzai) Ch'an and Gender: The Rhetoric of Equality and the Rhetoric of Heroism." In *Buddhism, Sexuality and Gender,* edited by Jose Ignacio Cabezon. Albany: State University of New York Press, 1992.

———. "Miao-tao and Her Teacher Ta-hui." In *Buddhism in the Sung Dynasty,* edited by Peter Gregory and Daniel Getz, pp. 188–219. Honolulu: University of Hawai'i Press, 1999.

———. "A Monk's Literary Education: Dahui's Friendship with Juefan Huihong," *Chung-Hwa Buddhist Journal* 13, no. 2 (2000): 369–384.

———. "Ta-hui and Lay Buddhists: Ch'an Sermons on Death." In *Buddhist and Taoist Practice in Medieval Chinese Society (Buddhist and Taoist Studies II),* edited by David W. Chappell. Honolulu: University of Hawai'i Press, 1987.

———. "Women Ch'an Masters: The Teacher Miao-tsung as Saint." In *Women Saints in World Religions,* edited by Arvind Sharma, pp. 180–204. Albany: State University of New York Press, 2000.

Li Li'an. "Mingmo Qingchu Chanzong de jiben zouxiang." *Zhongguo zhexue shi* 3 (1999): 83–86.

Li, Wai-yee. "Heroic Transformations: Women and National Trauma in Early Qing Literature." *Harvard Journal of Asiatic Studies* 9, no. 2 (December 1999): 363–364.

Li Yuzhen. *Tangdai de biqiuni.* Taiwan: Xuesheng shuju, 1989.

Lian Ruizhi. "Hanyue Fazang yu wan Ming Sanfeng zongpai de jianli." *Zhonghua Foxue xuebao* 9 (1996): 167–208.

———. "Qian Qianyi de fojiao shengya yu linian." *Zhongguo Foxue xuebao* 6 (1994): 317–370.

Lianfeng Chanshi yulu, 10 fasc. *J.* 38: 315–379.

Liao Cheng-Heng. "Huihong Juefan zai Mingdai: Songdai chanxue zai wan Ming de shuxie." *Zhongguo yanjiuyuan lishi Wenyan yanjiu suo ji kan* 75, no. 4 (2004): 797–837.

Lingrui chanshi Yanhua ji. 5 fasc. *J.* 35:741–760.

Lingrui ni Zukui Fu chanshi Miaozhan lu. 5 fasc. *J.* 35:715–740.

Little, Stephen, ed. *Taoism and the Arts of China.* Art Institute of Chicago/University of California Press, 2000.

Mann, Susan. *Precious Records: Women in China's Long Eighteenth Century.* Palo Alto, Calif.: Stanford University Press, 1997.

Mann, Susan, and Yu-yin Cheng, eds. *Under Confucian Eyes: Writing on Gender in Chinese History.* Berkeley: University of California Press, 2001.

McNamara, Jo Ann Kay. *Sisters in Arms: Catholic Nuns through Two Millennia.* Cambridge, Mass.: Harvard University Press, 1996.

McRae, John R. "Bracketing the Emergence of Encounter Dialogue: The Transformation of the Spiritual Path in Ch'an Buddhism." In *Paths to Liberation: The Mārga and Its Transformations in Buddhist Thought,* edited by Robert M. Gimello and Robert E. Buswell Jr. Honolulu: University of Hawai'i Press, 1992.

————. *Seeing through Zen: Encounter, Transformation, and Genealogy in Chinese Chan Buddhism.* Berkeley: University of California Press, 2003.

Meili zhi. 1824.

Miyun chanshi yulu. 12 fasc. *J.* 10:1–87.

Muren shenggao, 5 fasc. *J.* 35: 475–507.

Nanxun zhenzhi. 1863.

Nanxun zhi. 1921.

Naquin, Susan. *Peking: Temples and City Life, 1400–1900.* Berkeley: University of California Press, 2000.

————. "Sites, Saints, and Sights at the Tanzhe Monastery." *Cahiers d'Extrême-Asie* 10 (1998): 183–211.

Naquin, Susan, and Thomas Shiyu Li. "The Baoming Temple: Religion and the Throne in Ming and Qing China." *Harvard Journal of Asiatic Studies* 48, no. 1 (1988): 131–188.

Naquin, Susan, and Chün-fang Yü, eds. *Pilgrims and Sacred Sites in China.* Berkeley: University of California Press, 1992.

Ohnuma, Reiko. "The Gift of the Body and the Gift of the Dharma." *History of Religions* 37, no. 4 (1998): 321–359.

Pan Guangdan. *Ming-Qing liangdai Jiaxing de wangzu.* Shanghai: Renmin shudian chubanshe, 1991.

Paul, Diana Y. *Women in Buddhism: Images of the Feminine in the Mahāyāna Tradition.* Berkeley: University of California Press, 1985.

Peng Shaosheng. *Jushi zhuan.* 5 fasc. *Z.* no. 1646, vol. 88.

Peterson, Barbara Bennett, ed. *Notable Women of China: Shang Dynasty to the Early Twentieth Century.* Armonk and London: M. E. Sharpe, 2000.

Peterson, Willard J. *Bitter Gourd: Fang I-chih and the Impetus for Intellectual Change.* New Haven, Conn., and London: Yale University Press, 1997.

Pinghu xianzhi. 1745.

Poshan chanshi yulu. 20 fasc. *J.* 26:1–101.

Qian Qianyi. *Jianzhu Qian Muzhai quanji.* 163 fasc. Wujiang: Suihan zhai, 1910.

————. *Liechao shiji xiaozhuan.* Reprint, Shanghai: Gudian wenxue chubanshe, 1957. Originally published in 1698.

——. *Muzhai youxue ji, Siku quanshu* 78–79. Taipei: Taiwan Shangwu yinshu-guan, 1979.

Qin, Wen-jie. "The Buddhist Revival in Post-Mao China: Women Reconstruct Buddhism on Mt. Emei." Ph.D. diss., Harvard University, 2000.

Qiu Zhonglin. "Buxiao zhi xiao—Tang yilai gegu liaoqin xianxiang de shehuishi chutan." *Xin shixue* 6, no. 1 (1995): 49–94.

Rawski, Evelyn S. *The Last Emperors: A Social History of Qing Imperial Institutions.* Berkeley: University of California Press, 1998.

Ren Jiyu. *Zhongguo fojiao daguan.* Harbin: Harbin chubanshe, 1995.

Ruppert, Brian. "Buddhist Rainmaking in Early Japan: The Dragon King and the Ritual Careers of Esoteric Monks." *History of Religions* 42, no. 2 (2002): 143–174.

Sasaki, Ruth Fuller, and Yoshitaka Iriya. *The Recorded Sayings of Ch'an Master Lin-chi Hui-chao of Chen Prefecture.* Kyoto: Institute for Zen Studies, Hanazono College, 1975.

Sasaki, Ruth Fuller, Yoshitaka Iriya, and Dana R. Fraser. *A Man of Zen: The Recorded Sayings of Layman P'ang.* New York and Tokyo: Weatherhill, 1971 and 1976.

Sharf, Robert F. *Coming to Terms with Chinese Buddhism: A Reading of the Treasure Store Treatise.* Honolulu: University of Hawai'i Press, 2002.

——. "The Idolization of Enlightenment: On the Mummification of Ch'an Masters in Medieval China." *History of Religions* 32, no. 1 (1992): 1–31.

——. "On Pure Land Buddhism and Ch'an/Pure Land Syncretism in Medieval China." *T'oung Pao* 88, nos. 4–5 (2002): 282–332.

——. "The Zen of Japanese Nationalism." *History of Religions* 33, no. 1 (1993).

Shi Jianyi. "Hanyue Fazang zhi Chanfa yanjiu." *Zhonghua foxue bao* 11 (1998): 181–225.

Shi Shengyan. *Mingmo fojiao yanjiu.* Taipei: Tongchu chubanshe, 1987.

Shinsan dai Nihon zokuzōkyō. 90 vols. Tokyo: Kokusho kankōkai, 1975–1989. Originally published as *Dainihon zokuzōkyō,* 750 vols. (Kyoto: Zōkyō shoin, 1905–1912).

Siku quanshu. Wenyuange edition. 1500 vols. Taipei: Shangwu yinshuguan, 1983–1996.

Smith, Joanna F. Handlin. "Benevolent Societies: The Reshaping of Charity during the Late Ming and Early Ch'ing." *Journal of Asian Studies* 46, no. 2 (1987): 309–337.

——. "Liberating Animals in Ming-Qing China: Buddhist Inspiration and Elite Imagination." *Journal of Asian Studies* 58, no. 1 (1999): 51–84.

——. "Social Hierarchy and Merchant Philanthropy as Perceived in Several Late-Ming and Early-Qing Texts." *Journal of the Economic and Social History of the Orient* 41, no. 3 (1998): 417–451.

Smith, Sidonie. *A Poetics of Women's Autobiography: Marginality and the Fictions of Self-Representation.* Bloomington: Indiana University Press, 1987.

Songgu hexiang ji. 1 fasc. *J.* 28:565–572.

Spence, Jonathan D. *The Search for Modern China.* New York: W. W. Norton, 1999.

Spence, Jonathan D., and John E. Willis Jr. *From Ming to Ch'ing: Conquest, Regions and Continuity in Seventeenth-Century China.* New Haven, Conn., and London: Yale University Press, 1979.

Stevenson, Daniel B. "Text, Image and Transformation in the History of the *Shuilu Fahui,* the Buddhist Rite for Deliverance of Creatures of Water and Land." In *Cultural Intersections in Later Chinese Buddhism,* edited by Marsha Weidner. Honolulu: University of Hawai'i Press, 2001.

Strickman, Michel. "On the Alchemy of T'ao Hung-ching." In *Facets of Taoism: Essays in Chinese Religion,* edited by Holmes Welch and Anna Seidel. New Haven, Conn., and London: Yale University Press, 1979.

Su Meiwen. "Luanxiang zhong you xinsheng: Lun Mingmo Qingcu biqiuni zhe xingxiang yu chujing." *Zhonghua jishu xueyuan xuebao* 27 (2003): 227–243.

———. "Mingmo Qingchu nüxing chanshi yulu de chuban yu ru zang—jian lun: *Jiaxing zang* de ruzang wenti." *Taiwan zongjiao yanjiu* 4, no. 1 (2005) 113–174.

———. "Nüxing Chanshi de daoying: You 'Xiezhen yu mingyan' tanxi Qiyuan chanshi zhi xingxiang." *Foxue yanjiu zhongxin xuebao* 10 (2005): 253–286.

Sun Zongzeng. "Mingmo Chanzong zai Zhedong Xingsheng zhi yuanyou tantao." *Guoji Foxue yanjiu* 12 (1992): 141–176.

Taishō shinshō daizōkyō. Edited by Takakusu Junjirō et al. 100 vols. Tokyo: Daizōkyōkai shuppan. 1922–1933.

ter Haar, Barend J. *The White Lotus Teachings in Chinese Religious History.* Honolulu: University of Hawai'i Press, 1999.

Tiantong Hongjue Min chanshi yulu. 20 fasc. *J.* 26:287–307.

Tsai, Kathryn M. "The Chinese Buddhist Monastic Order for Women: The First Two Centuries." *Historical Reflections* 8, no. 3 (1981): 1–19.

———. *Lives of the Nuns: Biographies of Chinese Buddhist Nuns from the Fourth to Sixth Centuries.* Reprint ed. Honolulu: University of Hawai'i Press, 1994.

Wakeman, Frederic, Jr. "China and the Seventeenth-Century Crisis." *Late Imperial China* 7, no. 1 (1986): 1–26.

———. "Localism and Loyalism during the Ch'ing Conquest of Kiangnan." In *Conflict and Control in Late Imperial China,* edited by Frederick Wakeman Jr. and Carolyn Grant, pp. 43–85. Berkeley: University of California Press, 1975.

———. "Romantics, Stoics and Martyrs in Seventeenth-Century China. *Journal of Asian Studies* 43, no. 4 (1984): 631–666.

Wang Duanshu. *Mingyuan shiwei,* 1667.

Wang Qi, comp. *Chidu xinyu.* 2 vols. 1668. Reprint, Taipei: Guangwen, 1996.

Wang Shilu. *Ranzhi ji.* 1672. Partial copy in the Shanghai Municipal library.

Wanru chanshi yulu. 10 fasc. *J.* 26: 439–482.

Wanyan Yunzhu. *Guochao guixiu zhengshi ji.* 1831.

Watson, Burton, trans. *The Zen Teachings of Master Lin-chi: A Translation of the* Lin-chi Lu. New York: Columbia University Press, 1993.

Watson, James L. "Funeral Specialists in Cantonese Society: Pollution, Performance, and Social Hierarchy." In *Death Ritual in Late Imperial and Modern China,* edited by James L. Watson and Evelyn S. Rawski. Berkeley: University of California Press, 1998.

Weber, Alison. *Theresa of Avila and the Rhetoric of Femininity.* Princeton, N.J.: Princeton University Press, 1990.

Weidner, Marsha, ed. *Cultural Intersections in Later Chinese Buddhism.* Honolulu: University of Hawai'i Press, 2001.

———. *Latter Days of the Laws: Images of Chinese Buddhism 850–1850.* Lawrence, Kans.: Spencer Museum of Art, 1994.

Welch, Holmes. *The Buddhist Revival in China.* Cambridge, Mass.: Harvard University Press, 1968.

———. "Dharma Scrolls and the Succession of Abbots in Chinese Monasteries." *T'oung Pao* 50 (1963): 93–149.

———. *The Practice of Chinese Buddhism, 1900–1950.* Cambridge, Mass.: Harvard University Press, 1967.

Welter, Albert. "Lineage and Context in the *Patriarch's Hall Collection* and the *Transmission of the Lamp.* In *The Zen Canon: Understanding the Classic Texts,* edited by Steven Heine and Dale S. Wright, pp. 137–180. New York: Oxford University Press, 2004.

———. *Monks, Rulers, and Literati: The Political Ascendancy of Chan Buddhism.* New York: Oxford University Press, 2006.

Widmer, Ellen. *The Beauty and the Book: Women and Fiction in Nineteenth-Century China.* Harvard East Asian Monographs, Cambridge, Mass.: Harvard University, 2003.

Widmer, Ellen, and Kang-i Sun Chan, eds. *Writing Women in Late Imperial China.* Palo Alto, Calif.: Stanford University Press, 1997.

Winston-Allen, Anne. *Convent Chronicles: Women Writing about Reform in the Late Middle Ages.* University Park: Pennsylvania State University Press, 2004.

Wright, Dale S. *Philosophical Meditations on Zen Buddhism.* New York: Cambridge University Press, 2000.

Wu, Jiang. "Building a Dharma Transmission Monastery in Seventeenth-Century China: The Case of Mount Huangbo." *East Asian History* 31 (June 2006): 29–52.

———. *Enlightenment in Dispute: The Reinvention of Chan Buddhism in Seventeenth-Century China.* New York: Oxford University Press, 2008.

———. "Leaving for the Rising Sun: The Historical Background of Yinyuan Longqi's Migration to Japan in 1654." *Asia Major,* 3rd ser., 17, no. 2 (2004): 89–120.

———. "Orthodoxy, Controversy and the Transformation of Chan Buddhism in Seventeenth-Century China." Ph.D. diss., Harvard University, 2004.

Wu, Pei-Yi. *The Confucian's Progress: Autobiographical Writings in Traditional China.* Princeton, N.J.: Princeton University Press, 1990.

Wudeng quanshu. 120 fasc. Z. no. 1571, vols. 81 and 82.

Xiangyan Xixin Shui chanshi yulu. 2 fasc. *J.* 39:713–929.

Xingkong Tai chanshi yulu. 6 fasc. *J.* 39:747–767.

Xiuye Lin chanshi yulu. 3 fasc. *J.* 36:581–609.

Xu Naichang, ed., *Guixiu cichao.* Nanking, 1909.

Yang, Binbin. "Women and the Aesthetics of Illness: Poetry on Illness by Chinese Women Poets of the Qing." Ph.D. diss., Washington University in St. Louis, 2007.

Yang, Hsüan-chih. *A Record of Buddhist Monasteries in Lo-yang.* Translated by Wang, Yi-t'ung. Princeton, N.J.: Princeton University Press, 1984,

Yü, Chün-Fang. "Ming Buddhism," In *The Cambridge History of China,* vol. 8, part 2, 1368–1644, edited by Denis Twitchett and Frederick W. Mote, pp. 893–952. Cambridge: Cambridge University Press, 1988.

———. *The Renewal of Buddhism in China: Chu-hung and the Late Ming Synthesis.* New York: Columbia University Press, 1981.

Yu Jianhua, comp. *Zhongguo meishujia renming cidian.* Shanghai: Shanghai renmin meishu chubanshe, 1981.

Yuan'an Li chanshi yulu. 16 fasc. *J.* 37:335–408.

Zhang Geng. *Guochao huazheng xulu.* Jiangdu: Zhushi cangban, 1739.

Zhang Wenliang. "Hanyue Fazang lun Rulai Chan yu Zushi Chan." *Fayin* 3 (1995): 29–35.

Zhao Yuan. *Ming Qing zhiji shidafu yanjiu.* Beijing: Beijing daxue chubanshe, 1999.

Zhenhua. *Xu biqiuni zhuan.* In *Biqiuni zhuan quanji.* Taipei: Fojiao shuju, 1988.

Zhongguo Dazangjing di'er ji. Reprints of *Jiaxing xenzang, Jiaxing Xuzang, and Jiaxing you Xuzang.* Taipei: Xiuding Zhonghua dazang jinghui, 1962.

Zhongguo Fojiao congshu Xhanzong bian. Edited by Ren Jiyu. 12 vols. Nanjing: Jiangsu guji chubanshe, 1993.

Zhongguo Fojiao renming dacidian. Posthumous work by Zhenhua, edited by Zhen-chan and Wang Xin. 1999; reprint, Shanghai: Shanghai cishu chubanshe, 2002.

Zhu Hong. *Lianchi dashi chuanji.* Taipei: Zhonghua fojiao wenhua guan, 1973.

Zhu Yizun. *Jingzhiju shihua.* In *Xuxiu siku quanshu: Jibu* 23:760–761. Shanghai guji chubanshe, 1995–1999. Originally published in 1698.

Ziyong Ru chanshi yulu. 4 fasc. *J.* 39:819–832.

Zürcher, Erik. "Religieuses et Couvents dans l'Ancien Bouddhisme Chinois." In *Buddhism, Christianisme et Société Chinoise.* Paris: Julliard, 1990.

Index

About the Author

Beata Grant received her doctorate in Chinese language and literature from Stanford University and since 1989 has been teaching Chinese literature, religion, and women/gender studies at Washington University in St. Louis. Her abiding interdisciplinary interest in the interface between religion and literature is reflected in her first book, *Mount Lu Revisited: Buddhism in the Life and Writings of Su Shih (1036–1101)*, published by the University of Hawai'i Press in 1994. In subsequent publications, she has expanded her area of consideration to include women and gender. She has published numerous articles both on images of women in Chinese religious writing (including popular literature) and on writing by Buddhist nuns and laywomen of the Ming-Qing period in particular. In 2003 she published a book of translations entitled *Daughters of Emptiness: The Poetry of Chinese Buddhist Nuns* (Wisdom Publications), and she has also coauthored, with Wilt L. Idema, a major narrative anthology of women's writings (including writings by religious women) entitled *The Red Brush: Writing Women of Imperial China* (Harvard University Asia Center, 2004; second edition, 2007).